1999 Guide to DiRōNA Award Restaurants

DiRoNA
Published for Distinguished Restaurants of North America
456 Washington Street • Monterey • California • 93940 • USA
PH: (831) 649-6542 • FAX: (831) 372-4142
website address http://www.DiRoNA.com

Publisher: Mitch Kostuch, Editor: Deborah Waldner
Kostuch Publications Limited
1415 W. 22nd St., Tower Fl. • Oak Brook • IL • USA • 60521
PH: (630) 645-3877

website address:www.FoodserviceWorld.com

Canadian Address:
Suite 101, 23 Lesmill Rd. • Don Mills • ON • Canada • M3B 3P6
PH: (416) 447-0888

Printed in Canada

Table of Contents

THE UNITED STATES OF AMERICA

Table of Contents

CANADA

Table of Contents

DiRoNA Scholarship Program

The DiRoNA Award Scholarship Fund was initiated in 1989 and has helped many young entrepreneurs achieve their goals in the culinary world. Ted Balestreri, Scholarship Committee Chairman and Past DiRoNA Chairman states that "education is the best gift we can give to our youth." Distinguished Restaurants of North America is proud to offer assistance in the promotion of distinguished dining through the education of tomorrow's leaders.

DiRoNA Award Scholarships are presented to deserving individuals pursuing careers in the restaurant and hospitality industry. Recipients are selected through a review of applications from students throughout North America who exhibit a genuine interest in seeking an education in preparation for a professional foodservice career.

The DiRoNA Award Scholarship Fund is managed and administered for Distinguished Restaurants of North America by the National Restaurant Association Educational Foundation. Applicants can apply by contacting Bridgette de Jesus, the Scholarship Program Coordinator at:

National Restaurant Association
Educational Foundation
250 South Wacker Drive
Chicago, IL, 60606-5834
Ph: (800) 765-2122 (ext 748)

A total of $30,000 (15 scholarships valued at $2,000 each) will be awarded in 1999, in memory of Past DiRoNA Chairman Richard Swig.

Additional information can be obtained by contacting DiRoNA in Monterey, CA, at (831) 649-6542.

Dear Distinguished Diner,

Welcome to the 1999 Guide to Distinguished Restaurants of North America!

The DiRoNA Award is the only award which results from an independent and anonymous restaurant inspection. This Guide lists DiRoNA Award restaurants in alphabetical order by country, state and city.

Wine Spectator magazine recognizes The DiRoNA Guide as "*the* guide to fine dining." The National Restaurant Association recommends DiRoNA Award restaurants and the Guide as the most reliable source for exploring the best dining experiences in North America.

Distinguished Restaurants of North America's mission is to preserve and promote distinguished dining throughout the United States, Canada and Mexico. To qualify for the DiRoNA Award, a restaurant must be in business under the same ownership and concept for at least three years and pass a rigorous evaluation conducted anonymously by independent inspectors. The inspection examines the total dining experience from the reservation to departure, and emphasizes the quality of food and its presentation.

The Award itself is a die-cut figure of a whimsical 'happy diner.' The goals of Distinguished Restaurants of North America, in applying such standards to dining, are to motivate restaurants to strive for consistent excellence and to assist you in locating the ultimate experience in fine dining.

Happy Distinguished Dining!

Paul Athanas

Paul Athanas
Chairman

Distinguished Restaurants of North America is a non-profit organization who, by recognizing excellence in their field, seek to raise dining standards and promote distinguished dining throughout the United States, Canada and Mexico. The organization was founded in 1990 and is governed by an independent board of directors.

In 1992, the DiRoNA Award Program was launched, recognizing restaurants which exemplify the highest quality standards in all aspects of the dining experience, thus "The Award Of Excellence". The founding members were the 1989 recipients of the Travel Holiday Award, which was the last year that award was presented. Founding sponsors of the DiRoNA Award Program are American Express and Allied Domecq Spirits, U.S.A.

The DiRoNA Award Inspection Program is the ONLY independent and anonymous restaurant inspection program in North America. The DiRoNA Award recipients are selected through a rigorous inspection process. To qualify, a restaurant must be in business under the same ownership and concept for at least three years and pass a 75-point evaluation conducted anonymously by a specially trained, independent panel of qualified professionals and consumers of distinguished dining. The inspection process examines the total dining experience and is supervised by the DiRoNA Council of Inspection, Evaluation and Criteria. The Council also conducts an annual review of the process and requalifies the professional inspectors.

The DiRoNA designation remains in effect for three years, at which point the inspection process begins anew and the establishment is evaluated again, using the exact same criteria. If a restaurant undergoes a change of ownership or concept during the three years the Award is in effect, it forfeits the DiRoNA Award until such time as it has fulfilled the "three years in business" requirement and passes inspection.

The mission of Distinguished Restaurants of North America is to preserve and promote the ultimate in distinguished dining.

The DiRoNA Award results from an independent and anonymous restaurant inspection, administered by Harold Stayman, Director of Inspections. Mr. Stayman heads a team of 36 inspectors who are requalified and audited for Distinguished Restaurants of North America annually by Dr. Morris Gaebe, Chancellor of Johnson and Wales University. The inspectors are thoroughly oriented with the 75-point criteria, developed by Cornell University, which is the basis for all inspections. They have impeccable credentials and are experienced in fine dining.

Inspectors visit restaurants throughout North America at the direction of the Director of Inspections, who monitors thousands of restaurants each year. Candidates for inspections are identified through a multitude of resources, including requests for inspections that are submitted to DiRoNA headquarters by operators hoping to become DiRoNA members. With the exception of the Director of Inspections, the team of inspectors are unknown to the Board and DiRoNA Award Restaurants. Dr. Gaebe provides an annual report, verifying for the Board that he personally evaluates the Director of Inspections Annual Workshop for inspectors and each participating inspector.

A restaurant must be in business for three years before it is eligible for inspection, and once a restaurant earns the DiRoNA Award, it must be re-inspected within three years in order to maintain the membership.

A 75-point list of criteria are utilized to evaluate the restaurant on quality of overall environment, cuisine, beverages, and service. The physical property and the decor are evaluated, with comfort, cleanliness, room temperature and light levels observed.

The cuisine quality is the most important in the decision to confer the DiRoNA Award to a restaurant. The menu is examined for accuracy, variety of items, cooking techniques, creativity and originality, as well as for health and nutrition-oriented items. The food is evaluated on temperature, appearance, and quality of ingredients. Beverages offered by restaurants are evaluated on the basis of variety, availability, value and food affinity.

The service criteria evaluate guest interactions with the service staff starting from the reservation, greeting and seating, service throughout the meal, and assistance with departure. The staff's knowledge of the menu is tested and their friendliness, attentiveness, cleanliness and attire are appraised. Finally, the restaurant's procedures for handling the check are evaluated by verifying that the check is a consolidated bill which is accurate, legible and professionally presented.

W e've attempted to make the Guide to Distinguished Restaurants of North America as user-friendly as possible. Restaurants are listed alphabetically, by country, state and then by city. The first section is a complete listing of all DiRoNA Award winning restaurants. Some recipients provided materials for an expanded listing, which we've used in the second section. These listings include a color photo, information about the days the restaurant is open, which credit cards are accepted, the average cost of dinner for two (not including wine or gratuities), and substantial additional information. To relay this information in an easy-to-use format, we use a series of graphic symbols. The following table provides the user with the meaning of the symbols used throughout this book.

Credit Cards Accepted

American Express	AE
Visa	VC
Mastercard	MC
Carte Blanche	CB
Diners Club	DC
En Route	ER
JCB	J
Discover Card	DS

Dress Code

Upscale Casual

Coat & Tie Required

Parking

None Provided

Free

Paid Valet

Arrangement with Garage

Reservations Policy

Recommended

Required

Not Necessary

Dinner for two - no wine

$20 - $40	❶
$40 - $60	❷
$60 - $80	❸
$80 +	❹

Days open and meal occasions are signified by shaded spaces. White spaces indicate restaurant is closed.

	S	M	T	W	T	F	S
B							
L							
D							

Other Features

Outdoor Dining

Entertainment

Near Theatre

Private Room/Parties

Cigar/Cognac Events

Accommodations for Smoking

Officers

Paul Athanas, Chairman
Anthony's Pier 4; Boston, MA
John Folse, Vice Chairman
Lafitte's Landing; Donaldsonville, LA
*John Arena, President
DRNA; Toronto, Ontario, Canada
Kurt Knowles, Secretary
The Manor; West Orange, NJ
Alon Yu, Treasurer
Tommy Toy's; San Francisco, CA
*Christianne Ricchi
Ristorante i Ricchi; Washington, DC

Board of Directors

Richard Alberini
Alberini's; Niles, OH
*Ted Balestreri
Sardine Factory; Monterey, CA
Reinhard Barthel
Café 36; LaGrange, IL
James Blandi, Jr.
Le Mont; Pittsburgh, PA
Vincent Bommarito
Tony's; St. Louis, MO
Michael Carlevale
Prego Della Piazza; Toronto, Ontario
Vincent J. Catania
Dan'l Webster Inn; Sandwich, MA
Priscilla Cretier
Le Vichyssois; Lakemoor, IL
*Bert Cutino
Sardine Factory; Monterey, CA
Jack Czarnecki
Joel Palmer House; Dayton, OR
Remo d'Agliano
Raffaello; Carmel, CA
Jordi Escofet
La Cava; Mexico City, Mexico
Ralph Evans
Evans Farm Inn; McLean, VA
Mario Ferrari
Mario's; Nashville, TN

Dominic Galati
Dominic's; St. Louis, MO
Norbert Goldner
Café L'Europe; Palm Beach, FL
Wade Knowles
The Manor; West Orange, NJ
Tony May
San Domenico; New York, NY
Leonard Mirabile
Jasper's; Kansas City, MO
Christopher Passodelis
Pittsburgh, PA
Rick Powers
Beverly's; Coeur d'Alene, ID
David Stockman
Lawry's Restaurants; Pasadena, CA
Larry Work
Sam & Harry's; Washington, DC
Ernest Zingg
The Cellar; Fullerton, CA

Directors Emeritus

Jerry Burns
'21' Club; New York, NY
Ella Brennan
Commander's Palace; New Orleans, LA
Victor Gotti
Ernie's; San Francisco, CA
Warren F. Leruth
W.F. LeRuth Enterprises; Gretna, LA
Tom Margittai
The Four Seasons; New York, NY
Richard Marriott
Host Marriott Corp.; Washington, DC

Administration

David Armanasco, Director
Mary Chapman, Manager
Armanasco Public Relations, Inc.
Monterey, CA

*indicates Past Chairman

Wine Spectator

Distinguished Restaurants of North America is proud to include among its sponsors *Wine Spectator* which each year recognizes DiRoNA Award recipients in their Annual Dining Guide. Since 1981, *Wine Spectator's* Restaurant Awards Program has encouraged restaurants to strive for better quality wine programs. The program currently recognizes nearly 2000 restaurants worldwide for their wine lists.

Wine lists are judged for one of three awards — ranging from the *Award of Excellence*, to the *Best of Award of Excellence* and up to the *Grand Award*. New *Grand Award* winners are announced in the August 31 issue of *Wine Spectator*. *Award of Excellence* and *Best of Award of Excellence* winners are announced in the September 30th issue.

For complete information on entering the 1999 *Wine Spectator* Restaurant Awards Program, call *Wine Spectator* at (212) 684 4224 (ext 781).

About the Artist

Guy Buffet was born January 13, 1943, in the Montparnasse section of Paris where Marc Chagall, Pablo Picasso, Bartolomeo Modigliani and Henri Matisse had their studios. The Buffet family ran a restaurant business in the area. When he was 12, Guy's mother gave him art supplies, and shortly thereafter, Buffet paintings began to appear on the restaurant walls. The first sale of a Buffet original was to a visiting American when Guy was just 13. A year later, he was enrolled in the Beaux Arts de Toulon, an art school in the south of France. He went on to complete his formal studies at the Academy of Painting of the City of Paris, working nights as a busboy in the restaurant.

Artist: Guy Buffet

Today, Guy Buffet is famous for his whimsical fantasies. He has a remarkable ability to capture the essence of the moment and to visually articulate a sense of character and place. He is a recognized master of subjects such as chefs, sommeliers and wine makers. He is also widely respected for his paintings of historical events and significance. Corporations, private collectors, museums and special events committees from around the world continue to commission his work. He has homes in France and Maui, where he lives with his wife Laurence and their two children, Angel and Albert.

DiRoNA Appreciates...

Cards
FOUNDING SPONSOR

ALLIED DOMECQ
SPIRITS, USA
FOUNDING SPONSOR

NON-SMOKERS AND SMOKERS WELCOME
THE ACCOMMODATION PROGRAM
COURTESY OF PHILLIP MORRIS U.S.A.

SEAGRAM AMERICAS

Seagram Chateau & Estate
Wines Company

INFORMANT

National Restaurant Association
THE EDUCATIONAL FOUNDATION

JOHNSON & WALES
UNIVERSITY

Wine Spectator

ITALY'S #1 COFFEE

Superior Coffee

fantasia nel dessert

CURVWARE™

The one you know.

indicates expanded listing

UNITED STATES OF AMERICA

ALASKA

ANCHORAGE

Crow's Nest, The Hotel Captain Cook *page 94
4th at K St., Anchorage, AK, 99501
Ph: 907-276-6000 Fax: 907-343-2211 **Cuisine:** Contemporary American
Owner: Walter Hickel **Average Dinner for 2:** $80

Simon & Seafort's *page 94
420 L St., Anchorage, AK, 99501
Ph: 907-274-3502 Fax: 907-274-2487 **Cuisine:** Steak/Seafood
Average Dinner for 2: $60 **Closed:** Holidays

FAIRBANKS

The Pump House *page 95
796 Chena Pump Rd., Fairbanks, AK, 99708
Ph: 907-479-8452 Fax: 907-479-8432 **Cuisine:** Seafood
Owners: Vivian & Bill Bubbel **Average Dinner for 2:** $50

ARKANSAS

LITTLE ROCK

Alouette's *page 95
11401 N. Rodney Parham Rd., Little Rock, AR, 72212
Ph: 501-225-4152 Fax: 501-221-7920 **Cuisine:** French/Continental
Owner: Denis Seyer **Average Dinner for 2:** $40
Closed: Sunday, Monday

Ashley's at The Capital
111 W. Markham St., Little Rock, AR, 72201
Ph: 501-374-7474 Fax: 501-370-7089 **Cuisine:** Continental/Seafood
Average Dinner for 2: $75

ARIZONA

PHOENIX

A Different Pointe of View
11111 N. 7th St., Phoenix, AZ, 85020
Ph: 602-866-7500 Fax: 602-866-6358 **Cuisine:** Regional
Average Dinner for 2: $100 **Closed:** Sunday, Monday (seasonally)

Eddie's Grill
4747 N. 7th St., Phoenix, AZ, 85014
Ph: 602-241-1188 Fax: 602-241-1570 **Cuisine:** American
Owners: Larry Cohn & Eddie Matney **Average Dinner for 2:** $45

Roxsand
2594 E. Camelback Rd., Phoenix, AZ, 85016
Ph: 602-381-0444 Fax: 602-957-7558 **Cuisine:** Contemporary
Owners: Spyro & Roxsand Scocos **Average Dinner for 2:** $100
Closed: Christmas, New Years

Vincent Guerithault on Camelback
3930 E. Camelback Rd., Phoenix, AZ, 85018
Ph: 602-224-0225 Fax: 602-956-5400 **Cuisine:** Regional
Owner: Vincent Guerithault **Average Dinner for 2:** $100
Closed: Holidays

Wright's, The Arizona Biltmore Hotel
24th St. at Missouri, Phoenix, AZ, 85016
Ph: 602-954-2507 Fax: 602-381-7646 **Cuisine:** Regional
Average Dinner for 2: $110

SCOTTSDALE

The Chaparral, Marriott's Camelback Inn *page 96
5402 E. Lincoln Dr., Scottsdale, AZ, 85253
Ph: 602-948-1700 Fax: 602-905-7843 **Cuisine:** Continental
Average Dinner for 2: $100

The Latilla Room, The Boulders Resort *page 96
34631 N. Tom Darlington Dr., Carefree, AZ, 85377
Ph: 602-488-9009 Fax: 602-488-4118 **Cuisine:** Contemporary
American **Average Dinner for 2:** $80

Marquesa, The Scottsdale Princess
7575 E. Princess Dr., Scottsdale, AZ, 85255
Ph: 602-585-4848 Fax: 602-585-9895 **Cuisine:** Catalan
Average Dinner for 2: $85 **Closed:** Tuesday

Mary Elaine's, The Phoenician Resort *page 97
6000 E. Camelback Rd., Scottsdale, AZ, 85251
Ph: 602-941-8200 Fax: 602-437-2640 **Cuisine:** French
Average Dinner for 2: $200 **Closed:** Sunday

SEDONA

L' Auberge de Sedona *page 97
301 L' Auberge Lane, Sedona, AZ, 86336
Ph: 520-282-1661 Fax: 520-282-2885 **Cuisine:** French
Average Dinner for 2: $150

TUCSON

Anthony's in the Catalinas *page 98
6440 N. Campbell Ave., Tucson, AZ, 85718
Ph: 520-299-1771 Fax: 520-299-6635 **Cuisine:** Continental
Owner: Brooke Martino **Average Dinner for 2:** $70
Closed: Holidays

Janos
150 N. Main Ave., Tucson, AZ, 85701
Ph: 520-884-9426 Fax: 520-623-4172 **Cuisine:** Regional/French
Owners: Janos & Rebecca Wilder **Average Dinner for 2:** $90
Closed: Sunday, Monday (seasonally)

The Tack Room
7300 E. Vactor Ranch Trail, Tucson, AZ, 85715
Ph: 520-722-2800 Fax: 520-296-0464 **Cuisine:** Regional
Owners: D. Vactor & R. Tyler **Average Dinner for 2:** $130
Closed: Monday (seasonally)

The Ventana Room, Loews Ventana Canyon Resort *page 98
7000 N. Resort Dr., Tucson, AZ, 85750
Ph: 520-299-2020 Fax: 520-299-6832 **Cuisine:** Contemporary
American **Average Dinner for 2:** $140

CALIFORNIA

NORTHERN CALIFORNIA

BERKELEY

Chez Panisse
1517 Shattuck Ave., Berkeley, CA, 94709
Ph: 510-548-5525 Fax: 510-548-0140 **Cuisine:** Regional/French/Italian
Owner: Alice Waters **Average Dinner for 2:** $90 **Closed:** Sunday

DANVILLE

Bridges
44 Church St., Danville, CA, 94526
Ph: 925-820-7200 Fax: 925-820-9720 **Cuisine:** Californian/Asian
Owner: Kazuo Sugitani **Average Dinner for 2:** $70 **Closed:** Holidays

EMERYVILLE

Trader Vic's *page 100
9 Anchor Dr., Emeryville, CA, 94608
Ph: 510-653-3400 Fax: 415-653-9384 **Cuisine:** Island
Owners: The Bergeron Family **Average Dinner for 2:** $45
Closed: Holidays

GEYSERVILLE

Chateau Souverain Cafe at the Winery
400 Souverain Rd., Geyserville, CA, 95441
Ph: 707-433-3141 Fax: 707-433-5174 **Cuisine:** California
Average Dinner for 2: $65 **Closed:** Seasonally

LARKSPUR

The Lark Creek Inn *page 100
234 Magnolia Ave., Larkspur, CA, 94939
Ph: 415-924-7766 Fax: 415-924-7117 **Cuisine:** New American
Owners: Michael Dellar & Bradley Ogden **Average Dinner for 2:** $75
Closed: Christmas, New Years

LIVERMORE

Wente Vineyards Restaurant *page 101
5050 Arroyo Rd., Livermore, CA, 94550
Ph: 925-456-2400 Fax: 925-456-2401 **Cuisine:** Regional
Owners: The Wente Family **Average Dinner for 2:** $80
Closed: Holidays

MENLO PARK

Dal Baffo
878 Santa Cruz Ave., Menlo Park, CA, 94025
Ph: 650-325-1588 Fax: 650-326-2780 **Cuisine:** Continental/Italian
Owner: Vincenzo Lo Grasso **Average Dinner for 2:** $100
Closed: Sunday

RUTHERFORD

Auberge du Soleil *page 101
180 Rutherford Hill Rd., Rutherford, CA, 94573
Ph: 707-963-1211 Fax: 707-963-8764 **Cuisine:** Regional
Owner: Claude Rouas **Average Dinner for 2:** $120

SACRAMENTO

Biba *page 102
2801 Capital Ave., Sacramento, CA, 95816
Ph: 916-455-2422 Fax: 916-455-0542 **Cuisine:** Italian
Owner: Biba Caggiano **Average Dinner for 2:** $70 **Closed:** Sunday

SAN FRANCISCO

Acquerello *page 102
1722 Sacramento St., San Francisco, CA, 94109
Ph: 415-567-5432 Fax: 415-567-6432 **Cuisine:** Regional Italian
Owner: Giancarlo Paterlini **Average Dinner for 2:** $80
Closed: Sunday, Monday

Aqua *page 103
252 California St., San Francisco, CA, 94111
Ph: 415-956-9662 Fax: 415-956-5229 **Cuisine:** Seafood
Owner: Charles Condy **Average Dinner for 2:** $100 **Closed:** Sunday

The Carnelian Room *page 103
555 California St., San Francisco, CA, 94104
Ph: 415-433-7500 Fax: 415-433-5827 **Cuisine:** Contemporary
American **Average Dinner for 2:** $70 **Closed:** Christmas, New Years

The Dining Room, The Ritz-Carlton
600 Stockton St., San Francisco, CA, 94108
Ph: 415-296-7465 Fax: 415-291-0147 **Cuisine:** Contemporary French
Average Dinner for 2: $130 **Closed:** Sunday

Fleur de Lys
777 Sutter St., San Francisco, CA, 94109
Ph: 415-673-7779 Fax: 415-673-4619 **Cuisine:** Modern French
Owners: H. Keller & M. Rouas **Average Dinner for 2:** $140
Closed: Sunday

Fournou's Ovens, Renaissance Stanford Hotel *page 104
905 California St., San Francisco, CA, 94108
Ph: 415-989-3500 Fax: 415-986-8195 **Cuisine:** California
Average Dinner for 2: $85

Harris' Restaurant *page 104
2100 Van Ness Ave., San Francisco, CA, 94109
Ph: 415-673-1888 Fax: 415-673-8817 **Cuisine:** Steakhouse
Owner: Ann Lee Harris **Average Dinner for 2:** $80
Closed: Holidays

La Folie
2316 Polk St., San Francisco, CA, 94109
Ph: 415-776-5577 Fax: 415-776-3431 **Cuisine:** Continental
Average Dinner for 2: $100 **Closed:** Holidays

Le Central *page 105
453 Bush St., San Francisco, CA, 94108
Ph: 415-391-2233 Fax: 415-391-3615 **Cuisine:** French
Owner: Michel Bonnet **Average Dinner for 2:** $70 **Closed:** Sunday

Masa's, Hotel Vintage Court *page 105
648 Bush St., San Francisco, CA, 94108
Ph: 415-989-7154 Fax: 415-989-3141 **Cuisine:** French
Owner: Bill Kimpton **Average Dinner for 2:** $150
Closed: Sunday, Monday

Mason's, The Fairmont Hotel
950 California St., San Francisco, CA, 94108
Ph: 415-772-5233 Fax: 415-772-5440 **Cuisine:** American Grill
Average Dinner for 2: $90 **Closed:** Sunday, Monday

The North Beach Restaurant *page 106
1512 Stockton St., San Francisco, CA, 94133
Ph: 415-392-1700 Fax: 415-392-0230 **Cuisine:** Contemporary
Average Dinner for 2: $90 **Closed:** Holidays

Postrio
545 Post St., San Francisco, CA, 94102
Ph: 415-776-7825 Fax: 415-776-6702 **Cuisine:** California
Owner: Wolfgang Puck **Average Dinner for 2:** $100
Closed: Holidays

Silks
222 Sansome St., San Francisco, CA, 94104
Ph: 415-986-2020 Fax: 415-267-0403 **Cuisine:** French/Provencal
Average Dinner for 2: $80 **Closed:** Monday

Splendido
4 Embarcadero Center, San Francisco, CA, 94111
Ph: 415-986-3222 Fax: 415-434-3530 **Cuisine:** New Italian
Owner: Bill Kimpton **Average Dinner for 2:** $50

Stars *page 106
555 Golden Gate Ave., San Francisco, CA, 94102
Ph: 415-861-7827 Fax: 415-554-0351 **Cuisine:** American
Owner: Jeremiah Tower **Average Dinner for 2:** $70
Closed: Christmas

Tommy Toy's Haute Cuisine Chinoise *page 107
655 Montgomery St., San Francisco, CA, 94111
Ph: 415-397-4888 Fax: 415-397-0469 **Cuisine:** Chinese with French
Influence **Owner:** Alon Yu **Average Dinner for 2:** $75
Closed: Thanksgiving, Christmas

SAN JOSE

Emile's *page 107
545 S. 2nd St., San Jose, CA, 95112
Ph: 408-289-1960 Fax: 408-998-1245 **Cuisine:** Contemporary
Continental **Owner:** Emile Mooser **Average Dinner for 2:** $70
Closed: Sunday, Monday

Paolo's Restaurant *page 108
333 W. San Carlos St., San Jose, CA, 95110
Ph: 408-294-2558 Fax: 408-294-2595 **Cuisine:** Italian
Owner: Carolyn Allen **Average Dinner for 2:** $70 **Closed:** Sunday

SARATOGA

Le Mouton Noir *page 108
14560 Big Basin Way, Saratoga, CA, 95070
Ph: 408-867-7017 Fax: 408-867-5048 **Cuisine:** Contemporary
Average Dinner for 2: $60

The Plumed Horse *page 110
14555 Big Basin Way, Saratoga, CA, 95070
Ph: 408-867-4711 Fax: 408-867-6919 **Cuisine:** American/Continental
Owners: Klaus & Yvonne Pache **Average Dinner for 2:** $100
Closed: Sunday

ST. HELENA

The Restaurant at Meadowood
900 Meadowood Lane, St. Helena, CA, 94574
Ph: 707-963-3646 Fax: 707-963-9532 **Cuisine:** California
Owner: William Harlan **Average Dinner for 2:** $100

Terra
1345 Railroad Ave., St. Helena, CA, 94574
Ph: 707-963-8931 **Cuisine:** Continental
Owners: H. Sone & L. Doumani **Average Dinner for 2:** $70
Closed: Tuesday

YOUNTVILLE

Domaine Chandon
1 California Dr., Yountville, CA, 94599
Ph: 707-944-2892 Fax: 707-944-1123 **Cuisine:** French/California
Average Dinner for 2: $100 **Closed:** First 3 weeks of January

The French Laundry
6640 Washington St., Yountville, CA, 94559
Ph: 707-944-2380 Fax: 707-944-1974 **Cuisine:** American/French
Owner: Thomas Keller **Average Dinner for 2:** $140

SOUTHERN CALIFORNIA

ANAHEIM

Hasting's Grill *page 110
777 Convention Way, Anaheim, CA, 92802
Ph: 714-740-4422 Fax: 714-740-4252 **Cuisine:** California
Average Dinner for 2: $80

JW's Steakhouse, Anaheim Marriott Hotel *page 111
700 W. Convention Way, Anaheim, CA, 92802
Ph: 714-750-8000 Fax: 714-750-9100 **Cuisine:** Steakhouse
Average Dinner for 2: $100 **Closed:** Sunday

Mr. Stox *page 111
1105 E. Katella Ave., Anaheim, CA, 92805
Ph: 714-634-2994 Fax: 714-634-0561 **Cuisine:** California
Owners: The Marshall Family **Average Dinner for 2:** $45
Closed: Holidays

Thee White House *page 112
887 S. Anaheim Blvd., Anaheim, CA, 92805
Ph: 714-772-1381 Fax: 714-772-7062 **Cuisine:** Northern Italian
Owner: Bruno Serato **Average Dinner for 2:** $85

BEVERLY HILLS

The Dining Room, Regent Beverly Wilshire
9500 Wilshire Blvd., Beverly Hills, CA, 90212
Ph: 310-274-8179 Fax: 310-274-2851 **Cuisine:** California/Continental
Average Dinner for 2: $85

The Grill on the Alley *page 112
9560 Dayton Way, Beverly Hills, CA, 90210
Ph: 310-276-0615 Fax: 310-276-0284 **Cuisine:** Classic American
Owner: Bob Spivak **Average Dinner for 2:** $80

Maple Drive
345 N. Maple Dr., Beverly Hills, CA, 90210
Ph: 310-274-9800 Fax: 310-274-2782 **Cuisine:** California/American
Owners: Leonard Schwartz & Partners **Average Dinner for 2:** $90
Closed: Sunday

BREA

La Vie en Rose *page 113
240 S. State College Blvd., Brea, CA, 92821-5820
Ph: 714-529-8333 Fax: 714-529-2751 **Cuisine:** French/Provencal
Owner: Louis Laulhere **Average Dinner for 2:** $95
Closed: Sunday, Holidays

CALABASAS

Saddle Peak Lodge *page 113
419 Cold Canyon Rd., Calabasas, CA, 91302
Ph: 818-222-3888 Fax: 818-222-1054 **Cuisine:** American
Owner: Ann Graham Ehringer **Average Dinner for 2:** $95
Closed: Monday, Tuesday

DANA POINT

The Dining Room, Ritz-Carlton
33533 Ritz-Carlton Dr., Dana Point, CA, 92629
Ph: 714-240-2000 Fax: 714-240-5044 **Cuisine:** French/Mediterranean
Average Dinner for 2: $110 **Closed:** Sunday, Monday

FULLERTON

The Cellar *page 114
305 N. Harbor Blvd., Fullerton, CA, 92832
Ph: 714-525-5682 Fax: 714-525-3853 **Cuisine:** Modern French
Owners: Gertrude & Ernest Zingg **Average Dinner for 2:** $80
Closed: Sunday, Monday

GLENDALE

Gennaro's
1109 N. Brand Blvd., Glendale, CA, 91202
Ph: 818-243-6231 Fax: 818-246-6627 **Cuisine:** Italian
Owner: Gennaro Rosato **Average Dinner for 2:** $75

IRVINE

Chanteclair *page 114
18912 MacArthur Blvd., Irvine, CA, 92612
Ph: 949-752-8001 Fax: 949-955-1394 **Cuisine:** French Provencal
Owner: John Kookootsedes **Average Dinner for 2:** $65
Closed: Holidays

LA JOLLA

Cindy Black's
5721 La Jolla Blvd., La Jolla, CA, 92037
Ph: 619-456-6299 Fax: 619-456-0390 **Cuisine:** California
Average Dinner for 2: $60 **Closed:** Sunday, Monday

George's at the Cove *page 115
1250 Prospect St., La Jolla, CA, 92037
Ph: 619-454-4244 Fax: 619-454-5458 **Cuisine:** California
Owner: George Hauer **Average Dinner for 2:** $80

The Marine Room, La Jolla Beach & Tennis Club *page 115
2000 Spindrift Dr., La Jolla, CA, 92037
Ph: 619-459-7222 Fax: 619-551-4673 **Cuisine:** California/Pacific Rim
Average Dinner for 2: $80

The Sky Room
1132 Prospect St., La Jolla, CA, 92037
Ph: 619-454-0771 Fax: 619-456-3921 **Cuisine:** French
Average Dinner for 2: $90

Top O' The Cove
1216 Prospect St., La Jolla, CA, 92037
Ph: 619-454-7779 Fax: 619-454-3783 **Cuisine:** Continental
Owner: R. R. Zappardino **Average Dinner for 2:** $100

LOS ANGELES

Bernard's *page 116
506 S. Grand Ave., Los Angeles, CA, 90071
Ph: 213-612-1580 Fax: 213-612-1628 **Cuisine:** Continental
Average Dinner for 2: $120 **Closed:** Sunday, Monday

Campanile
624 S. La Brea Ave., Los Angeles, CA, 90036
Ph: 213-938-1447 Fax: 213-935-5480
Cuisine: California/Mediterranean **Average Dinner for 2:** $80
Closed: Sunday, Holidays

Diaghilev, Wyndham Belage Hotel
1020 N. San Vincent Blvd., West Hollywood, CA, 90069
Ph: 310-854-1111 Fax: 310-854-0926 **Cuisine:** Franco-Russian
Average Dinner for 2: $140

The Dynasty Room
930 Hilgard Ave., Los Angeles, CA, 90024
Ph: 310-208-8765 Fax: 310-824-0355 **Cuisine:** Continental
Average Dinner for 2: $120

Fenix at the Argyle
8358 Sunset Blvd., West Hollywood, CA, 90069
Ph: 213-848-6677 Fax: 213-654-9287 **Cuisine:** California
Average Dinner for 2: $120 **Closed:** Holidays

The Gardens *page 116
300 S. Doheny Dr., Los Angeles, CA, 90048
Ph: 310-273-2222 Fax: 310-274-3891 **Cuisine:** California
Average Dinner for 2: $100

L' Orangerie
903 N. La Cienega Blvd., Los Angeles, CA, 90069
Ph: 310-652-9770 Fax: 310-652-8870 **Cuisine:** Modern French
Owner: Gerard Ferry **Average Dinner for 2:** $140
Closed: Monday

Le Dome
8720 Sunset Blvd., Los Angeles, CA, 90069
Ph: 310-659-6919 Fax: 310-659-5429 **Cuisine:** French/Provencal
Owner: Eddy Kerkhofs **Average Dinner for 2:** $80
Closed: Sunday

Le Petit Chateau *page 117
4615 Lankershim Blvd., North Hollywood, CA, 91602
Ph: 818-769-1812 Fax: 818-769-3431 **Cuisine:** French
Owners: Andrew & Christine Higgs **Average Dinner for 2:** $65

Matsuhisa
129 N. La Cienega Blvd., West Hollywood, CA, 90211
Ph: 310-659-9639 Fax: 310-659-0492 **Cuisine:** Japanese
Average Dinner for 2: $130 **Closed:** Holidays

Patina
5955 Melrose Ave., Los Angeles, CA, 90038
Ph: 213-467-1108 Fax: 213-467-1924 **Cuisine:** Modern French
Owner: Joachim Splichal **Average Dinner for 2:** $120

The Restaurant at the Hotel Bel Air
701 Stone Canyon Rd., Los Angeles, CA, 90077
Ph: 310-472-1211 Fax: **Cuisine:** American/Continental
Average Dinner for 2: $100

Spago
1114 Horn Ave., West Hollywood, CA, 90069
Ph: 310-652-4025 Fax: 310-657-0927 **Cuisine:** California
Owner: Wolfgang Puck **Average Dinner for 2:** $90

MALIBU

Granita
23725 W. Malibu Rd., Malibu, CA, 90265
Ph: 310-456-0488 Fax: 310-456-8317 **Cuisine:** California
Owner: Wolfgang Puck **Average Dinner for 2:** $75

MARINA DEL REY

Café Del Rey *page 117
4451 Admiralty Way, Marina del Rey, CA, 90292
Ph: 310-823-6395 Fax: 310-821-3734 **Cuisine:** California/Pacific
Rim **Average Dinner for 2:** $75 **Closed:** Thanksgiving, Christmas

NEWPORT BEACH

Pascal
1000 N. Bristol St., Newport Beach, CA, 92660
Ph: 714-752-0107 Fax: 714-752-4942 **Cuisine:** French/Provencal
Owners: Mimi & Pascal Olhats **Average Dinner for 2:** $75
Closed: Sunday

Pavilion, The Four Seasons Hotel *page 118
690 Newport Center Dr., Newport Beach, CA, 92660
Ph: 949-760-4920 Fax: 949-760-8073 **Cuisine:** California
Average Dinner for 2: $80

Ritz Restaurant and Garden *page 118
880 Newport Center Dr., Newport Beach, CA, 92660
Ph: 949-720-1800 Fax: 949-720-8753 **Cuisine:**
American/Continental **Average Dinner for 2:** $60

PALM DESERT

LG's Prime Steak House *page 119
74225 Hwy 111, Palm Desert, CA, 92260
Ph: 760-779-9799 Fax: 760-779-1979 **Cuisine:** Steakhouse
Average Dinner for 2: $70 **Closed:** Holidays

PALM SPRINGS

Le Vallauris
385 W. Tahquitz Canyon Way, Palm Springs, CA, 92262
Ph: 619-325-5059 Fax: 619-325-7602 **Cuisine:** French
Owners: P. Bruggemans & M. Despras **Average Dinner for 2:** $80

RANCHO MIRAGE

The Dining Room, Ritz-Carlton
68-900 Frank Sinatra Dr., Rancho Mirage, CA, 92270
Ph: 619-321-8282 Fax: 760-770-7605 **Cuisine:** Continental
Average Dinner for 2: $130

Wally's Desert Turtle
71-775 Hwy 111, Rancho Mirage, CA, 92270
Ph: 760-568-9321 Fax: 760-568-9713 **Cuisine:** Continental
Owner: Michael Botello **Average Dinner for 2:** $90
Closed: Seasonally

RANCHO SANTA FE

Mille Fleurs *page 119
6009 Paseo Delicias, Rancho Santa Fe, CA, 92067
Ph: 619-756-3085 Fax: 619-756-9945 **Cuisine:** California/French
Owner: Bertrand Hug **Average Dinner for 2:** $100

SAN DIEGO

El Bizcocho, Rancho Bernardo Inn *page 120
17550 Bernardo Oaks Dr., San Diego, CA, 92128
Ph: 619-675-8550 Fax: 619-675-8443 **Cuisine:** French
Average Dinner for 2: $100

Grant Grill, U.S. Grant Hotel *page 120
326 Broadway, San Diego, CA, 92101
Ph: 619-239-6806 Fax: 619-239-9517 **Cuisine:** American
Average Dinner for 2: $80

Mister A's Restaurant
2550 5th Ave., San Diego, CA, 92103
Ph: 619-239-1377 Fax: 619-544-0744 **Cuisine:** Continental
Average Dinner for 2: $75 **Closed:** Holidays

Star of the Sea *page 120
1360 N. Harbor Dr., San Diego, CA, 92110
Ph: 619-232-7408 Fax: 619-232-1877
Cuisine: California/Continental **Owners:** Ghio, Weber & Mascari
Average Dinner for 2: $75 **Closed:** Holidays

SANTA BARBARA

Downey's *page 121
1305 State St., Santa Barbara, CA, 93101
Ph: 805-966-5006 Fax: 805-966-5000 **Cuisine:** Contemporary
Regional **Owner:** John Downey **Average Dinner for 2:** $80
Closed: Monday

SANTA MONICA

Michael's
1147 3rd St., Santa Monica, CA, 90403
Ph: 310-451-0843 Fax: 310-394-1830 **Cuisine:** Contemporary
American **Owner:** Michael McCarty **Average Dinner for 2:** $70
Closed: Sunday, Monday

Valentino
3115 Pico Blvd., Santa Monica, CA, 90405
Ph: 310-829-4313 Fax: 310-315-2791 **Cuisine:** Italian
Owner: Piero Selvaggio **Average Dinner for 2:** $100

VENICE

72 Market Street Oyster Bar & Grill *page 122
72 Market St., Venice, CA, 90291
Ph: 310-392-8720 Fax: 310-392-8665 **Cuisine:** American
Owners: Tony Bill, Dudley Moore & Roland Gibert
Average Dinner for 2: $90

MONTEREY PENINSULA

CARMEL

The Covey, Quail Lodge Resort *page 122
8205 Valley Greens Dr., Carmel, CA, 93923
Ph: 831-624-1581 Fax: 831-624-3726
Cuisine: American/Continental **Average Dinner for 2:** $70

The French Poodle *page 123
NW corner of Junipero & 5th St., Carmel, CA, 93921
Ph: 408-624-8643 Fax: 408-625-6264 **Cuisine:** Classical French
Owners: Richard & Anamaria Zoellin **Average Dinner for 2:** $80
Closed: Sunday

Pacific's Edge, Highlands Inn *page 123
Highway 1, Carmel, CA, 93921
Ph: 831-624-3801 Fax: 831-626-1574 **Cuisine:** California
Average Dinner for 2: $100

Raffaello *page 124
Mission St. between Ocean & 7th, Carmel, CA, 93921
Ph: 831-624-1541 Fax: 831-624-9411 **Cuisine:** Northern Italian
Owner: Remo d'Agliano **Average Dinner for 2:** $60
Closed: Tuesday

MONTEREY

Fresh Cream *page 124
100 Heritage Harbor, Monterey, CA, 93940
Ph: 408-375-9798 Fax: 408-375-2283 **Cuisine:** French/California
Owners: Ted Balestreri & Bert Cutino **Average Dinner for 2:** $80
Closed: Christmas Eve

Sardine Factory *page 125
701 Wave St., Monterey, CA, 93940
Ph: 831-373-3775 Fax: 831-373-4241 **Cuisine:** Seafood
Average Dinner for 2: $80 **Closed:** Holidays

PEBBLE BEACH

Club XIX, The Lodge at Pebble Beach *page 125
17 Mile Dr., Pebble Beach, CA, 93953
Ph: 831-625-8519 Fax: 831-622-8746 **Cuisine:** French
Average Dinner for 2: $100

COLORADO

ASPEN

Pinons Restaurant
105 S. Mill St., Aspen, CO, 81611
Ph: 970-920-2021 Fax: 970-920-9035 **Cuisine:** American
Owner: Paul Chanin **Average Dinner for 2:** $100
Closed: Seasonally

The Restaurant at the Little Nell Hotel *page 127
675 E. Durant Ave., Aspen, CO, 81611
Ph: 970-920-6330 Fax: 970-920-6328 **Cuisine:** Regional
Average Dinner for 2: $90

Syzygy *page 127
520 E. Hyman Ave., Aspen, CO, 81611
Ph: 970-925-3700 Fax: 970-925-5593 **Cuisine:** International
Owner: Walter Harris **Average Dinner for 2:** $50
Closed: Seasonally

Beano's Cabin
Beaver Creek Mountain, Avon, CO, 81620
Ph: 970-949-5750 Fax: 970-845-5769 **Cuisine:** Contemporary
American **Average Dinner for 2:** $150 **Closed:** Seasonally

Mirabelle
55 Village Rd., Beaver Creek, CO, 81620
Ph: 970-949-7728 Fax: 970-845-9578 **Cuisine:** French/Belgian
Owner: Luc Meyer **Average Dinner for 2:** $80 **Closed:** Sunday

BOULDER

Flagstaff House Restaurant *page 128
1138 Flagstaff Rd., Boulder, CO, 80302
Ph: 303-442-4640 Fax: 303-442-8924
Cuisine: American/Continental **Owners:** The Monette Family
Average Dinner for 2: $120 **Closed:** Thanksgiving, Christmas

DENVER

The Broker *page 128
821 17th St., Denver, CO, 80202
Ph: 303-292-5065 Fax: 303-292-2652 **Cuisine:** Steakhouse
Owners: E. Novak & G. Fritzler **Average Dinner for 2:** $70
Closed: Christmas

Cliff Young's *page 129
700 E.17th Ave., Denver, CO, 80203-1405
Ph: 303-831-8900 Fax: 303-831-0360
Cuisine: Contemporary Continental **Owner:** J. Stewart Jackson
Average Dinner for 2: $110 **Closed:** Sunday

Palace Arms, The Brown Palace Hotel
321 17th St., Denver, CO, 80202
Ph: 303-297-3111 Fax: 303-297-3928 **Cuisine:** Continental
Average Dinner for 2: $90

Strings
1700 Humboldt St., Denver, CO, 80218
Ph: 303-831-7310 Fax: 303-860-8812
Cuisine: Contemporary American
Owner: Noel Cunningham **Average Dinner for 2:** $80

Tante Louise *page 129
4900 E. Colfax Ave., Denver, CO, 80220
Ph: 303-355-4488 Fax: 303-321-6312 **Cuisine:** Modern French
Average Dinner for 2: $60 **Closed:** Sunday

EDWARDS

Restaurant Picasso
2205 Cordillera Way, Edwards, CO, 81632
Ph: 970-926-2200 Fax: 970-926-2486 **Cuisine:** Continental
Owners: Felix & Jane Posen **Average Dinner for 2:** $120

KEYSTONE

The Keystone Ranch
PO Box 38, Keystone, CO, 80435
Ph: 970-468-4187 Fax: 970-468-4028 **Cuisine:** American
Average Dinner for 2: $100 **Closed:** Seasonally

VAIL

The Left Bank, The Sitzmark Lodge
183 Gore Creek Dr., Vail, CO, 81657
Ph: 970-476-3696 Fax: 970-476-3723 **Cuisine:** French/American
Owners: Luc & Elizabeth Meyer **Average Dinner for 2:** $100
Closed: Wednesday

Ludwig's, Sonnenalp Resort *page 130
20 Vail Rd., Vail, CO, 81657
Ph: 970-476-5656 Fax: 970-476-8066 **Cuisine:** Bavarian
Average Dinner for 2: $90

Sweet Basil
193 E. Gore Creek Dr., Vail, CO, 81657
Ph: 970-476-0125 Fax: 970-476-0137 **Cuisine:** American
Owner: Kevin Clair **Average Dinner for 2:** $90

Wildflower, The Lodge at Vail *page 130
174 E. Gore Creek Dr., Vail, CO, 81657
Ph: 970-476-5011 Fax: 970-476-7425 **Cuisine:** American
Owner: Scott Englemann **Average Dinner for 2:** $130
Closed: Seasonally

CONNECTICUT

GREENWICH

Restaurant Jean-Louis
61 Lewis St., Greenwich, CT, 06830
Ph: 203-622-8450 Fax: 203-622-5845 **Cuisine:** French
Owner: Jean-Louis Gerin **Average Dinner for 2:** $120
Closed: Sunday

MANCHESTER

Cavey's *page 131
45 E. Center St., Manchester, CT, 06040
Ph: 860-643-2751 Fax: 860-649-0344
Cuisine: French/Northern Italian
Owners: Steven & Kate Cavagnaro **Average Dinner for 2:** $100
Closed: Sunday, Monday

RIDGEFIELD

The Inn at Ridgefield
20 W. Lane, Ridgefield, CT, 06877
Ph: 203-438-8282 Fax: 203-431-3614 **Cuisine:** American
Average Dinner for 2: $100

The Stonehenge Inn
Route 7, Ridgefield, CT, 06877
Ph: 203-438-6511 Fax: 203-438-2478 **Cuisine:** French/American
Owner: Douglas Seville **Average Dinner for 2:** $80
Closed: Monday

DELAWARE

WILMINGTON

Columbus Inn *page 131
2216 Pennsylvania Ave., Wilmington, DE, 19806
Ph: 302-571-1492 Fax: 302-571-1111 **Cuisine:** American
Average Dinner for 2: $45 **Closed:** Christmas, New Years

DISTRICT OF COLUMBIA

WASHINGTON

1789 Restaurant *page 132
1226 36th St. N.W., Washington, DC, 20007
Ph: 202-965-1789 Fax: 202-337-1541 **Cuisine:** American
Owner: Clydes Restaurant Group **Average Dinner for 2:** $80
Closed: Christmas

701 Pennsylvania Avenue *page 132
701 Pennsylvania Ave. N.W., Washington, DC, 20004
Ph: 202-393-0701 Fax: 202-393-6493 **Cuisine:** American
Owner: Ashok Bajaj **Average Dinner for 2:** $75 **Closed:** Sunday

The Bombay Club *page 133
815 Connecticut Ave. N.W., Washington, DC, 20006
Ph: 202-659-3727 Fax: 202-659-5012 **Cuisine:** Indian
Owner: Ashok Bajaj **Average Dinner for 2:** $110

Galileo *page 133
1110 21st St. N.W., Washington, DC, 20036
Ph: 202-293-7191 Fax: 202-331-9364 **Cuisine:** Italian
Owner: Roberto Donna **Average Dinner for 2:** $120

i Ricchi *page 134
1220 19th St. N.W., Washington, DC, 20036
Ph: 202-835-0459 Fax: 202-872-1220 **Cuisine:** Tuscan
Owners: C. Russo Ricchi & F. Ricchi **Average Dinner for 2:** $120
Closed: Sunday

Kinkead's
2000 Pennsylvania Ave. N.W., Washington, DC, 20006
Ph: 202-296-7700 Fax: 202-296-7688 **Cuisine:** Seafood
Owner: Robert Kinkead **Average Dinner for 2:** $110

Melrose, The Park Hyatt Hotel *page 134
24th at M St. N.W., Washington, DC, 20037
Ph: 202-955-3899 Fax: 202-408-6118 **Cuisine:** International
Average Dinner for 2: $75

Morrison Clark Inn *page 135
Massachusetts Ave. & 11th St. N.W., Washington, DC, 20001
Ph: 202-898-1200 Fax: 202-289-8576 **Cuisine:** Regional
Average Dinner for 2: $85

Nora
2132 Florida Ave. N.W., Washington, DC, 20008
Ph: 202-462-5143 Fax: 202-234-6232
Cuisine: Organic International **Owners:** N. Pouillon & S. Damato
Average Dinner for 2: $80 **Closed:** Sunday

The Prime Rib *page 135
2020 K Street N.W., Washington, DC, 20006
Ph: 202-466-8811 Fax: 202-466-2010 **Cuisine:** American
Owner: C. Peter BeLer **Average Dinner for 2:** $110
Closed: Sunday

Sam & Harry's *page 135
1200 19th St. N.W., Washington, DC, 20036
Ph: 202-296-4333 Fax: 202-785-1070 **Cuisine:** American
Owners: M. Sternberg & L. Work **Average Dinner for 2:** $110
Closed: Sunday

Vidalia *page 136
1990 M St. N.W., Washington, DC, 20036
Ph: 202-659-1990 Fax: 202-223-8572 **Cuisine:** Regional
Owners: Jeffrey & Sallie Buben **Average Dinner for 2:** $100

The Willard Room, Willard Intercontinental Hotel
1401 Pennsylvania Ave. N.W., Washington, DC, 20004
Ph: 202-637-7440 Fax: 202-637-7326
Cuisine: American/Continental **Average Dinner for 2:** $100

FLORIDA

NORTH FLORIDA AND THE PANHANDLE

DESTIN

Elephant Walk, The Resort at Sandestin *page 138
9300 Hwy 98 W., Destin, FL, 32541
Ph: 850-267-4800 Fax: 850-267-6120 **Cuisine:** American
Average Dinner for 2: $65

Marina Café *page 138
404 E. Hwy. 98, Destin, FL, 32540
Ph: 850-837-7960 Fax: 850-837-3047
Cuisine: Mediterranean/Creole
Average Dinner for 2: $75 **Closed:** Holidays

GRAYTON BEACH

Criolla's
170 E. Scenic Highway 30-A, Grayton Beach, FL, 32459
Ph: 850-267-1267 Fax: 850-231-4568 **Cuisine:** Caribbean Creole
Owner: John Earles **Average Dinner for 2:** $80 **Closed:** Sunday

JACKSONVILLE

La Cena Ristorante *page 139
6271-7 Saint Augustine Rd., Jacksonville, FL, 32217
Ph: 904-737-5350 Fax: 904-733-7980 **Cuisine:** Italian
Owner: Jerry Moran **Average Dinner for 2:** $45
Closed: Sunday, Monday

CENTRAL FORIDA

ALTAMONTE SPRINGS

Maison & Jardin
430 S. Wymore Rd., Altamonte Springs, FL, 32714
Ph: 407-862-4410 Fax: 407-862-0557 **Cuisine:** Continental
Owner: William R. Beuret **Average Dinner for 2:** $95
Closed: Sundays (seasonally)

Ruth's Chris Steak House *page 140
999 Douglas Ave., Altamonte Springs, FL, 32714
Ph: 407-682-6444 Fax: 407-682-7055 **Cuisine:** Steakhouse
Owner: Ruth V. Furtel **Average Dinner for 2:** $80
Closed: Thanksgiving, Christmas

LONGWOOD

Peter Scott's *page 140
1811 W. State Rd. 434, Longwood, FL, 32750
Ph: 407-834-4477 Fax: 407-834-2414
Cuisine: American/Continental
Average Dinner for 2: $60 **Closed:** Sunday, Monday

ORLANDO

Atlantis, Renaissance Orlando Resort *page 141
6677 Sea Harbor Dr., Orlando, FL, 32821
Ph: 407-351-5555 Fax: 407-363-9247 **Cuisine:** French/Seafood
Average Dinner for 2: $105 **Closed:** Sunday

Christini's Ristorante Italiano *page 141
7600 Dr. Phillips Blvd., Orlando, FL, 32819
Ph: 407-345-8770 Fax: 407-345-8700 **Cuisine:** Northern Italian
Average Dinner for 2: $70 **Closed:** Holidays

Dux at The Peabody Orlando *page 142
9801 International Dr., Orlando, FL, 32819
Ph: 407-345-4550 Fax: 407-363-1505 **Cuisine:** International
Average Dinner for 2: $95 **Closed:** Sunday

Haifeng, Renaissance Orlando Resort *page 142
6677 Sea Harbor Dr., Orlando, FL, 32821
Ph: 407-351-5555 Fax: 407-351-9991 **Cuisine:** Asian
Average Dinner for 2: $60 **Closed:** Holidays

La Coquina, The Hyatt Regency Hotel *page 143
1 Grand Cypress Blvd., Orlando, FL, 32836
Ph: 407-239-1234 Fax: 407-239-3800
Cuisine: Contemporary American
Average Dinner for 2: $120 **Closed:** Monday

Manuel's on the 28th *page 143
380 State Lane, Orlando, FL, 32801
Ph: 407-246-6580 Fax: 407-246-6575 **Cuisine:** Continental
Owner: Manny Garcia **Average Dinner for 2:** $100
Closed: Sunday, Monday

Victoria & Albert's
4401 Grand Floridian Way, Orlando, FL, 32830
Ph: 407-824-1089 Fax: 407-824-1053 **Cuisine:** American
Average Dinner for 2: $220

WEST COAST OF FLORIDA

LONGBOAT KEY

The Colony Beach and Tennis Resort *page 144
1620 Gulf of Mexico Dr., Longboat Key, FL, 34228
Ph: 941-383-5558 Fax: 941-387-0250 **Cuisine:** Regional
Owner: M. Klauber **Average Dinner for 2:** $100

Euphemia Haye
5540 Gulf of Mexico Dr., Longboat Key, FL, 34228
Ph: 941-383-3633 Fax: 941-387-8336 **Cuisine:** Continental
Owners: Ray & D'arcy Arpke **Average Dinner for 2:** $90

NAPLES

The Dining Room, Ritz-Carlton
280 Vanderbilt Beach Rd., Naples, FL, 34108
Ph: 941-598-3300 Fax: 941-598-6691
Cuisine: Continental **Average Dinner for 2:** $130

Lafite *page 144
475 Seagate Dr., Naples, FL, 33940
Ph: 941-597-3232 Fax: 941-597-7168 **Cuisine:** Regional
Average Dinner for 2: $100

Restaurant on the Bay by Marie-Michelle *page 145
4236 Gulf Shore Blvd. N., Naples, FL, 34103
Ph: 941-263-0900 Fax: 941-267-0850 **Cuisine:** Mediterranean
Owner: Marie-Michelle Rey **Average Dinner for 2:** $65
Closed: Sundays in Off-Season

Sign of the Vine
980 Solana Rd., Naples, FL, 33940
Ph: 941-261-6745 Fax: **Cuisine:** American/Continental
Owners: John & Nancy Christiansen **Average Dinner for 2:** $100
Closed: Sunday

Villa Pescatore
8920 N. Tamiami Tr., Naples, FL, 34108
Ph: 941-597-8119 Fax: 941-597-8332 **Cuisine:** Italian
Average Dinner for 2: $65

SARASOTA

Café L'Europe *page 145
431 St. Armands Circle, Sarasota, FL, 34236
Ph: 941-388-4415 Fax: 941-388-2362 **Cuisine:** Continental
Owner: Titus Letshert **Average Dinner for 2:** $75

Michael's on East *page 146
1212 E. Ave S., Sarasota, FL, 34239
Ph: 941-366-0007 Fax: 941-953-3463
Cuisine: Contemporary American
Owner: Michael Klaubner **Average Dinner for 2:** $75

TAMPA

Armani's, The Hyatt Regency Westshore *page 146
6200 Courtney Campbell Causeway, Tampa, FL, 33607
Ph: 813-281-9165 Fax: 813-281-9168 **Cuisine:** Northern Italian
Average Dinner for 2: $85 **Closed:** Sunday, Holidays

Bern's Steak House *page 147
1208 S. Howard Ave., Tampa, FL, 33606
Ph: 813-251-2421 Fax: 813-251-5001 **Cuisine:** American
Owner: David Laxer **Average Dinner for 2:** $65
Closed: Christmas Day

SOUTH FLORIDA

AVENTURA

Chef Allen's *page 147
19088 N.E. 29th Ave., Aventura, FL, 33180
Ph: 305-935-2900 Fax: 305-935-9062 **Cuisine:** International
Owner: Allen Susser **Average Dinner for 2:** $95
Closed: Super Bowl Sunday

BOCA RATON

Chef Reto's
41 E. Palmetto Park Rd., Boca Raton, FL, 33432
Ph: 561-395-0633 Fax: 561-395-5074 **Cuisine:** Regional
Owner: Reto Demarmels **Average Dinner for 2:** $75

La Finestra
171 E. Palmetto Park Rd., Boca Raton, FL, 33432
Ph: 561-392-1838 Fax: 561-392-0632 **Cuisine:** Northern Italian
Owner: Tony Pepas **Average Dinner for 2:** $75 **Closed:** Sunday

La Vieille Maison
770 E Palmetto Park Rd., Boca Raton, FL, 33432
Ph: 561-391-6701 Fax: 561-368-4507 **Cuisine:** French Provencal
Average Dinner for 2: $90

Maxaluna Tuscan Grill
5050 Town Center Cr., Boca Raton, FL, 33486
Ph: 561-391-7177 Fax: 561-392-9308 **Cuisine:** Italian
Owner: Dennis Max **Average Dinner for 2:** $85
Closed: Thanksgiving

CORAL GABLES

Caffe Abbracci
318 Aragon Ave., Coral Gables, FL, 33133
Ph: 305-441-0700 Fax: 305-442-0061 **Cuisine:** Northern Italian
Owner: Nino Pernetti **Average Dinner for 2:** $70

Christy's
3101 Ponce de Leon Blvd., Coral Gables, FL, 33134
Ph: 305-446-1400 Fax: 305-446-3257 **Cuisine:** Steak/Seafood
Owner: Michael Namour **Average Dinner for 2:** $40

Giacosa
394 Giralda Ave., Coral Gables, FL, 33134
Ph: 305-445-5858 Fax: 305-445-6973 **Cuisine:** Italian
Owner: Alfredo Alvarez **Average Dinner for 2:** $70

Le Festival
2120 Salzedo St., Coral Gables, FL, 33134
Ph: 305-442-8545 Fax: 305-445-5563 **Cuisine:** French
Owners: Rodolfo Gil & Rafael Cuenca **Average Dinner for 2:** $90
Closed: Sunday

Norman's
21 Almeria Ave., Coral Gables, FL, 33134
Ph: 305-446-6767 Fax: 305-446-7909
Cuisine: Contemporary American
Owner: Norman Van Aken **Average Dinner for 2:** $75
Closed: Sunday

Restaurant St. Michel *page 148
162 Alcazar Ave., Coral Gables, FL, 33134
Ph: 305-444-1666 Fax: 305-529-0074
Cuisine: Contemporary American
Owner: Stuart Bornstein **Average Dinner for 2:** $80

Ristorante La Bussola *page 148
264 Giraldo Ave., Coral Gables, FL, 33134
Ph: 305-445-8783 Fax: 305-441-6435 **Cuisine:** Northern Italian
Owner: Elizabeth Giordano **Average Dinner for 2:** $90

FORT LAUDERDALE

Burt & Jacks *page 149
Berth 23 - Port Everglades, Ft. Lauderdale, FL, 33335
Ph: 954-522-5225 Fax: 954-522-2048 **Cuisine:** American
Owners: Jack Jackson & Burt Reynolds
Average Dinner for 2: $75 **Closed:** Christmas Day

Eduardo de San Angel *page 149
2822 E. Commercial Blvd., Ft. Lauderdale, FL, 33308
Ph: 954-772-4731 Fax: 954-772-0794 **Cuisine:** Mexican
Owners: Jose, Luis & Rafael Pria **Average Dinner for 2:** $90
Closed: Sunday, Monday

il Tartufo on Las Olas *page 150
2400 E. Las Olas Blvd., Ft. Lauderdale, FL, 33301
Ph: 954-767-9190 Fax: 954-767-9821 **Cuisine:** Italian
Owner: Gianni Minervini **Average Dinner for 2:** $60

Sheffield's *page 150
3030 Holiday Dr., Ft. Lauderdale, FL, 33316
Ph: 954-766-6100 Fax: 954-766-6165 **Cuisine:** Continental
Average Dinner for 2: $90 **Closed:** Holidays

MANALAPAN

The Grill, The Ritz-Carlton
100 S. Ocean Blvd., Manalapan, FL, 33462
Ph: 561-533-6000 Fax: 561-588-4202
Cuisine: American Continental **Average Dinner for 2:** $120

MIAMI

Le Pavillon
100 Chopin Plaza, Miami, FL, 33131
Ph: 305-372-4494 Fax: 305-372-4477 **Cuisine:** Continental
Average Dinner for 2: $100 **Closed:** Holidays

MIAMI BEACH

The Forge
432 Arthur Godfrey Rd., Miami Beach, FL, 33140
Ph: 305-538-8533 Fax: 305-538-7733 **Cuisine:** Steak/Seafood
Average Dinner for 2: $80 **Closed:** Holidays

PALM BEACH

Café L'Europe *page 151
331 S. County Rd., Palm Beach, FL, 33480-4443
Ph: 561-655-4020 Fax: 561-659-6619 **Cuisine:** French/American
Owners: Norbert & Lidia Goldner **Average Dinner for 2:** $125

The Restaurant, The Four Seasons Hotel
2800 S. Ocean Blvd., Palm Beach, FL, 33480
Ph: 561-533-3750 Fax: 561-586-3393 **Cuisine:** American/Caribbean
Owners: L. Sachs & R. Malesardi **Average Dinner for 2:** $150
Closed: Monday

PALM BEACH GARDENS

Café Chardonnay *page 151
4533 PGA Blvd., Palm Beach Gardens, FL, 33418
Ph: 561-627-2662 Fax: 561-627-3413 **Cuisine:** American
Owners: Frank & Gigi Eucalitto **Average Dinner for 2:** $70
Closed: Christmas, Thanksgiving

PEMBROKE PINES

Capriccio *page 152
2424 N. University Dr., Pembroke Pines, FL, 33024
Ph: 954-432-7001 Fax: 954-432-7560 **Cuisine:** Italian
Average Dinner for 2: $45

POMPANO BEACH

Darrel & Oliver's Café Maxx *page 152
2601 E. Atlantic Blvd., Pompano Beach, FL, 33062
Ph: 954-782-0606 Fax: 954-782-0648 **Cuisine:** Regional
Owners: Oliver Saucy & Darrel Broeck **Average Dinner for 2:** $80
Closed: Holidays

VERO BEACH

Café du Soir
21 Royal Palm Blvd., Vero Beach, FL, 32960
Ph: 561-569-4607 **Cuisine:** French
Owners: Yannick & Valerie Martin **Average Dinner for 2:** $70
Closed: Sunday, Monday

FLORIDA KEYS

ISLAMORADA

Atlantic's Edge, Cheeca Lodge
Mile Marker 82, Islamorada, FL, 33036
Ph: 800-327-2888 Fax: 305-664-2893 **Cuisine:** Seafood
Average Dinner for 2: $75

Marker 88 *page 153
Mile Marker 88, Overseas Hwy., Islamorada, FL, 33036
Ph: 305-852-9315 Fax: 305-852-9069 **Cuisine:** Continental/Seafood
Owner: Andre Mueller **Average Dinner for 2:** $70
Closed: Monday

KEY WEST

Café des Artistes
1007 Simonton St., Key West, FL, 33040
Ph: 305-294-7100 Fax: 305-296-5504 **Cuisine:** French
Owner: Timothy Ryan **Average Dinner for 2:** $90

Café Marquesa, The Marquesa Hotel
600 Fleming St., Key West, FL, 33040
Ph: 305-292-1244 Fax: 305-294-2121 **Cuisine:** International
Average Dinner for 2: $90

Louie's Backyard
700 Waddell Ave., Key West, FL, 33040
Ph: 305-294-1061 Fax: 605-294-0002 **Cuisine:** American
Owners: Phil & Pat Tenney **Average Dinner for 2:** $85
Closed: Christmas

Square One
1075 Duval St., Key West, FL, 33040
Ph: 305-296-4300 Fax: 305-292-5039
Cuisine: Contemporary American
Owner: Michael Stewart **Average Dinner for 2:** $60

GEORGIA

ATLANTA

103 West *page 153
103 W. Paces Ferry Rd. N.W., Atlanta, GA, 30305
Ph: 404-233-5993 Fax: 404-240-6619
Cuisine: American/Continental
Owner: Pano Karatassos **Average Dinner for 2:** $90
Closed: Sunday

1848 House *page 154
780 S. Cobb Dr., Marietta, GA, 30060
Ph: 770-428-1848 Fax: 770-427-5886
Cuisine: Contemporary Southern
Owner: William B. Dunaway **Average Dinner for 2:** $75
Closed: Monday

Abruzzi Ristorante
2355 Peachtree Rd. N.E., Atlanta, GA, 30305
Ph: 404-261-8186 Fax: **Cuisine:** Regional Italian
Owner: Nicola Pertucci **Average Dinner for 2:** $80
Closed: Sunday

Bone's Restaurant *page 154
3130 Piedmont Rd., Atlanta, GA, 30305
Ph: 404-237-2663 Fax: 404-233-5704 **Cuisine:** Steak/Seafood
Owners: Richard Lewis & Susan DeRose
Average Dinner for 2: $100 **Closed:** Holidays

Chops *page 155
70 W. Paces Ferry Rd., Atlanta, GA, 30305
Ph: 404-262-2675 Fax: 404-240-6645 **Cuisine:** Steakhouse
Owner: Pano Karatassos **Average Dinner for 2:** $90

Chopstix
4279 Roswell Rd., Atlanta, GA, 30342
Ph: 404-255-4868 Fax: 404-255 **Cuisine:** International
Average Dinner for 2: $100

Ciboulette
1529 Piedmont Ave. N.E., Atlanta, GA, 30324
Ph: 404-874-7600 Fax: 404-875-7074 **Cuisine:** Modern French
Average Dinner for 2: $80

City Grill
50 Hurt Plaza, Atlanta, GA, 30303
Ph: 404-524-2489 Fax: 404-529-9474 **Cuisine:** Regional
Average Dinner for 2: $75 **Closed:** Sunday, Holidays

The Dining Room, Ritz-Carlton Buckhead *page 155
3434 Peachtree Rd. N.E., Atlanta, GA, 30326
Ph: 404-237-2700 Fax: 404-262-2888 **Cuisine:** French
Average Dinner for 2: $110 **Closed:** Sunday

La Grotta Ristorante Italiano *page 156
2637 Peachtree Rd. N.E., Atlanta, GA, 30305
Ph: 404-231-1368 Fax: 404-231-1274 **Cuisine:** Northern Italian
Owner: Sergio Favalli **Average Dinner for 2:** $60

Nava
3060 Peachtree Rd., Ste. 160, Atlanta, GA, 30305
Ph: 404-237-2060 Fax: 404-240-1831 **Cuisine:** Southwestern
Owner: P. Karatassos **Average Dinner for 2:** $55

Nikolai's Roof, Atlanta Hilton and Towers *page 156
255 Courtland St. N.E., Atlanta, GA, 30303
Ph: 404-221-6362 Fax: 404-221-6811 **Cuisine:** French/Continental
Average Dinner for 2: $130

Pano's and Paul's *page 157
1232 W. Paces Ferry Rd N.W., Atlanta, GA, 30327
Ph: 404-261-3662 Fax: 404-261-4512 **Cuisine:** Seafood
Owner: P. Karatossos **Average Dinner for 2:** $100
Closed: Sunday

Pricci *page 157
500 Pharr Rd. at Maple Dr., Atlanta, GA, 30305
Ph: 404-237-2941 Fax: 404-261-0058 **Cuisine:** Italian
Owner: P. Karatassos **Average Dinner for 2:** $75
Closed: Holidays

The Restaurant, Ritz-Carlton
181 Peachtree Rd. N.E., Atlanta, GA, 30303
Ph: 404-659-0400 Fax: **Cuisine:** Modern French
Average Dinner for 2: $120 **Closed:** Sunday

Riviera Restaurant
519 E. Paces Ferry Rd. N.E., Atlanta, GA, 30306
Ph: 404-262-7112 Fax: 404-262-7335 **Cuisine:** French/Continental
Average Dinner for 2: $80 **Closed:** Sunday, Monday

Veni Vidi Vici *page 158
41 14th St., Atlanta, GA, 30309
Ph: 404-875-8424 Fax: 404-875-6533 **Cuisine:** Northern Italian
Owner: P. Karatassos **Average Dinner for 2:** $45
Closed: Holidays

SAVANNAH

45 South at the Pirate's House
20 E. Broad St., Savannah, GA, 31401
Ph: 912-233-1881 Fax: 912-233-5757 **Cuisine:** American
Owner: Sander Hollander **Average Dinner for 2:** $80
Closed: Sunday, Holidays

Elizabeth on 37th *page 158
105 E. 37th St., Savannah, GA, 31401
Ph: 912-236-5547 Fax: 912-232-1095 **Cuisine:** Regional
Owners: Elizabeth & Michael Terry **Average Dinner for 2:** $75

HAWAII

ISLAND OF KAUAI

KAPAA

A Pacific Café
4-831 Kuhio Highway, Kapaa, HI, 96746
Ph: 808-822-0013 Fax: 808-822-0054 **Cuisine:** Pacific Rim
Owner: Jean-Marie Josselin **Average Dinner for 2:** $75
Closed: Christmas

ISLAND OF MAUI

KAPALUA

The Anuenue Room, Ritz-Carlton Kapalua
One Ritz-Carlton Dr., Kapalua, Maui, HI, 96761
Ph: 808-669-6200 Fax: 808-665-0026 **Cuisine:** Hawaiian/Provencal
Average Dinner for 2: $165 **Closed:** Sunday, Monday.

LAHAINA

Swan Court
200 Nohea Kai Dr., Lahaina, Maui, HI, 96761
Ph: 808-661-1234 Fax: 808-667-4499 **Cuisine:** Continental
Average Dinner for 2: $90

WAILEA

Raffles
3550 Wailea Alanui Dr., Wailea Maui, HI, 96753
Ph: 808-879-4900 Fax: 808-874-5370 **Cuisine:** Regional
Average Dinner for 2: $85 **Closed:** Holidays

Seasons, The Four Seasons Resort
3900 Wailea Alanui Dr., Wailea, HI, 96753
Ph: 808-874-8000 Fax: 808-874-2222 **Cuisine:** Regional
Average Dinner for 2: $130 **Closed:** Sunday, Monday

ISLAND OF OAHU

HONOLULU

Bali-By-The-Sea, Hilton Hawaiian Village
2005 Kalia Rd., Honolulu, HI, 96815
Ph: 808-949-4321 Fax: 808-947-7926 **Cuisine:** Continental
Average Dinner for 2: $90 **Closed:** Sunday

La Mer, The Halekulani Hotel
2199 Kalia Rd., Honolulu, HI, 96815-198
Ph: 808-923-2311 Fax: 808-922-5111 **Cuisine:** French
Average Dinner for 2: $200

Roy's Restaurant
6600 Kalanianaole Hwy., Honolulu, HI, 96825
Ph: 808-396-7697 Fax: 808-396-8706 **Cuisine:** Pacific Rim
Average Dinner for 2: $60

IDAHO

COEUR D' ALENE

Beverly's *page 160
115 Front St., Coeur d'Alene, ID, 83814
Ph: 208-765-4000 Fax: 208-664-7276 **Cuisine:** Regional
Owners: D. Hagadone & J. Jaeger **Average Dinner for 2:** $75

ILLINOIS

ARLINGTON HEIGHTS

Le Titi de Paris *page 160
1015 W. Dundee Rd., Arlington Heights, IL, 60004
Ph: 847-506-0222 Fax: 847-506-0474 **Cuisine:** French
Owners: Pierre & Judith Pollin **Average Dinner for 2:** $100
Closed: Sunday, Monday

CHICAGO

Ambria *page 161
2300 N. Lincoln Park W., Chicago, IL, 60614
Ph: 773-472-5959 Fax: 773-472-9077 **Cuisine:** French
Owner: Gabino Sotelino **Average Dinner for 2:** $120
Closed: Sunday

Arun's
4156 N. Kedzie Ave., Chicago, IL, 60618
Ph: 773-539-1909 Fax: 773-539-2125 **Cuisine:** Thai
Owner: Arun Sampanthavivat **Average Dinner for 2:** $150
Closed: Monday

Bistro 110 *page 161
110 E. Pearson St., Chicago, IL, 60611
Ph: 312-266-3110 Fax: 312-266-3116 **Cuisine:** French/American
Owners: Doug Roth & Larry Levy **Average Dinner for 2:** $60
Closed: Thanksgiving, Christmas

Charlie Trotter's
816 W. Armitage, Chicago, IL, 60614
Ph: 773-248-6228 Fax: 773-248-6088
Cuisine: Contemporary American
Owner: Charlie Trotter **Average Dinner for 2:** $250
Closed: Sunday, Monday

CoCo Pazzo *page 162
300 W. Hubbard St., Chicago, IL, 60610
Ph: 312-836-0900 Fax: 312-836-0257 **Cuisine:** Italian
Owner: Jack Weiss **Average Dinner for 2:** $100

The Dining Room, Ritz-Carlton
160 E. Pearson St., Chicago, IL, 60611
Ph: 312-266-1000 Fax: 312-266-9623 **Cuisine:** Modern French
Average Dinner for 2: $120

Entre Nous, The Fairmont Hotel
200 N. Columbus Dr., Chicago, IL, 60601
Ph: 312-565-8000 Fax: 312-856-9020 **Cuisine:** Regional/French
Average Dinner for 2: $60 **Closed:** Sunday

Everest *page 162
440 S. LaSalle St., 40th Fl., Chicago, IL, 60605
Ph: 312-663-8920 Fax: 312-663-8802 **Cuisine:** French
Owner: Philippe Tosques **Average Dinner for 2:** $140
Closed: Sunday, Monday

Gordon *page 163
500 N. Clark St., Chicago, IL, 60610
Ph: 312-467-9780 Fax: 312-467-1671 **Cuisine:** Contemporary
Owner: Gordon Sinclair **Average Dinner for 2:** $60
Closed: Holidays

La Strada *page 163
155 N. Michigan Ave., Chicago, IL, 60601
Ph: 312-565-2200 Fax: 312-565-2216 **Cuisine:** Italian
Owner: Michael Mormando **Average Dinner for 2:** $70
Closed: Sunday

Nick's Fishmarket
1 First National Plaza, Chicago, IL, 60603
Ph: 312-621-0200 Fax: 312-621-1118 **Cuisine:** Steak/Seafood
Owner: Steve Karpf **Average Dinner for 2:** $80 **Closed:** Sunday

Printer's Row
550 S. Dearborn St., Chicago, IL, 60605
Ph: 312-461-0780 Fax: 312-461-0624 **Cuisine:** American
Owner: Michael Foley **Average Dinner for 2:** $70
Closed: Sunday, Holidays

Restaurant Suntory
13 E. Huron St., Chicago, IL, 60611
Ph: 312-664-3344 Fax: 312-664-4421 **Cuisine:** Japanese
Average Dinner for 2: $50 **Closed:** Christmas, New Years

Seasons, The Four Seasons
120 E. Delaware Pl., Chicago, IL, 60611
Ph: 312-649-2349 Fax: 312-280-9184 **Cuisine:** American
Average Dinner for 2: $80

Spiaggia *page 164
980 N. Michigan Ave., Chicago, IL, 60611
Ph: 312-280-2750 Fax: 312-943-8560 **Cuisine:** New Italian
Owner: Levy Restaurants **Average Dinner for 2:** $65
Closed: Holidays

Vivere *page 164
71 W. Monroe St., Chicago, IL, 60603
Ph: 312-332-4040 Fax: 312-332-2656 **Cuisine:** Regional Italian
Owners: The Capitanini Family **Average Dinner for 2:** $65
Closed: Sunday, Holidays

Yoshi's Cafe
3257 N. Halstead, Chicago, IL, 60657
Ph: 773-248-6160 Fax: 773-327-6014 **Cuisine:** Japanese
Average Dinner for 2: $70 **Closed:** Holidays

GENEVA

302 West
302 W. State St., Geneva, IL, 60134
Ph: 630-232-9302 **Cuisine:** Contemporary American
Owners: Joel & Catherine Findlay **Average Dinner for 2:** $90
Closed: Sunday, Monday

HIGHLAND PARK

Carlos' *page 165
429 Temple Ave., Highland Park, IL, 60035
Ph: 847-432-0770 Fax: 847-432-2047 **Cuisine:** French
Owners: Debbie & Carlos Nieto **Average Dinner for 2:** $130
Closed: Tuesday

LA GRANGE

Café 36 *page 165
36 S. La Grange Rd., La Grange, IL, 60525
Ph: 708-354-5722 Fax: 708-354-5042 **Cuisine:** French
Owner: Reinhard Barthel **Average Dinner for 2:** $60
Closed: Holidays

LAKEMOOR

Le Vichyssois *page 166
220 W. Rte. 120, Lakemoor, IL, 60050
Ph: 815-385-8221 Fax: 815-385-8223 **Cuisine:** French
Owners: Bernard & Priscilla Cretier **Average Dinner for 2:** $55
Closed: Monday, Tuesday

LOCKPORT

Tallgrass
1006 S. State St., Lockport, IL, 60441
Ph: 815-838-5566 Fax: 815-838-8917 **Cuisine:** Modern French
Owners: R.D. Burcenski & J.T. Alves **Average Dinner for 2:** $110
Closed: Monday, Tuesday

NAPERVILLE

Montparnasse
200 E. 5th Ave., Naperville, IL, 60563
Ph: 630-961-8203 Fax: 630-961-0992 **Cuisine:** French
Average Dinner for 2: $95 **Closed:** Sunday

ROSEMONT

Carlucci *page 166
6111 N. River Rd., Rosemont, IL, 60018
Ph: 847-518-0990 Fax: 847-518-0999 **Cuisine:** Italian
Owner: Joseph Carlucci **Average Dinner for 2:** $85
Closed: Holidays

Nick's Fishmarket
10275 W. Higgins Rd., Rosemont, IL, 60018
Ph: 847-298-8200 Fax: 847-298-3755 **Cuisine:** Seafood
Owner: Steve Karpf **Average Dinner for 2:** $80

WHEELING

Le Français
269 S. Milwaukee Ave., Wheeling, IL, 60090
Ph: 847-541-7470 Fax: 847-541-7489 **Cuisine:** Classical French
Owners: Roland & Mary Beth Liccioni **Average Dinner for 2:** $160
Closed: Sunday

INDIANA

CARMEL

The Glass Chimney *page 168
12901 Old Meridian St., Carmel, IN, 46032
Ph: 317-844-0921 Fax: 317-574-1360 **Cuisine:** French/Continental
Owner: Dieter Puska **Average Dinner for 2:** $60 **Closed:** Sunday

INDIANAPOLIS

The Restaurant at the Canterbury Hotel *page 168
123 S. Illinois St., Indianapolis, IN, 46225
Ph: 317-634-3000 Fax: 317-685-2519 **Cuisine:** Continental
Owner: Don Fortunato **Average Dinner for 2:** $100

KENTUCKY

LOUISVILLE

Le Relais *page 169
2817 Taylorsville Rd., Louisville, KY, 40205
Ph: 502-451-9020 Fax: 502-459-3112 **Cuisine:** French/Provencal
Owner: Anthony Dike **Average Dinner for 2:** $60 **Closed:** Monday

Lilly's
1147 Bardstown Rd., Louisville, KY, 40204
Ph: 502-451-0447 Fax: 502-458-7546 **Cuisine:** Regional
Owners: Kathy & Will Cary **Average Dinner for 2:** $55
Closed: Sunday, Monday

Vincenzo's *page 169
150 S. 5th St., Louisville, KY, 40202
Ph: 502-580-1350 Fax: 502-580-1355 **Cuisine:** Northern Italian
Owners: Vincenzo & Agostino Gabrielli **Average Dinner for 2:** $80
Closed: Sunday, Holidays

LOUISIANA

DONALDSONVILLE

Lafitte's Landing Restaurant at Bittersweet Plantation *page 170
404 Claiborne Ave., Donaldsonville, LA, 70346
Ph: 225-473-1232 Fax: 225-473-1161 **Cuisine:** Regional
Owner: John Folse **Average Dinner for 2:** $60 **Closed:** Monday

LACOMBE

La Provence
25020 Hwy.190 E., Lacombe, LA, 70445
Ph: 504-626-7662 Fax: 504-626-9598 **Cuisine:** Provencal
Owner: Chris Kerageorgiou **Average Dinner for 2:** $60
Closed: Monday, Tuesday

LAKE CHARLES

Café Margaux
765 Bayou Pines E., Lake Charles, LA, 70605
Ph: 318-433-2902 Fax: 318-494-0606 **Cuisine:** French
Owner: D.C. Flynt **Average Dinner for 2:** $65
Closed: Sunday, Holidays

NEW ORLEANS

Arnaud's
2730 Magazine St., New Orleans, LA, 70130
Ph: 504-523-5433 Fax: 504-581-7908 **Cuisine:** French Creole
Owners: Jane & Archie Casbarian **Average Dinner for 2:** $80
Closed: Holidays

Bayona *page 170
430 Dauphine St., New Orleans, LA, 70112
Ph: 504-525-4455 Fax: 504-522-0589
Cuisine: French/Mediterranean
Owners: Susan Spicer & Regina Keever **Average Dinner for 2:** $70
Closed: Holidays

Brigtsen's *page 171
723 Bante St., New Orleans, LA, 70118
Ph: 504-861-7610 Fax: 504-866-7397 **Cuisine:** French Creole
Owners: Frank & Marna Brigtsen **Average Dinner for 2:** $45
Closed: Sunday, Monday

Broussard's *page 171
819 Rue Conti, New Orleans, LA, 70112
Ph: 504-581-3866 Fax: 504-581-3873 **Cuisine:** French Creole
Owners: Gunter & Evelyn Preuss **Average Dinner for 2:** $60

Christian's *page 172
3835 Iberville St., New Orleans, LA, 70119
Ph: 504-482-4924 Fax: 504-482-6852 **Cuisine:** French Creole
Owner: Hank Bergeron **Average Dinner for 2:** $60
Closed: Sunday, Monday

Commander's Palace
1403 Washington Ave., New Orleans, LA, 70130
Ph: 504-899-8221 Fax: 504-891-3242 **Cuisine:** French Creole
Owners: The Brennan Family **Average Dinner for 2:** $90
Closed: Christmas, Mardi Gras

Emeril's
800 Tchoupitoulas St., New Orleans, LA, 70130
Ph: 504-528-9393 Fax: 504-523-5888 **Cuisine:** Regional
Owner: Emeril Lagasse **Average Dinner for 2:** $120
Closed: Sunday, Holidays

The Grill Room, Windsor Court Hotel *page 172
300 Gravier St., New Orleans, LA, 70130
Ph: 504-522-1992 Fax: 504-596-4513
Cuisine: Contemporary American **Average Dinner for 2:** $125

Louis XVI *page 173
730 Bienville St., New Orleans, LA, 70130
Ph: 504-581-7000 Fax: 504-524-8925
Cuisine: Classical French **Average Dinner for 2:** $80

Nola
534 St. Louis St., New Orleans, LA, 70130
Ph: 504-522-6652 Fax: 504-524-6178 **Cuisine:** French Creole
Owner: Emeril Lagasse **Average Dinner for 2:** $70

Sazerac Bar & Grill, The Fairmont Hotel
123 Baronne St., New Orleans, LA, 70112
Ph: 504-529-4733 Fax: 504-529-4806
Cuisine: Continental/Creole **Average Dinner for 2:** $70
Closed: Sunday

SHREVEPORT

Monsieur Patou
855 Pierremont Rd., Ste.135, Shreveport, LA, 71106
Ph: 318-868-9822
Cuisine: French **Owners:** Patou and Horia Muriel Hebert
Average Dinner for 2: $65 **Closed:** Sunday

MAINE

KENNEBUNKPORT

The White Barn Inn *page 173
37 Beach St., Kennebunkport, ME, 04046
Ph: 207-967-2321 Fax: 207-967-1100
Cuisine: Regional **Owner:** Laurie Bongiorno
Average Dinner for 2: $125 **Closed:** Seasonally

MARYLAND

ANNAPOLIS

Northwoods
609 Melvin Ave., Annapolis, MD, 21401
Ph: 410-269-6775 Fax: 410-268-0930
Cuisine: Continental **Owners:** Russell & Leslie Brown
Average Dinner for 2: $60 **Closed:** Holidays

BALTIMORE

The Brass Elephant
924 N. Charles St., Baltimore, MD, 21201
Ph: 410-547-8480 Fax: 410-783-2933
Cuisine: Italian/Continental **Owner:** John C. Elsby
Average Dinner for 2: $70

Hampton's, the Harbor Court Hotel *page 174
550 Light St., Baltimore, MD, 21202
Ph: 410-234-0550 Fax: 410-659-5925
Cuisine: Contemporary American **Average Dinner for 2:** $100
Closed: Monday

The Prime Rib *page 174
1101 N. Calvert St., Baltimore, MD, 21202
Ph: 410-539-1804
Cuisine: Steak/Seafood **Owner:** C. Peter BeLer
Average Dinner for 2: $80

BETHESDA

Tragara *page 175
4935 Cordell Ave., Bethesda, MD, 20814
Ph: 301-951-4935 Fax: 301-951-0401
Cuisine: Northern Italian **Owner:** Claude Amsellem
Average Dinner for 2: $75 **Closed:** Holidays

FINKSBURG

Rudy's 2900
2900 Baltimore Blvd., Finksburg, MD, 21048
Ph: 410-833-5777
Cuisine: Continental **Owners:** Rudolph and Gayle Speckamp
Average Dinner for 2: $70 **Closed:** Monday

MIDDLETON

The Stone Manor Country Club *page 175
5820 Carroll Boyer Rd., Middleton, MD, 21769
Ph: 301-473-5454 Fax: 301-371-5622
Cuisine: Regional **Average Dinner for 2:** $90 **Closed:** Monday

POTOMAC

Old Angler's Inn
10801 MacArthur Blvd., Potomac, MD, 20654
Ph: 301-365-2425 Fax: 301-983-0630
Cuisine: Contemporary American **Owner:** Olympia Regis
Average Dinner for 2: $80 **Closed:** Monday

SPARKS

Milton Inn, The
14833 York Rd., Sparks, MD, 21152
Ph: 410-771-4366 Fax: 410-771-4184 **Cuisine:** Regional American
Owners: Todd Meginness & Brian Boston
Average Dinner for 2: $85 **Closed:** Christmas, New Years

ST. MICHAELS

208 Talbot *page 176
208 N. Talbot St., St. Michaels, MD, 21663
Ph: 410-745-3838 Fax: 410-745-6041
Cuisine: Regional American **Owners:** C. Chiaruttini & P. Milne
Average Dinner for 2: $110 **Closed:** Seasonally

The Inn at Perry Cabin *page 176
308 Watkins Lane, St. Michaels, MD, 21663
Ph: 410-745-2200 Fax: 410-745-3348
Cuisine: Continental **Owner:** Sir Bernard Ashley
Average Dinner for 2: $120

MASSACHUSETTS

BOSTON

Anthony's Pier 4 *page 177
140 Northern Ave., Boston, MA, 02210
Ph: 617-482-6262 Fax: 617-426-2324 Cuisine: American
Owners: Anthony Athanas & Sons **Average Dinner for 2:** $60
Closed: Christmas

Aujourd'hui, The Four Seasons
200 Boylston St., Boston, MA, 02116
Ph: 617-451-1392 Fax: 617-351-2251
Cuisine: Contemporary American **Average Dinner for 2:** $170

The Bay Tower *page 177
60 State St., Boston, MA, 02109
Ph: 617-723-1666 Fax: 617-723-7887
Cuisine: Contemporary American **Average Dinner for 2:** $125
Closed: Sunday

Biba *page 178
272 Boylston St., Boston, MA, 02116
Ph: 617-426-7878 Fax: 617-426-9253
Cuisine: Contemporary American **Owner:** Lydia Shire
Average Dinner for 2: $100 **Closed:** Holidays

Café Budapest *page 178
90 Exeter St., Boston, MA, 02116
Ph: 617-266-1979 Fax: 617-266-1395 **Cuisine:** Hungarian
Owner: Livia Rev-Kury **Average Dinner for 2:** $125
Closed: Christmas

The Dining Room, Ritz-Carlton *page 179
15 Arlington St., Boston, MA, 02117
Ph: 617-536-5700 Fax: 617-536-9340 **Cuisine:** French
Average Dinner for 2: $120

Galleria Italiana Ristorante *page 179
177 Tremont St., Boston, MA, 02111
Ph: 617-423-2092 Fax: 617-423-4436 **Cuisine:** Regional Italian
Owners: Rita d'Angelo & Marisa Iocco **Average Dinner for 2:** $60
Closed: Monday

Grill 23 & Bar *page 180
161 Berkeley St., Boston, MA, 02116
Ph: 617-542-2255 Fax: 617-542-5114 **Cuisine:** American
Average Dinner for 2: $100 **Closed:** Holidays

Hamersley's Bistro *page 180
553 Tremont St., Boston, MA, 02116
Ph: 617-423-2700 Fax: 617-423-7710
Cuisine: American/Continental **Owners:** Gordon & Fiona Hamersley
Average Dinner for 2: $100

Icarus *page 181
3 Appleton St., Boston, MA, 02116
Ph: 617-426-1790 Fax: 617-426-2150 **Cuisine:** Regional
Owner: John Bellott **Average Dinner for 2:** $80

Julien, The Hotel Meridien Boston *page 181
250 Franklin St., Boston, MA, 02110
Ph: 617-451-1900 Fax: 617-423-2844
Cuisine: French/Provencal **Average Dinner for 2:** $140
Closed: Sunday, Holidays

L' Espalier *page 182
30 Gloucester St., Boston, MA, 02115-2509
Ph: 617-262-3023 Fax: 617-375-9297
Cuisine: Contemporary French **Owners:** Frank and Catherine
McClelland **Average Dinner for 2:** $130 **Closed:** Sunday

Locke-Ober Café
3 Winter Place, Boston, MA, 02108
Ph: 617-542-1340 Fax: 617-542-6452
Cuisine: Continental **Average Dinner for 2:** $75

Maison Robert *page 182
45 School St., Boston, MA, 02108
Ph: 617-227-3370 Fax: 617-227-5977 **Cuisine:** French
Owner: Lucien Robert **Average Dinner for 2:** $85 **Closed:** Sunday

Seasons, The Regal Bostonian Hotel *page 183
Corner of North & Blackstone, Boston, MA, 02109
Ph: 617-523-4119 Fax: 617-523-2593
Cuisine: Regional **Average Dinner for 2:** $110

Top of the Hub *page 183
800 Boylston St., Boston, MA, 02119
Ph: 617-536-1775 Fax: 617-859-8298
Cuisine: American/Continental **Average Dinner for 2:** $45

CAMBRIDGE

Rialto, The Charles Hotel
One Bennett St., Cambridge, MA, 02138
Ph: 617-661-5050 Fax: 617-661-5053 **Cuisine:** Continental
Owner: Michela Larson **Average Dinner for 2:** $50
Closed: Holidays

Salamander Restaurant *page 184
1 Athenaeum St., Cambridge, MA, 02142
Ph: 617-225-2121 Fax: 617-494-8871 **Cuisine:** Asian
Owner: Stan Frankenthaler **Average Dinner for 2:** $80
Closed: Sunday

LEICESTER

The Castle Restaurant *page 184
1230 Main St., Leicester, MA, 01524
Ph: 508-892-9090 Fax: 508-892-3620 **Cuisine:** Continental
Owner: Stanley J. Nicas **Average Dinner for 2:** $70
Closed: Monday

LENOX

Wheatleigh, The Wheatleigh Hotel *page 185
Hawthorne Rd., Lenox, MA, 01240
Ph: 413-637-0610 Fax: 413-637-4507 **Cuisine:** French
Owners: Susan & Linfield Simon **Average Dinner for 2:** $180

TYNGSBORO

Silks at Stonehedge Inn *page 185
160 Pawtucket Blvd., Tyngsboro, MA, 01879
Ph: 978-649-4400 Fax: 978-649-9256 **Cuisine:** Modern French
Owners: L. Bozkurt & G. Campbell **Average Dinner for 2:** $100
Closed: Monday

CAPE COD

BREWSTER

Chillingsworth *page 186
2449 Main St., Brewster, MA, 02631
Ph: 508-896-3640 Fax: 508-896-7540
Cuisine: Modern French/Seafood **Owners:** Robert & Patricia Rabin
Average Dinner for 2: $120 **Closed:** Monday

SANDWICH

Dan'l Webster Inn *page 186
149 Main St., Sandwich, MA, 02563
Ph: 508-888-3622 Fax: 508-888-5156
Cuisine: Regional **Owners:** The Catania Family
Average Dinner for 2: $55 **Closed:** Christmas

SIASCONSET   (NANTUCKET)

The Chanticleer *page 187
9 New St., Siasconset, MA, 02564
Ph: 508-257-6231 Fax: 508-257-4154
Cuisine: Classical French **Owner:** Jean-Charles Beuret
Average Dinner for 2: $140 **Closed:** Monday

MICHIGAN

DETROIT

Opus One *page 187
565 E. Larned St., Detroit, MI, 48226
Ph: 313-961-7766 Fax: 313-961-9243
Cuisine: Contemporary American
Owners: Kokas, Mandziara & Bletzas
Average Dinner for 2: $90 **Closed:** Sunday

The Rattlesnake Club
300 River Pl., Detroit, MI, 48207
Ph: 313-567-4400 Fax: 313-567-2063
Cuisine: Contemporary American **Owner:** Jimmy Schmidt
Average Dinner for 2: $100 **Closed:** Sunday

Van Dyke Place
649 Van Dyke Ave., Detroit, MI, 48214
Ph: 313-821-2620 Fax: 313-821-0633 **Cuisine:** American
Owner: John McCarthy **Average Dinner for 2:** $80
Closed: Sunday, Monday

The Whitney
4421 Woodward Ave., Detroit, MI, 48201
Ph: 313-832-5700 Fax: 313-832-2159 **Cuisine:** American
Owner: John McCarthy **Average Dinner for 2:** $100
Closed: Holidays

ELLSWORTH

The Rowe, The Michigan Country Inn
6303 County Rd. 48, Ellsworth, MI, 49729
Ph: 616-588-7351 Fax: 616-588-2365 **Cuisine:** Regional/Provencal
Owner: Albert Westhoven **Average Dinner for 2:** $100

Tapawingo
9502 Lake St., Ellsworth, MI, 49729
Ph: 616-588-7971 Fax: 616-588-6175
Cuisine: Contemporary American
Owner: Harlan Peterson **Average Dinner for 2:** $90

FARMINGTON HILLS

Café Cortina *page 188
30715 W.10 Mile Rd., Farmington Hills, MI, 48836
Ph: 248-474-3033 Fax: 248-474-9064 **Cuisine:** Italian
Owners: Adrian & Rina Tonon **Average Dinner for 2:** $60
Closed: Sunday

SOUTHFIELD

The Golden Mushroom *page 188
18100 W. Ten Mile Rd., Southfield, MI, 48075
Ph: 248-559-4230 Fax: 248-559-7312
Cuisine: Continental **Owner:** Reid Ashton
Average Dinner for 2: $120 **Closed:** Sunday

WEST BLOOMFIELD

The Lark *page 189
6430 Farmington Rd., West Bloomfield, MI, 48322
Ph: 248-661-4466 Fax: 248-661-8891 **Cuisine:** French
Owners: Jim & Mary Lark **Average Dinner for 2:** $110
Closed: Sunday, Monday, Holidays

MINNESOTA

MINNEAPOLIS

The 510 Restaurant
510 Groveland Ave., Minneapolis, MN, 55403
Ph: 612-874-6440 Fax: 612-874-0791
Cuisine: American/Continental **Owner:** Craig Schutte
Average Dinner for 2: $55 **Closed:** Sunday

D'Amico Cucina *page 189
100 N. 6th St., Minneapolis, MN, 55403
Ph: 612-338-2401 Fax: 612-337-5130 **Cuisine:** Italian
Owners: Richard & Larry D'Amico **Average Dinner for 2:** $90

Goodfellow's *page 190
40 S. 7th St., Minneapolis, MN, 55402
Ph: 612-332-4800 Fax: 612-332-1274
Cuisine: Regional **Owners:** John Dayton & Wayne Kostroski
Average Dinner for 2: $100 **Closed:** Sunday

The Rosewood Room, The Crowne Plaza Northstar Hotel *page 190
618 2nd Ave. S., Minneapolis, MN, 55402
Ph: 612-338-2288 Fax: 612-338-6194 **Cuisine:** Continental
Average Dinner for 2: $70 **Closed:** Sunday, Monday

MISSISSIPPI

GULFPORT

Vrazel's *page 191
3206 W. Beach Blvd., Gulfport, MS, 39501
Ph: 228-863-2229 Fax: 228-863-2240 **Cuisine:** French Creole
Owners: William & Louise Vrazel **Average Dinner for 2:** $45
Closed: Sunday

ROBINSONVILLE

Fairbanks Steakhouse *page 191
1150 Casino Strip Blvd., Robinsonville, MS, 38664
Ph: 800-871-0711 Fax: 601-357-7800 **Cuisine:** Steakhouse
Average Dinner for 2: $90 **Closed:** Holidays

MISSOURI

KANSAS CITY

American Restaurant
200 E. 25th St., Kansas City, MO, 64108
Ph: 816-426-1133 Fax: 816-426-1190 **Cuisine:** Contemporary
American **Average Dinner for 2:** $100 **Closed:** Sunday

Café Allegro
1815 W. 39th St., Kansas City, MO, 64111
Ph: 816-561-3663 Fax: 816-756-3265 **Cuisine:** Contemporary
Owner: Stephen E. Cole **Average Dinner for 2:** $75
Closed: Sunday

The Peppercorn Duck Club, Hyatt Regency Hotel
2345 McGee St., Kansas City, MO, 64108
Ph: 816-435-4199 Fax: 816-435-4190 **Cuisine:** American
Average Dinner for 2: $70 **Closed:** Holidays

ST. ALBANS

Malmaison
St. Albans Rd., St. Albans, MO, 63073
Ph: 314-458-0131 Fax: 314-458-4803 **Cuisine:** French
Owner: Gilbert Andujar **Average Dinner for 2:** $70
Closed: Monday, Tuesday

ST. LOUIS

Al's Restaurant *page 192
1200 N. First St., St. Louis, MO, 63102
Ph: 314-421-6399 **Cuisine:** Continental/Italian
Owner: Albert Barroni **Average Dinner for 2:** $100
Closed: Sunday, Holidays

Benedetto's *page 192
10411 Clayton Rd., Frontenac, MO, 63131
Ph: 314-432-8585 Fax: 314-432-3199 **Cuisine:** Italian
Owner: Benedetto Buzzetta **Average Dinner for 2:** $70

Café de France *page 193
410 Olive St., St Louis, MO, 63102
Ph: 314-231-2204 Fax: 314-231-0391 **Cuisine:** French
Owner: Monique Keraval **Average Dinner for 2:** $60
Closed: Sunday

Dominic's *page 193
5101 Wilson Ave., St Louis, MO, 63110
Ph: 314-771-1632 Fax: 314-771-1695 **Cuisine:** Italian
Owner: Giovanni Galati **Average Dinner for 2:** $75
Closed: Sunday, Holidays

Faust's, Adam's Mark Hotel
4th & Chestnut St., St Louis, MO, 63102
Ph: 314-342-4690 Fax: 314-241-9839
Cuisine: Contemporary American **Owner:** Fred Kummer
Average Dinner for 2: $65

Fio's La Fourchette
7515 Forsyth St., St Louis, MO, 63105
Ph: 314-863-6866 **Cuisine:** French/Continental
Owners: Lisa & Fio Antognini **Average Dinner for 2:** $100
Closed: Sunday, Monday

G. P. Agostino's *page 194
15846 Manchester Rd., Ellisville, MO, 63011
Ph: 314-391-5480 Fax: 314-391-3892 **Cuisine:** Italian
Owners: Agostino Restaurants Inc. **Average Dinner for 2:** $40
Closed: Holidays

Giovanni's
5201 Shaw Ave., St Louis, MO, 63110
Ph: 314-772-5958 Fax: 314-772-0343 **Cuisine:** Italian
Owner: Giovanni Gabriele **Average Dinner for 2:** $100
Closed: Holidays

Giovanni's Little Place
14650 Manchester Rd., Ballwin, MO, 63011
Ph: 314-227-7230 Fax: 314-227-9917 **Cuisine:** Italian
Owner: Giovanni Gabriele **Average Dinner for 2:** $100
Closed: Sunday

John Mineo's
13490 Clayton Rd., St Louis, MO, 63131
Ph: 314-434-5244 Fax: 314-434-0714 **Cuisine:** Regional Italian
Owner: John Mineo **Average Dinner for 2:** $75

Seventh Inn   *page 194
100 Seven Trails Dr., Ballwin, MO, 63011
Ph: 314-227-6686 Fax: 314-227-6595 **Cuisine:** Continental
Owner: Ron Schrader **Average Dinner for 2:** $70
Closed: Sunday, Monday

Station Grill, Hyatt Regency Hotel
1 Union Station, St Louis, MO, 63103
Ph: 314-231-1234 Fax: 314-923-3971 **Cuisine:** Steak/Seafood
Owner: Paul Verciglio **Average Dinner for 2:** $60

The Grill Room, Ritz-Carlton   *page 195
100 Carondelet Plaza, St. Louis, MO, 63105
Ph: 314-863-6300 Fax: 314-719-1428 **Cuisine:** American
Average Dinner for 2: $80

Tony's   *page 195
410 Market St., St Louis, MO, 63102
Ph: 314-231-7007 Fax: 314-231-4740 **Cuisine:** Italian
Owner: Vincent J. Bommarito **Average Dinner for 2:** $100
Closed: Sunday

MONTANA

BILLINGS

Juliano's
2912 7th Ave. N., Billings, MT, 59101
Ph: 406-248-6400 **Cuisine:** Contemporary American
Average Dinner for 2: $50 **Closed:** Sunday

BOZEMAN

The Gallatin Gateway Inn *page 196
Highway 191, Bozeman, MT, 59715
Ph: 406-763-4672 **Cuisine:** American
Owner: Catherine Wrather **Average Dinner for 2:** $45

NEBRASKA

OMAHA

Le Cafe De Paris
1228 S. 6th St., Omaha, NE, 68108
Ph: 402-344-0227 **Cuisine:** French
Owner: Ivan Konsul **Average Dinner for 2:** $90
Closed: Sunday, Holidays

NEVADA

LAKE TAHOE

Llewellyn's, Harvey's Resort Hotel & Casino *page 196
U.S. Highway 50 & Stateline Ave., Lake Tahoe, NV, 89449
Ph: 702-588-2411 Fax: 702-586-6775 **Cuisine:** Continental
Average Dinner for 2: $75

The Summit
15 Highway 50, Stateline, NV, 89449
Ph: 702-588-6611 Fax: 702-586-6601 **Cuisine:** Continental
Average Dinner for 2: $85

LAS VEGAS

André's *page 197
401 S. 6th St., Las Vegas, NV, 89101
Ph: 702-385-5016 Fax: 702-384-8574 **Cuisine:** Classical French
Owner: Andre Rochat **Average Dinner for 2:** $100
Closed: Holidays

Fiore Rotisserie & Grille *page 197
3700 W. Flamingo Rd., Las Vegas, NV, 89103
Ph: 702-252-7702 Fax: 702-247-7932
Cuisine: Contemporary American **Average Dinner for 2:** $70

Melange *page 198
3400 Las Vegas Blvd. S., Las Vegas, NV, 89109
Ph: 702-791-7111 Fax: 702-791-7437 **Cuisine:** Continental
Average Dinner for 2: $100

Michael's
3595 Las Vegas Blvd. S., Las Vegas, NV, 89109
Ph: 702-737-7111 **Cuisine:** Continental
Average Dinner for 2: $200

Monte Carlo, The Desert Inn *page 198
3145 Las Vegas Blvd. S., Las Vegas, NV, 89109
Ph: 702-733-4400 Fax: 702-733-4675 **Cuisine:** French/Continental
Average Dinner for 2: $200 **Closed:** Tuesday, Wednesday

Palace Court, Caesars Palace
3570 Las Vegas Blvd. S., Las Vegas, NV, 89109
Ph: 702-731-7731 Fax: 702-731-7331 **Cuisine:** French
Average Dinner for 2: $160

Piero's *page 199
355 Convention Center Dr., Las Vegas, NV, 89109
Ph: 702-369-2305 Fax: 702-735-5699 **Cuisine:** Northern Italian
Owner: Fred Glusman **Average Dinner for 2:** $175
Closed: Holidays

RENO

Harrah's Steak House *page 199
219 N. Center St., Reno, NV, 89504
Ph: 702-786-3232 Fax: 702-788-3049 **Cuisine:** Steakhouse
Average Dinner for 2: $80 **Closed:** Seasonally

NEW HAMPSHIRE

BEDFORD

The Bedford Village Inn *page 200
2 Village Inn Lane, Bedford, NH, 03110
Ph: 603-472-2001 Fax: 603-472-2868 **Cuisine:** Regional
Owner: Jack Carnevale **Average Dinner for 2:** $75

NEW JERSEY

ABSECON

Ram's Head Inn *page 200
9 W. White Horse Pike, Absecon, NJ, 08201
Ph: 609-652-1700 Fax: 609-748-1588 **Cuisine:** Continental
Owner: Harry Knowles **Average Dinner for 2:** $70
Closed: Monday

ATLANTIC CITY

Peregrines', Atlantic City Hilton Hotel
Casino, Boston & Boardwalk, Atlantic City, NJ, 08401
Ph: 609-340-7200 Fax: 609-340-4858 **Cuisine:** International
Average Dinner for 2: $120 **Closed:** Monday, Tuesday, Wednesday

Scheherazade, Trump Taj Mahal *page 201
1000 Boardwalk at Virginia Ave., Atlantic City, NJ, 08401
Ph: 609-449-6840 Fax: 609-449-6842 **Cuisine:** Continental
Average Dinner for 2: $100

MEDFORD

Beau Rivage *page 201
128 Taunton Blvd., Medford, NJ, 08055
Ph: 609-983-1999 Fax: 609-988-1136 **Cuisine:** Classical French
Average Dinner for 2: $75 **Closed:** Monday

NEW BRUNSWICK

Panico's *page 202
103 Church St., New Brunswick, NJ, 08901
Ph: 732-545-6100 Fax: 732-545-7346 **Cuisine:** Italian
Owner: Frank Panico **Average Dinner for 2:** $100
Closed: Sunday

TRENTON

Diamond's *page 202
132 Kent St., Trenton, NJ, 08611
Ph: 609-393-1000 Fax: 609-393-1672 **Cuisine:** Italian/Continental
Owners: Anthony & Thomas Zucchetti **Average Dinner for 2:** $80

WEST ORANGE

Highlawn Pavilion *page 203
Eagle Rock Reservation, West Orange, NJ, 07052
Ph: 973-731-3463 Fax: 973-731-0034 **Cuisine:** American
Owner: Harry Knowles **Average Dinner for 2:** $45

The Manor *page 203
111 Prospect Ave., West Orange, NJ, 07052
Ph: 973-731-2360 Fax: 973-731-4838 **Cuisine:** Continental
Owner: Harry Knowles **Average Dinner for 2:** $85
Closed: Monday

WHITEHORSE

The Ryland Inn
Route 22 W., Whitehouse, NJ, 08888
Ph: 908-534-4011 Fax: 908-534-6592 **Cuisine:** American/French
Owner: Craig Shelton **Average Dinner for 2:** $140
Closed: Holidays

NEW MEXICO

ALBUQUERQUE

Rancher's Club of New Mexico *page 204
1901 University Blvd. N.E., Albuquerque, NM, 87102
Ph: 505-884-2500 Fax: 505-837-1715 **Cuisine:** Steakhouse
Average Dinner for 2: $100

Stephens
14th & Central Ave. N.W., Albuquerque, NM, 87102
Ph: 505-842-1773 Fax: 505-842-8268 **Cuisine:** Contemporary
American **Owners:** Bill & Nancy Anixter
Average Dinner for 2: $95 **Closed:** Holidays

SANTA FE

Coyote Café
132 W. Water St., Santa Fe, NM, 87501
Ph: 505-983-1615 Fax: 505-989-9026
Cuisine: Contemporary Southwestern
Owner: Mark Miller **Average Dinner for 2:** $90

Santacafé
231 Washington Ave., Santa Fe, NM, 87501
Ph: 505-984-1788 Fax: 505-986-0110 **Cuisine:** Regional
Owners: R. Morean & J. Ebbinghaus **Average Dinner for 2:** $80
Closed: New Years

TAOS

Villa Fontana *page 204
Hwy 522, Taos, NM, 87571
Ph: 505-758-5800 Fax: 505-758-0301 **Cuisine:** Northern Italian
Owners: Carlo & Siobhan Gislimberti **Average Dinner for 2:** $100
Closed: Sunday

NEW YORK

NEW YORK CITY-BROOKLYN

The River Café *page 206
1 Water St., Brooklyn, NY, 11201
Ph: 718-522-5200 Fax: 718-875-0037
Cuisine: American/Continental
Owner: Michael O'Keefe **Average Dinner for 2:** $140

NEW YORK CITY-MANHATTAN

The 21 Club *page 206
21 W. 52nd St., New York, NY, 10019
Ph: 212-582-7200 Fax: 212-581-7138
Cuisine: Contemporary American **Owner:** Orient Express Hotels
Average Dinner for 2: $140 **Closed:** Sunday

Alison on Dominick Street
38 Dominick St., New York, NY, 10013
Ph: 212-727-1188 Fax: 212-727-1005 **Cuisine:** French
Owner: Alison Becker-Hurt **Average Dinner for 2:** $130
Closed: Holidays

An American Place
2 Park Ave. at 32nd Street, New York, NY, 10016
Ph: 212-684-2122 Fax: 212-684-3599 **Cuisine:** Regional
Owner: Larry Forgione **Average Dinner for 2:** $80
Closed: Sunday, Holidays

Aquavit *page 207
13 W. 54th St., New York, NY, 10019
Ph: 212-307-7311 Fax: 212-957-9043 **Cuisine:** Scandinavian
Owner: Hakan Swahn **Average Dinner for 2:** $125

Aureole
34 E. 61st St., New York, NY, 10021
Ph: 212-319-1660 Fax: 212-755-3126 **Cuisine:** American
Owner: Charles Palmer **Average Dinner for 2:** $170
Closed: Sunday

Barbetta *page 207
321 W. 46th St., New York, NY, 10036
Ph: 212-246-9171 Fax: 212-246-1279 **Cuisine:** Italian
Owner: Laura Miaoglio **Average Dinner for 2:** $90
Closed: Sunday

The Box Tree
250 E. 49th St., New York, NY, 10017
Ph: 212-758-8320 **Cuisine:** French
Owner: Augustein Paege **Average Dinner for 2:** $185

Café des Artistes
33 W. 67th St., New York, NY, 10023
Ph: 212-877-3500 Fax: 212-877-6263 **Cuisine:** French
Owners: Jenifer & George Lang **Average Dinner for 2:** $150

Café Pierre
5th Ave. & 61st St., New York, NY, 10021
Ph: 212-940-8185 Fax: 212-750-0541 **Cuisine:** Classical French
Average Dinner for 2: $80

Chanterelle
2 Harrison St., New York, NY, 10013
Ph: 212-966-6960 **Cuisine:** French
Owners: David & Karen Waltuck **Average Dinner for 2:** $150
Closed: Sunday

Cité *page 208
120 W. 51st St., New York, NY, 10020
Ph: 212-956-7100 Fax: 212-956-7157 **Cuisine:** French/Steakhouse
Owner: Alan Stillman **Average Dinner for 2:** $90 **Closed:** Holidays

Daniel
20 E. 76th St., New York, NY, 10021
Ph: 212-288-0033 Fax: 212-737-0612 **Cuisine:** French
Owner: Daniel Boulud **Average Dinner for 2:** $200
Closed: Sunday

Dawat
210 E. 58th St., New York, NY, 10022
Ph: 212-355-7555 Fax: 212-355-1735 **Cuisine:** Indian
Owner: Laxmi Malhotra **Average Dinner for 2:** $60

Felidia Ristorante
243 E. 58th St., New York, NY, 10022
Ph: 212-758-1479 Fax: 212-935-7687 **Cuisine:** Italian
Owners: Lidia & Felix Bastianich **Average Dinner for 2:** $130
Closed: Sunday

The Four Seasons
99 E. 52nd St., New York, NY, 10022
Ph: 212-754-9494 Fax: 212-754-1077 **Cuisine:** Continental
Average Dinner for 2: $130 **Closed:** Sunday

Gotham Bar & Grill
12 E.12th St., New York, NY, 10003
Ph: 212-620-4020 Fax: 212-627-7810 **Cuisine:** American
Average Dinner for 2: $150 **Closed:** Holidays

Gramercy Tavern
42 E. 20th St., New York, NY, 10003
Ph: 212-477-0777 Fax: 212-477-1160
Cuisine: American **Owners:** Danny Meyer & Tom Colicchio
Average Dinner for 2: $120 **Closed:** Holidays

Il Monello
1460 2nd Ave., New York, NY, 10021
Ph: 212-535-9310 Fax: 212-535-8516 **Cuisine:** Northern Italian
Owner: Adi Giovanetti **Average Dinner for 2:** $55
Closed: Christmas, New Years

Il Nido
251 E. 53rd St., New York, NY, 10022
Ph: 212-753-8450 **Cuisine:** Northern Italian
Owner: Adi Giovanetti **Average Dinner for 2:** $175

JoJo
160 E. 64th St., New York, NY, 10021
Ph: 212-223-5656 Fax: 212-755-9038 **Cuisine:** Modern French
Average Dinner for 2: $80 **Closed:** Sunday

La Caravelle *page 208
33 W. 55th St., New York, NY, 10019
Ph: 212-586-4252 Fax: 212-956-8269 **Cuisine:** French
Owners: Andre & Rita Jammet **Average Dinner for 2:** $130
Closed: Sunday

La Colombe d'Or
134 E. 26th St., New York, NY, 10010
Ph: 212-689-0666 Fax: 212-689-2952 **Cuisine:** French
Average Dinner for 2: $100

La Côte Basque
60 W. 55th St., New York, NY, 10019
Ph: 212-688-6525 Fax: 212-758-3361 **Cuisine:** French
Owner: Jean-Jacques Rachou **Average Dinner for 2:** $140

La Grenouille
3 E. 52nd St., New York, NY, 10022
Ph: 212-752-1495 Fax: 212-593-4964 **Cuisine:** Classical French
Owners: Gisele and Philippe Masson **Average Dinner for 2:** $190

La Reserve
4 W. 49th St., New York, NY, 10020
Ph: 212-247-2993 Fax: 212-247-2959 **Cuisine:** French
Owner: Jean-Louis Missud **Average Dinner for 2:** $170
Closed: Sunday

Le Bernardin
155 W. 51st St., New York, NY, 10019
Ph: 212-489-1515 Fax: 212-265-1615 **Cuisine:** French
Owners: Maguy LeCoze & Eric Ripert **Average Dinner for 2:** $140
Closed: Sunday

Le Madri
168 W. 18th St., New York, NY, 10011
Ph: 212-727-8022 Fax: 212-727-3168 **Cuisine:** Italian
Average Dinner for 2: $100 **Closed:** Holidays

Le Périgord
405 E. 52nd St., New York, NY, 10022
Ph: 212-755-6244 Fax: 212-486-3906 **Cuisine:** French
Owner: Georges Briquet **Average Dinner for 2:** $100
Closed: Christmas, New Years

Le Regence, Hotel Plaza Athenee
37 E. 64th St., New York, NY, 10021
Ph: 212-606-4647 Fax: 212-772-0958 **Cuisine:** French
Average Dinner for 2: $160

Les Celebrites
160 Central Park S., New York, NY, 10019
Ph: 212-484-5113 Fax: 212-484-4427 **Cuisine:** Continental
Average Dinner for 2: $100 **Closed:** Holidays

Lespinasse, The St. Regis Hotel
2 E. 55th St., New York, NY, 10022
Ph: 212-753-4500 Fax: 212-787-3447 **Cuisine:** French/Asian
Average Dinner for 2: $300 **Closed:** Sunday

The Manhattan Ocean Club *page 209
57 W. 58th St., New York, NY, 10019
Ph: 212-371-7777 Fax: 212-371-9362 **Cuisine:** Seafood
Owner: Alan Stillman **Average Dinner for 2:** $110
Closed: Holidays

March
405 E. 58th St., New York, NY, 10022
Ph: 212-754-6272 Fax: 212-838-5108
Cuisine: Contemporary American
Owners: Wayne Nish & Joseph Scalice
Average Dinner for 2: $140

Montrachet
239 W. Broadway, New York, NY, 10013
Ph: 212-219-2777 Fax: 212-274-9508 **Cuisine:** Modern French
Average Dinner for 2: $100 **Closed:** Sunday

Nicola's
146 E. 84th St., New York, NY, 10028
Ph: 212-249-9850 Fax: 212-772-7564 **Cuisine:** Italian
Average Dinner for 2: $80 **Closed:** Holidays

One if by Land, Two if by Sea
17 Barrow St., New York, NY, 10014
Ph: 212-228-0822 Fax: 212-206-7855
Cuisine: American/Continental
Average Dinner for 2: $55 **Closed:** Holidays

Palio *page 209
151 W. 51st St., New York, NY, 10019
Ph: 212-245-4850 Fax: 212-397-7814 **Cuisine:** Italian
Owner: Maria Pia Hellrigl **Average Dinner for 2:** $120
Closed: Sunday, Holidays

Park Avenue Café *page 210
100 E. 63rd St., New York, NY, 10021
Ph: 212-644-1900 Fax: 212-688-0373
Cuisine: Contemporary American
Average Dinner for 2: $60 **Closed:** Holidays

Periyali
35 W. 20th St., New York, NY, 10011
Ph: 212-463-7890 Fax: 212-924-9403 **Cuisine:** Greek
Average Dinner for 2: $80 **Closed:** Sundays and Holidays

Petrossian
182 W. 58th St., New York, NY, 10019
Ph: 212-245-2214 Fax: 212-245-2812 **Cuisine:** Continental
Owner: Armen Petrossian **Average Dinner for 2:** $95

The Post House *page 210
28 E. 63rd St., New York, NY, 10021
Ph: 212-935-2888 Fax: 212-371-9264 **Cuisine:** Steakhouse
Owner: Alan Stillman **Average Dinner for 2:** $130
Closed: Holidays

The Rainbow Room
30 Rockefeller Plaza 65th Fl., New York, NY, 10112
Ph: 212-632-5000 Fax: 212-632-5010
Cuisine: Contemporary American **Owner:** Joseph Baum
Average Dinner for 2: $140 **Closed:** Monday

Remi
145 W. 53rd St., New York, NY, 10019
Ph: 212-581-4242 Fax: 212-581-7182 **Cuisine:** Modern Venetian
Owners: Francesco Antonucci and Adam Tihany
Average Dinner for 2: $80

Restaurant Raphael *page 211
33 W. 54th St., New York, NY, 10019
Ph: 212-582-8993 Fax: 212-582-8993 **Cuisine:** French
Owners: Raphael & Mira Edery **Average Dinner for 2:** $100
Closed: Sunday

San Domenico
240 Central Park S., New York, NY, 10019
Ph: 212-265-5959 Fax: 212-397-0844 **Cuisine:** Italian
Owner: Tony May **Average Dinner for 2:** $65

Smith & Wollensky *page 212
44th St. at 3rd. Ave., New York, NY, 10022
Ph: 212-753-1530 Fax: 212-751-5446 **Cuisine:** Steakhouse
Owner: Alan Stillman **Average Dinner for 2:** $100
Closed: Holidays

Sparks Steakhouse *page 212
210 E. 46th St., New York, NY, 10017
Ph: 212-687-4855 Fax: 212-557-7409 **Cuisine:** Steakhouse
Average Dinner for 2: $55 **Closed:** Sunday

Terrace Restaurant
400 W. 119th St., New York, NY, 10027
Ph: 212-666-9490 Fax: 212-666-3471
Cuisine: American/Continental **Owner:** Nada Bernic
Average Dinner for 2: $70 **Closed:** Sunday, Monday

Union Square Café
21 E. 16th St., New York, NY, 10003
Ph: 212-243-4020 Fax: 212-627-2673
Cuisine: American/Continental
Owner: Danny Meyer **Average Dinner for 2:** $100

Vong
200 E. 54th St., New York, NY, 10022
Ph: 212-486-9592 Fax: 212-980-3745 **Cuisine:** French/Thai
Owner: Jean-Georges Vongerichten **Average Dinner for 2:** $80
Closed: Christmas, New Years

NEW YORK CITY-QUEENS

Il Toscano Ristorante
42-05 235th St., Douglaston, NY, 11363
Ph: 718-631-0300 Fax: 718-225-5223 **Cuisine:** Italian
Owner: Mauro Privelgi **Average Dinner for 2:** $80
Closed: Monday

HUDSON VALLEY

PIERMONT

Xaviar's
506 Piermont Ave., Piermont, NY, 10968
Ph: 914-359-7007 Fax: 914-424-3124 **Cuisine:** American
Owner: Peter Kelly **Average Dinner for 2:** $100
Closed: Monday, Tuesday

LONG ISLAND

HUNTINGTON

Piccolo   *page 213
215 Wall St., Huntington, NY, 11743
Ph: 516-424-5592 Fax: 516-421-5555 **Cuisine:** Italian/Continental
Owners: Dean & Dino Philippis **Average Dinner for 2:** $70
Closed: Monday

OYSTER BAY

Mill River Inn
160 Mill River Rd., Oyster Bay, NY, 11771
Ph: 516-922-7768 **Cuisine:** Regional
Owners: K. Stephens & R. Raudkivi **Average Dinner for 2:** $65

ROSLYN

Jolly Fisherman & Steakhouse
25 Main St., Roslyn, NY, 11576
Ph: 516-621-0055 Fax: 516-621-2126 **Cuisine:** Seafood/Steakhouse
Owner: Steven Scheiner **Average Dinner for 2:** $75
Closed: Monday

SAG HARBOR

The American Hotel
Main St., Sag Harbor, NY, 11963
Ph: 516-725-3535 Fax: 516-725-3573 **Cuisine:** Classical French
Average Dinner for 2: $100

ST. JAMES

Mirabelle
404 N. Country Rd., St James, NY, 11780
Ph: 516-584-5999 Fax: 516-751-1089 **Cuisine:** Classical French
Owners: Guy & Maria Reuge **Average Dinner for 2:** $100
Closed: Monday

UPSTATE NEW YORK

EAST AMHERST

Il Fiorentino *page 213
8485 Transit Rd., East Amherst, NY, 14051
Ph: 716-625-4250 Fax: 716-689-0476 **Cuisine:** Italian
Owners: Sandra & Giancarlo Bruni **Average Dinner for 2:** $50

CHESTERTOWN

Friends Lake Inn *page 214
963 Friends Lake Rd., Chestertown, NY, 12817
Ph: 518-494-4751 Fax: 518-494-4616 **Cuisine:** New American
Owner: Sharon Taylor **Average Dinner for 2:** $85

ELMIRA HEIGHTS

Pierce's 1894 Restaurant *page 214
228 Oakwood Ave., Elmira Heights, NY, 14903
Ph: 607-734-2022 Fax: 607-734-2024 **Cuisine:** Continental
Owners: The Pierce Family **Average Dinner for 2:** $50
Closed: Monday

ROCHESTER

The Rio *page 215
2828 Alexander St., Rochester, NY, 14607
Ph: 716-473-2806 Fax: 716-473-2809 **Cuisine:** Continental
Average Dinner for 2: $80 **Closed:** Sunday

STORMVILLE

Harralds
3110 Rt. 52, Stormville, NY, 12582
Ph: 914-878-6595 Fax: **Cuisine:** International
Owner: Eva Durrschmidt **Average Dinner for 2:** $130
Closed: Sunday, Monday, Tuesday

SYRACUSE

Pascale Wine Bar and Restaurant
204 W. Fayette St., Syracuse, NY, 13202
Ph: 315-471-3040 Fax: **Cuisine:** Contemporary American
Owners: Neil & Chuck Pascale **Average Dinner for 2:** $50
Closed: Sunday

TROY

The Tavern at Sterup Square *page 215
2113 Rte. 7, Troy, NY, 12180
Ph: 518-663-5800 Fax: 518-663-9261 **Cuisine:** International
Average Dinner for 2: $60

WESTCHESTER COUNTY

GRANITE SPRINGS

Maxime's
Old Tomahawk St., Granite Springs, NY, 10527
Ph: 914-248-7200 **Cuisine:** Classical French
Average Dinner for 2: $80 **Closed:** Monday, Tuesday

RYE

La Panetiere
530 Milton Rd., Rye, NY, 10580
Ph: 914-967-8140 Fax: 914-921-0654 **Cuisine:** French
Owner: Jacques Loupiac **Average Dinner for 2:** $150

NORTH CAROLINA

ASHEVILLE

23 Page Restaurant, Haywood Park Hotel *page 216
One Battery Park Ave., Asheville, NC, 28801
Ph: 828-252-3685 Fax: 704-252-8102 **Cuisine:** American
Owners: Aletha Roper & Broc Fountain
Average Dinner for 2: $60 **Closed:** Holidays

Horizons *page 216
290 Macon Ave., Asheville, NC, 28804
Ph: 828-252-2711 Fax: 828-253-7053 **Cuisine:** American
Average Dinner for 2: $80

CHARLOTTE

The LampLighter *page 217
1065 E. Morehead St., Charlotte, NC, 28202-2920
Ph: 704-372-5343 Fax: 704-372-5354
Cuisine: American/Continental **Owner:** Woody Fox
Average Dinner for 2: $85 **Closed:** Holidays

PITTSBORO

The Fearrington House *page 217
2000 Fearrington Village Ctr., Pittsboro, NC, 27312
Ph: 919-542-2121 Fax: 919-542-4202 **Cuisine:** Regional
Owners: Roy & Jenny Fitch **Average Dinner for 2:** $120
Closed: Monday

RALEIGH

The Angus Barn *page 218
9401 Glenwood Ave., Raleigh, NC, 27628
Ph: 919-787-3505 Fax: 919-783-5568 **Cuisine:** American
Owner: Van Eure **Average Dinner for 2:** $70
Closed: Thanksgiving, Christmas

OHIO

BEACHWOOD

Ristorante Giovanni's
25550 Chagrin Blvd., Beachwood, OH, 44122
Ph: 216-831-8625 Fax: 216-831-4338 **Cuisine:** Northern Italian
Owner: Carl Quagliata **Average Dinner for 2:** $90
Closed: Sunday

CINCINNATI

Maisonette *page 218
114 E. 6th St., Cincinnati, OH, 45202
Ph: 513-721-2260 Fax: 513-287-7785 **Cuisine:** French
Owners: The Comisar Family **Average Dinner for 2:** $130
Closed: Sunday

Palace Restaurant, The Cincinnatian Hotel *page 219
601 Vine St., Cincinnati, OH, 45202
Ph: 513-381-3000 Fax: 513-381-2659 **Cuisine:** Regional
Average Dinner for 2: $85

CLEVELAND

The Baricelli Inn *page 219
2203 Cornell Rd., Cleveland, OH, 44106
Ph: 216-791-6500 Fax: 216-791-9131 **Cuisine:** Continental
Owner: Paul Minnillo **Average Dinner for 2:** $100
Closed: Sunday

Classics, The Omni International Hotel
2065 E. 96th St., Cleveland, OH, 44106
Ph: 216-791-1300 Fax: 216-231-3329 **Cuisine:** Continental
Average Dinner for 2: $100 **Closed:** Sunday, Holidays

Sammy's *page 220
1400 W. 10th St., Cleveland, OH, 44113
Ph: 216-523-5560 Fax: 216-523-1873
Cuisine: Contemporary American **Owners:** R. DiOrio & D.M. Fugo
Average Dinner for 2: $110 **Closed:** Sunday

COLUMBUS

The Refectory *page 220
1092 Bethel Rd., Columbus, OH, 43220
Ph: 614-451-9774 Fax: 614-451-4434 **Cuisine:** Classical French
Owner: Kamal Boulos **Average Dinner for 2:** $60 **Closed:** Sunday

DAYTON

L' Auberge *page 221
4120 Far Hills Ave., Dayton, OH, 45429
Ph: 937-299-5536 Fax: 937-299-9129 **Cuisine:** Contemporary
Owner: Josef Reif **Average Dinner for 2:** $60 **Closed:** Sunday

NILES

Alberini's Restaurant *page 221
1201 Youngstown-Warren Rd., Niles, OH, 44446
Ph: 330-652-5895 Fax: 330-652-7041 **Cuisine:** Italian
Owners: The Alberini Family **Average Dinner for 2:** $45
Closed: Sunday, Holidays

OREGON

EUGENE

Chanterelle *page 222
207 E. 5th Ave., Ste. 109, Eugene, OR, 97401
Ph: 541-484-4065 **Cuisine:** European
Owner: Ralf Schmidt **Average Dinner for 2:** $50
Closed: Sunday, Monday

GLENEDEN BEACH

The Dining Room at the Salishan Lodge
7760 N. Hwy 101, Gleneden Beach, OR, 97388
Ph: 541-764-2371 Fax: 541-764-3663 **Cuisine:** Regional
Average Dinner for 2: $50

PORTLAND

Atwater's Restaurant & Bar *page 222
11 S.W. 5th Ave., Portland, OR, 97204
Ph: 503-275-3600 Fax: 503-275-8587
Cuisine: Contemporary American
Average Dinner for 2: $45 **Closed:** Christmas, New Years

The Couch Street Fish House
105 N.W. 3rd Ave., Portland, OR, 97209
Ph: 503-224-9729 Fax: 503-721-0820 **Cuisine:** Steak/Seafood
Owner: Sherwood Dudley **Average Dinner for 2:** $95
Closed: Sunday

The Heathman Hotel Restaurant *page 223
1001 S.W. Broadway, Portland, OR, 97205
Ph: 503-790-7752 Fax: 503-790-7112 **Cuisine:** French
Average Dinner for 2: $75

Zefiro *page 223
500 N.W. 21st Ave., Portland, OR, 97209
Ph: 503-226-3394 Fax: 503-226-4744 **Cuisine:** International
Owners: B. Carey & C. Israel **Average Dinner for 2:** $65
Closed: Sunday

PENNSYLVANIA

DOYLESTOWN

Sign of the Sorrel Horse
4424 Old Eastern Rd., Doylestown, PA, 18901
Ph: 215-230-9999 Fax: 215-230-8053 **Cuisine:** French/Continental
Average Dinner for 2: $70 **Closed:** Monday, Tuesday

EAST PETERSBURG

Haydn Zug's *page 224
1987 State St., East Petersburg, PA, 17520
Ph: 717-569-5746 Fax: 717-569-8450 **Cuisine:** American
Owners: The Lee Family **Average Dinner for 2:** $50
Closed: Sunday, Monday, Holidays

ERWINNA

EverMay on-the-Delaware *page 224
River Rd. Bucks County, Erwinna, PA, 18920
Ph: 610-294-9100 Fax: 610-294-8249 **Cuisine:** Continental
Owners: Bill & Danielle Moffly **Average Dinner for 2:** $125
Closed: Monday through Thursday

FARMINGTON

The Golden Trout, Mimico on Woodland Resort
Route 40 E., Farmington, PA, 15437
Ph: 724-329-8555 Fax: 724-329-6098 **Cuisine:** American
Average Dinner for 2: $80 **Closed:** Holidays

GREENSBURG

Vallozzi's *page 225
Rte. 30 East, Greensburg, PA, 15601
Ph: 412-836-7663 Fax: 412-836-7917 **Cuisine:** Italian
Owner: Ernest Vallozzi **Average Dinner for 2:** $55
Closed: Sunday

HAZLETON

Scatton's
1008 N. Vine St., Hazleton, PA, 18201
Ph: 717-455-6630 **Cuisine:** Northern Italian
Owners: Larry & Susie Dull **Average Dinner for 2:** $50
Closed: Sunday

NEW HOPE

La Bonne Auberge *page 225
Hammerstein Way - Village 2, New Hope, PA, 18938
Ph: 215-862-2462 Fax: 215-862-9105 **Cuisine:** Classical French
Owner: Gerard Caronello **Average Dinner for 2:** $80
Closed: Monday, Tuesday

PHILADELPHIA

Ciboulette, The Bellevue Building *page 226
200 S. Broad St., Philadelphia, PA, 19102
Ph: 215-790-1210 Fax: 215-790-1209 **Cuisine:** Modern French
Average Dinner for 2: $80

Circa
1518 Walnut St., Philadelphia, PA, 19102
Ph: 215-545-6800 Fax: 215-545-7683 **Cuisine:** American
Owner: David Mantelmacher **Average Dinner for 2:** $65

Deux Cheminées
1221 Locust St., Philadelphia, PA, 19107
Ph: 215-790-0200 Fax: 215-790-0202 **Cuisine:** French
Owner: Fritz Blank **Average Dinner for 2:** $150
Closed: Sunday, Monday

DiLullo Centro
1407 Locust St., Philadelphia, PA, 19102
Ph: 215-546-2000 Fax: 215-546-8639 **Cuisine:** Italian
Owner: Antonio Schiavone **Average Dinner for 2:** $80
Closed: Sunday

Founder's, Park Hyatt Philadelphia
Broad & Walnut St., Philadelphia, PA, 19102
Ph: 215-790-2814 Fax: 215-893-9868
Cuisine: Continental American/Asian **Average Dinner for 2:** $125

Fountain Restaurant, The Four Seasons
1 Logan Square, Philadelphia, PA, 19103
Ph: 215-963-1500 Fax: 215-963-2748 **Cuisine:** International
Average Dinner for 2: $140

The Garden
1617 Spruce St., Philadelphia, PA, 19103
Ph: 215-546-4455 Fax: 215-546-1753
Cuisine: American/Continental **Owner:** Kathleen Mulhern
Average Dinner for 2: $90 **Closed:** Sunday

La Famiglia
8 S. Front St., Philadelphia, PA, 19106
Ph: 215-922-2803 Fax: 215-922-7495 **Cuisine:** Italian
Owners: The Sena Family **Average Dinner for 2:** $180
Closed: Monday

Le Bec-Fin
1523 Walnut St., Philadelphia, PA, 19102
Ph: 215-567-1000 Fax: 215-568-1151 **Cuisine:** French
Owner: Georges Perrier **Average Dinner for 2:** $240
Closed: Sunday

Monte Carlo Living Room *page 226
150 South St., Philadelphia, PA, 19147
Ph: 215-925-2220 Fax: 215-925-9956 **Cuisine:** Italian
Average Dinner for 2: $100 **Closed:** Holidays

Ristorante La Buca *page 227
711 Locust St., Philadelphia, PA, 19106
Ph: 215-928-0556 Fax: 215-928-1175 **Cuisine:** Northern Italian
Owner: Guiseppe Giuliani **Average Dinner for 2:** $60
Closed: Sunday

Saloon
750 S. 7th St., Philadelphia, PA, 19147
Ph: 215-627-1811 Fax: 215-627-6765 **Cuisine:** Northern Italian
Owner: Richard Santore **Average Dinner for 2:** $100
Closed: Sunday

Striped Bass
1500 Walnut St., Philadelphia, PA, 19102
Ph: 215-732-4444 Fax: 215-732-4433 **Cuisine:** Seafood
Owner: Neil Stein **Average Dinner for 2:** $100

Susanna Foo
1512 Walnut St., Philadelphia, PA, 19102
Ph: 215-545-2666 Fax: 215-546-9106
Cuisine: Chinese with French Influence
Owners: Ensin & Susanna Foo **Average Dinner for 2:** $85

PITTSBURGH

Hyeholde Restaurant *page 227
190 Hyeholde Dr., Corapolis, PA, 15108
Ph: 412-264-3116 Fax: 412-264-5723 **Cuisine:** American
Owners: Quentin & Barbara McKenna
Average Dinner for 2: $75 **Closed:** Sunday

Le Mont *page 228
1114 Grandview Ave., Pittsburgh, PA, 15211
Ph: 412-431-3100 Fax: 412-431-1204 **Cuisine:** Contemporary
American **Owner:** Jim Blandi Jr. **Average Dinner for 2:** $90
Closed: Holidays

WEST CHESTER

The Dilworthtown Inn *page 228
1390 Old Wilmington Pike, West Chester, PA, 19382
Ph: 610-399-1390 Fax: 610-399-1504 **Cuisine:** Continental
Owners: James Barnes & Robert Rafetto
Average Dinner for 2: $75

RHODE ISLAND

PORTSMOUTH

Sea Fare Inn *page 229
3352 E. Main Rd., Portsmouth, RI, 02871
Ph: 401-683-0577 Fax: 401-683-2910 **Cuisine:** Regional
Owners: Anna & George Karousos **Average Dinner for 2:** $100
Closed: Monday

PROVIDENCE

Al Forno
577 S. Main St., Providence, RI, 02903
Ph: 401-273-9760 Fax: 401-331-1462 **Cuisine:** Italian
Owners: J. Killeen & G.Germon **Average Dinner for 2:** $75
Closed: Sunday, Monday

SOUTH CAROLINA

ANDERSON

1109 South Main *page 229
1109 S. Main St., Anderson, SC, 29621
Ph: 864-225-1109 Fax: 864-225-3884 **Cuisine:** Continental
Owners: Peter and Myrna Ryter **Average Dinner for 2:** $60
Closed: Sunday, Christmas, New Years

CHARLESTON

Louis's Restaurant & Bar *page 230
200 Meeting St., Charleston, SC, 29403
Ph: 843-853-2550 Fax: 843-722-9485 **Cuisine:** Regional
Owner: Louis Osteen **Average Dinner for 2:** $80

Magnolias *page 230
185 E. Bay St., Charleston, SC, 29401
Ph: 803-577-7771 Fax: 803-722-0035 **Cuisine:** Continental
Owner: Tom Parsell **Average Dinner for 2:** $55

TENNESSEE

BRISTOL

The Troutdale Dining Room *page 231
412 6th St., Bristol, TN, 37620
Ph: 423-968-9099 **Cuisine:** American
Owners: Carol & Barry Serber **Average Dinner for 2:** $75
Closed: Sunday

KNOXVILLE

The Orangery *page 231
5412 Kingston Pike, Knoxville, TN, 37919
Ph: 423-588-2964 Fax: 423-588-5499
Cuisine: Contemporary American **Owner:** Karen Kendrick
Average Dinner for 2: $90 **Closed:** Sunday

Regas Restaurant *page 232
318 N. Gay St. N.W., Knoxville, TN, 37917
Ph: 423-637-9805 Fax: 423-546-5031 **Cuisine:** American
Owner: William Regas **Average Dinner for 2:** $65

MEMPHIS

Chez Philippe, The Peabody Hotel *page 232
149 Union Ave., Memphis, TN, 38103
Ph: 901-529-4188 Fax: 901-529-3639 **Cuisine:** International
Average Dinner for 2: $75 **Closed:** Sunday, Holidays

La Tourelle *page 233
2146 Monroe Ave., Memphis, TN, 38104
Ph: 901-726-5771 Fax: 901-272-0492 **Cuisine:** French
Owner: Glenn Hayes **Average Dinner for 2:** $100

Restaurant Raji
712 W. Brookhaven Cir., Memphis, TN, 38117
Ph: 901-685-8723 Fax: 901-767-2226 **Cuisine:** French and Indian
Fusion **Average Dinner for 2:** $100

NASHVILLE

Arthur's *page 233
1001 Broadway, Nashville, TN, 37203
Ph: 615-255-1494 Fax: 615-255-1496 **Cuisine:** Continental
Owner: Sheila Thrailkill **Average Dinner for 2:** $110

Mario's *page 234
2005 Broadway, Nashville, TN, 37203
Ph: 615-327-3232 Fax: 615-321-2675 **Cuisine:** Northern Italian
Owner: Mario Ferrari **Average Dinner for 2:** $120
Closed: Holidays

The Wild Boar *page 234
2014 Broadway, Nashville, TN, 37203
Ph: 615-329-1313 Fax: 615-329-4930 **Cuisine:** Modern French
Average Dinner for 2: $120 **Closed:** Sunday, Holidays

TEXAS

DALLAS

Café Pacific *page 235
24 Highland Park Village, Dallas, TX, 75205
Ph: 214-526-1170 Fax: 214-526-0332
Cuisine: Contemporary American
Owner: Jack Knox **Average Dinner for 2:** $70 **Closed:** Sunday

The French Room, Hotel Adolphus *page 235
1321 Commerce St., Dallas, TX, 75202
Ph: 214-742-8200 Fax: 214-651-3683 **Cuisine:** French
Average Dinner for 2: $140 **Closed:** Sunday, Monday

Laurels, Sheraton Park Central Hotel
12720 Merit Dr., Dallas, TX, 75251
Ph: 972-851-2021 Fax: 972-851-2033 **Cuisine:** Contemporary
Average Dinner for 2: $100 **Closed:** Sunday

The Mansion on Turtle Creek
2821 Turtle Creek Blvd., Dallas, TX, 75219
Ph: 214-559-2100 Fax: 214-526-5345 **Cuisine:** Regional
Average Dinner for 2: $140

Old Warsaw
2610 Maple Ave., Dallas, TX, 75201
Ph: 214-528-0032 Fax: 214-871-1965 **Cuisine:** French/Continental
Owner: Al Heidari **Average Dinner for 2:** $120

The Pyramid Room, Fairmont Hotel
1717 N. Akard St., Dallas, TX, 75201
Ph: 214-720-2020 Fax: 214-871-7555 **Cuisine:** Continental
Average Dinner for 2: $80

The Riviera
7709 Inwood Rd., Dallas, TX, 75209
Ph: 214-351-0094 Fax: 214-351-3344 **Cuisine:** Continental
Owner: Franco Bertolasi **Average Dinner for 2:** $130
Closed: Holidays

HOUSTON

Brennan's of Houston
3300 Smith St., Houston, TX, 77006
Ph: 713-522-9711 Fax: 713-522-9142 **Cuisine:** Regional
Owners: The Brennan Family **Average Dinner for 2:** $95
Closed: Christmas

Cafe Annie
1728 Post Oak Blvd., Houston, TX, 77056
Ph: 713-840-1111 Fax: 713-840-1558 **Cuisine:** Regional
Average Dinner for 2: $80 **Closed:** Sunday, Holidays

Chez Nous   *page 236
217 South Ave. G, Humble, TX, 77338
Ph: 281-446-6717 Fax: 281-446-8612 **Cuisine:** French
Owner: Gerard Brach **Average Dinner for 2:** $85
Closed: Sunday

De Ville, Four Seasons Hotel   *page 236
1300 Lamar St., Houston, TX, 77010
Ph: 713-652-6250 Fax: 713-650-1203 **Cuisine:** French
Average Dinner for 2: $85

Empress *page 237
5419-A FM 1960 W., Houston, TX, 77069
Ph: 281-583-8021 Fax: 281-583-8095 **Cuisine:** French/Asian
Owner: Scott Chen **Average Dinner for 2:** $60 **Closed:** Sunday

La Colombe d'Or
3410 Montrose Blvd., Houston, TX, 77006
Ph: 713-524-7999 Fax: 713-524-8923 **Cuisine:** French
Owner: Steve Zimmerman **Average Dinner for 2:** $100

La Reserve, The Omni Houston Hotel *page 237
4 Riverway Dr., Houston, TX, 77056
Ph: 713-871-8181 Fax: 713-871-8116 **Cuisine:** French
Average Dinner for 2: $90 **Closed:** Sunday

Maxim's *page 238
3755 Richmond Ave., Houston, TX, 77046
Ph: 713-877-8899 Fax: 713-877-8855 **Cuisine:** French/Continental
Owner: Ronnie Berman **Average Dinner for 2:** $50
Closed: Sunday

The Rivoli *page 238
5636 Richmont St., Houston, TX, 77057
Ph: 713-789-1900 Fax: 713-266-5265 **Cuisine:** Continental
Owner: Rose Cantu **Average Dinner for 2:** $70 **Closed:** Sunday

Rotisserie for Beef and Bird *page 239
2200 Wilcrest St., Houston, TX, 77042
Ph: 713-977-9524 Fax: 713-977-9568 **Cuisine:** Steak/Seafood
Owner: Joe Mannke **Average Dinner for 2:** $80 **Closed:** Sunday

Tony's *page 239
1801 Post Oak Blvd., Houston, TX, 77056
Ph: 713-622-6778 Fax: **Cuisine:** Northern Italian
Owner: Tony Vallone **Average Dinner for 2:** $120
Closed: Sunday

UTAH

PARK CITY

Grappa Italian Restaurant
151 Main St., Park City, UT, 84060
Ph: 435-645-0636 Fax: 435-647-0844 **Cuisine:** Northern Italian
Owners: J. & L. Brill & B.White **Average Dinner for 2:** $80

Riverhorse Cafe *page 240
540 Main St., Park City, UT, 84060
Ph: 435-649-3536 Fax: 435-649-7983
Cuisine: Contemporary American
Owner: Jerry Gilomen **Average Dinner for 2:** $80

SALT LAKE CITY

Fresco Italian Cafe
1513 S. 1500 E., Salt Lake City, UT, 84117
Ph: 801-486-1300 Fax: 801-487-5379 **Cuisine:** Northern Italian
Owner: David Harries **Average Dinner for 2:** $60

The Metropolitan
173 W. Broadway, Salt Lake City, UT, 84101
Ph: 801-364-3472 Fax: 801-364-8671
Cuisine: Contemporary American **Owner:** Karen Olsen
Average Dinner for 2: $80 **Closed:** Sunday, Monday

VERMONT

KILLINGTON

Hemingway's *page 240
Route 4, Killington, VT, 05751
Ph: 802-422-3886 Fax: 802-422-3468
Cuisine: Contemporary American **Owners:** Linda & Ted Fondulas
Average Dinner for 2: $100 **Closed:** Monday, Tuesday

MANCHESTER

Colonnade Room, The Equinox
Historic Route 7A, Manchester, VT, 05254
Ph: 802-362-4700 Fax: 802-362-1595 **Cuisine:** Regional
Average Dinner for 2: $95 **Closed:** Sunday, Monday

WEST DOVER

The Inn at Sawmill Farm *page 241
Rte. 100 & Crosstown Rd., West Dover, VT, 05356
Ph: 802-464-8131 Fax: 802-464-1130
Cuisine: American/Continental
Owners: The Williams Family **Average Dinner for 2:** $100
Closed: Seasonally

VIRGINIA

ALEXANDRIA

La Bergerie *page 241
218 N. Lee St., Alexandria, VA, 22314
Ph: 703-683-1007 Fax: 703-519-6114 **Cuisine:** French/Basque
Owners: Jean & Bernard Campagne **Average Dinner for 2:** $75
Closed: Sunday, Holidays

GREAT FALLS

L' Auberge Chez Francois   *page 243
332 Springvale Rd., Great Falls, VA, 22066
Ph: 703-759-3800 Fax: 703-759-5966 **Cuisine:** French/Alsatian
Owner: Francois Haeringer **Average Dinner for 2:** $75
Closed: Monday

LEON

Prince Michel Restaurant   *page 243
Rte. 29 South, Leon, VA, 22725
Ph: 540-547-9720 Fax: 540-547-3088 **Cuisine:** French
Owner: Jean DeDucq **Average Dinner for 2:** $70
Closed: Monday through Wednesday

MCLEAN

Evans Farm Inn *page 244
1696 Chain Bridge Rd., McLean, VA, 22101
Ph: 703-356-8000 Fax: 703-821-3396 **Cuisine:** Continental
Owners: Ralph & Maria Evans **Average Dinner for 2:** $60
Closed: Christmas

RICHMOND

Lemaire, The Jefferson Hotel *page 244
Franklin & Adams St., Richmond, VA, 23220
Ph: 804-788-8000 Fax: 804-649-4624 **Cuisine:** Southern Regional
Average Dinner for 2: $100

ROANOKE

The Library
3117 Franklin Rd. S.W., Roanoke, VA, 24014
Ph: 540-985-0811 Fax: **Cuisine:** French
Owner: Lowell Hill **Average Dinner for 2:** $80
Closed: Sunday, Holidays

ROSSLYN

Tivoli *page 245
1700 N. Moore St., Rosslyn, VA, 22209
Ph: 703-524-8900 Fax: 703-524-4971 **Cuisine:** Italian
Owner: American Restaurants Corp. **Average Dinner for 2:** $65
Closed: Sunday

WASHINGTON

The Inn at Little Washington
Middle and Main St., Washington, VA, 22747
Ph: 540-675-3800 Fax: 540-675-3100
Cuisine: American/Continental **Owners:** P. O'Connell & R. Lynch
Average Dinner for 2: $200 **Closed:** Tuesday

WILLIAMSBURG

The Dining Room at Ford's Colony *page 245
240 Ford's Colony Dr., Williamsburg, VA, 23188
Ph: 757-258-4107 Fax: 757-258-4168 **Cuisine:** Regional
Owner: Richard J. Ford **Average Dinner for 2:** $75
Closed: Monday

Regency Dining Room, The Williamsburg Inn
136 Francis St., Williamsburg, VA, 23185
Ph: 757-229-1000 Fax: 757-220-7096 **Cuisine:** American
Average Dinner for 2: $110

WASHINGTON

SEATTLE

Campagne
86 Pine St., Seattle, WA, 98101
Ph: 206-728-2800 Fax: 206-448-0631 **Cuisine:** French/Provencal
Owners: Peter & Maria Lewis **Average Dinner for 2:** $100

Canlis *page 246
2576 Aurora Ave. N., Seattle, WA, 98109
Ph: 206-283-3313 Fax: 206-283-1766 **Cuisine:** Regional
Owners: Chris & Alice Canlis **Average Dinner for 2:** $100
Closed: Sunday

Fullers, Sheraton Seattle Hotel
1400 6th Ave., Seattle, WA, 98101
Ph: 206-447-5544 Fax: 206-287-5508 **Cuisine:** Northwest
Average Dinner for 2: $90 **Closed:** Sunday

The Georgian Room
411 University, Seattle, WA, 98101
Ph: 206-621-7889 Fax: 206-623-2271 **Cuisine:** Continental
Average Dinner for 2: $100 **Closed:** Sunday

Kaspar's
19 W. Harrison, Seattle, WA, 98119
Ph: 206-298-0123 Fax: 206-298-0146 **Cuisine:** Pacific Northwest
Owners: Marcus & Nancy Donier **Average Dinner for 2:** $60
Closed: Sunday, Monday

Place Pigalle Restaurant *page 246
81 Pike St., Seattle, WA, 98101
Ph: 206-624-1756 Fax: 206-285-4245 **Cuisine:** Regional
Owner: Bill Frank **Average Dinner for 2:** $75 **Closed:** Sunday

Ray's Boathouse
6049 Seaview Ave. N.W., Seattle, WA, 98107
Ph: 206-789-3770 Fax: 206-781-1960 **Cuisine:** Regional Seafood
Owners: Wohlers, Lasher & Gingrich **Average Dinner for 2:** $60

Reiner's *page 247
1106 8th Ave., Seattle, WA, 98101
Ph: 206-624-2222 Fax: 206-624-2519
Cuisine: Continental, Pacific Northwest
Owners: Hanspeter & Margret Aebersold
Average Dinner for 2: $45 **Closed:** Sunday, Monday

Rover's *page 247
2808 E. Madison St., Seattle, WA, 98112
Ph: 206-325-7442 Fax: 206-325-1092 **Cuisine:** Regional/French
Owner: Thierry Rautureau **Average Dinner for 2:** $120
Closed: Sunday, Monday

SNOQUALMIE

The Salish Dining Room
6501 Railroad Ave. S.E., Snoqualmie, WA, 98065
Ph: 206-888-2556 Fax: 206-888-2533 **Cuisine:** American
Average Dinner for 2: $75

WEST VIRGINIA

WHITE SULPHUR SPRINGS

The Main Dining Room, Greenbrier Resort *page 248
U.S. Route 60, White Sulphur Springs, WV, 24986
Ph: 304-536-1110 Fax: 304-536-7854
Cuisine: American/Continental
Average Dinner for 2: $140

WISCONSIN

KOHLER

Immigrant Restaurant *page 248
444 Highland Dr., Kohler, WI, 53044
Ph: 920-457-8888 Fax: 920-457-7011 **Cuisine:** Contemporary
Average Dinner for 2: $100 **Closed:** Sunday, Monday

MILWAUKEE

Karl Ratzsch's *page 249
320 E. Mason St., Milwaukee, WI, 53202
Ph: 414-276-2720 Fax: 414-276-3038
Cuisine: German/Continental **Owner:** Josef Ratzsch
Average Dinner for 2: $55 **Closed:** Holidays

Sanford
1547 N. Jackson St., Milwaukee, WI, 53202
Ph: 414-276-9608 Fax: 414-278-8509
Cuisine: Contemporary American
Owners: Sanford & Angela D'Amato **Average Dinner for 2:** $50
Closed: Sunday

WYOMING

JACKSON HOLE

The Granary, The Spring Creek Resort *page 249
1800 Spirit Dance Rd., Jackson Hole, WY, 83001
Ph: 307-733-8833 Fax: 307-733-1524 **Cuisine:** Regional
Average Dinner for 2: $60

Snake River Grill
84 E. Broadway, Jackson Hole, WY, 83001
Ph: 307-733-0557 Fax: 307-733-5767 **Cuisine:** American
Owner: Alan Hirschfield **Average Dinner for 2:** $55
Closed: Seasonally

CANADA

ALBERTA

CALGARY

The Conservatory, The Bow Valley Delta Hotel *page 251
209 4th Ave. S.E., Calgary, AB, T2G 0C6
Ph: 403-205-5433 Fax: 403-266-0007 Cuisine: Continental
Average Dinner for 2: $100 **Closed:** Sunday

La Chaumière *page 251
139 17th Ave. S.W., Calgary, AB, T2S 0A1
Ph: 403-228-5690 Fax: 403-228-4448 Cuisine: French
Owner: Joseph de Angelis **Average Dinner for 2:** $65
Closed: Sunday

Owl's Nest, The Westin Hotel
320 4th Ave. S.W., Calgary, AB, T2P 2S6
Ph: 403-266-1611 Fax: 403-265-7908 **Cuisine:** French/Continental
Average Dinner for 2: $80 **Closed:** Sunday

The Dining Room at the Post Hotel *page 252
200 Pipestone St., Lake Louise, AB, T0L 1E0
Ph: 403-522-3989 Fax: 403-522-3966 **Cuisine:** International
Owner: George Schwarz **Average Dinner for 2:** $110
Closed: Seasonally

BRITISH COLUMBIA

SOOKE

The Sooke Harbour House *page 252
1528 Whiffen Spit Rd., Sooke, BC, V0S 1N0
Ph: 250-642-3421 Fax: 250-642-6988 **Cuisine:** Regional
Owners: Sinclair & Fredricka Philip **Average Dinner for 2:** $90
Closed: January

VANCOUVER

5 Sails, The Pan Pacific Hotel *page 253
999 Canada Pl., Ste. 300, Vancouver, BC, V6C 3B5
Ph: 604-662-8111 Fax: 604-662-3815 **Cuisine:** Regional
Average Dinner for 2: $130

Caffe De Medici *page 253
1025 Robson St. Ste. 109, Vancouver, BC, V6E 1A9
Ph: 604-669-9322 Fax: 604-669-3771 **Cuisine:** Northern Italian
Owner: Gino Punzo **Average Dinner for 2:** $80
Closed: Christmas, New Years

Chartwell, The Four Seasons
791 W. Georgia St., Vancouver, BC, V6C 2T4
Ph: 604-689-9333 Fax: 604-689-3466 **Cuisine:** Regional
Average Dinner for 2: $100

Imperial Chinese Seafood Restaurant *page 254
355 Burrard St., Vancouver, BC, V6C 2G8
Ph: 604-688-8191 Fax: 604-688-8466 **Cuisine:** Chinese
Owner: K. L. Wong **Average Dinner for 2:** $65

MANITOBA

WINNIPEG

Dubrovnik's
390 Assiniboine Ave., Winnipeg, MB, R3C 0Y1
Ph: 204-944-0594 Fax: 204-957-7750
Cuisine: Contemporary French
Owner: Milan Bodiroga **Average Dinner for 2:** $100
Closed: Holidays

ONTARIO

CAMBRIDGE

Langdon Hall Country House Hotel *page 254
Langdon Dr. at Blair Rd., Cambridge, ON, N3H 4R8
Ph: 519-622-5048 Fax: 519-622-3158
Cuisine: Contemporary Canadian
Owners: Mary Beaton & William Bennett
Average Dinner for 2: $75

JORDAN

On The Twenty Restaurant & Wine Bar *page 255
3836 Main St., Jordan, ON, LOR 1SO
Ph: 905-562-7313 Fax: 905-562-3348 **Cuisine:** Regional
Owner: Helen Young **Average Dinner for 2:** $80
Closed: Monday

KING CITY

Hogan's Inn at Four Corners *page 255
12998 Keele St., King City, ON, LOG 1KO
Ph: 905-833-5311 Fax: 905-833-2912 **Cuisine:** Continental
Average Dinner for 2: $60 **Closed:** Sunday

MCKELLAR

The Inn at Manitou *page 256
McKellar Centre Rd., McKellar, ON, POG 1CO
Ph: 705-389-2171 Fax: 705-389-3818
Cuisine: Contemporary French **Owner:** Ben Wise
Average Dinner for 2: $100 **Closed:** Seasonally

OTTAWA

Le Jardin
127 York St., Ottawa, ON, K1N 5T4
Ph: 613-241-1424 Fax: 613-241-8911 **Cuisine:** French
Owner: Beyhan Tosun **Average Dinner for 2:** $55

TORONTO

360 Restaurant at the CN Tower *page 256
301 Front St. W., Toronto, ON, M5V 2T6
Ph: 416-362-5411 Fax: 416-601-4712 **Cuisine:** Regional
Average Dinner for 2: $90 **Closed:** Christmas

Accolade, The Crowne Plaza Hotel
225 Front St. W., Toronto, ON, M5V 2X3
Ph: 416-597-1400 Fax: 416-597-8165 **Cuisine:** French/Continental
Average Dinner for 2: $90

Auberge du Pommier
4150 Yonge St., Toronto, ON, M2P 2C6
Ph: 416-222-2220 Fax: 416-222-2580 **Cuisine:** French
Owners: Peter Oliver & Michael Bonacini
Average Dinner for 2: $100 **Closed:** Sunday

Biagio Ristorante *page 257
155 King St. E., Toronto, ON, M5C 1G9
Ph: 416-366-4040 Fax: 416-366-4765 **Cuisine:** Northern Italian
Average Dinner for 2: $75 **Closed:** Sunday, Holidays

Centro Grill & Wine Bar *page 257
2472 Yonge St., Toronto, ON, M4P 2H5
Ph: 416-483-2211 Fax: 416-483-2641 **Cuisine:** Contemporary
Owners: Tony Longo & Marc Thuet **Average Dinner for 2:** $120
Closed: Sunday

Chiaro's, The King Edward Hotel *page 258
37 King St. E., Toronto, ON, M5C 1E9
Ph: 416-863-4126 Fax: 416-863-4127 **Cuisine:** International
Average Dinner for 2: $90 **Closed:** Sunday

La Fenice *page 258
319 King St. W., Toronto, ON, M5V 1J5
Ph: 416-585-2377 Fax: 416-585-2709 **Cuisine:** Italian
Owner: Luigi Orgera **Average Dinner for 2:** $60 **Closed:** Sunday

North 44º
2537 Yonge St., Toronto, ON, M4P 2H9
Ph: 416-487-4897 Fax: 416-487-2179
Cuisine: Contemporary North American
Owner: Mark McEwan **Average Dinner for 2:** $90
Closed: Sunday

Prego Della Piazza *page 259
150 Bloor St. W., Toronto, ON, M5S 2X9
Ph: 416-920-9900 Fax: 416-920-9949 **Cuisine:** Italian
Owner: Michael Carlevale **Average Dinner for 2:** $80

Pronto Ristorante
692 Mt. Pleasant Rd., Toronto, ON, M4S 2N3
Ph: 416-486-1111 Fax: 416-486-1142 **Cuisine:** Contemporary
Average Dinner for 2: $40

Scaramouche
1 Benvenuto Pl., Toronto, ON, M4V 2L1
Ph: 416-961-8011 Fax: 416-961-1922
Cuisine: Contemporary French
Owners: M.Yoltes, C.Korte, K. Froggett
Average Dinner for 2: $120 **Closed:** Sunday, Holidays

Truffles, Four Seasons Hotel
21 Avenue Rd., Toronto, ON, M5R 2G1
Ph: 416-928-7331 Fax: 416-964-2301 **Cuisine:** International
Average Dinner for 2: $100 **Closed:** Sunday

Signatures, The Intercontinental Hotel *page 260
220 Bloor St. W., Toronto, ON, M5S 1T8
Ph: 416-324-5885 Fax: 416-324-5920 **Cuisine:** Regional
Average Dinner for 2: $70

QUEBEC

BEAUPRE

Auberge La Camarine
10947 Blvd. Sainte Anne, Beaupré, PQ, G0A 1B0
Ph: 418-827-1958 Fax: 418-827-5430 **Cuisine:** International
Owners: Andre & Francine Roy **Average Dinner for 2:** $65

CAREGNAN

Au Tourant de la Rivière
5070 Salaberry, Caregnan, PQ, G3L 3P9
Ph: 514-658-7372 Fax: 514-658-7372 **Cuisine:** French
Owner: Jacques Robert **Average Dinner for 2:** $80
Closed: Sunday, Monday

HULL

Cafe Henry Burger *page 261
69 Laurier St., Hull, PQ, J8X 3V7
Ph: 819-777-5646 Fax: 819-777-0832 **Cuisine:** French
Owner: Robert Bourassa **Average Dinner for 2:** $50
Closed: Holidays

MONTREAL

The Beaver Club, The Queen Elizabeth Hotel *page 261
900 René Lévesque Blvd. W., Montréal, PQ, H3B 4A5
Ph: 514-861-3511 Fax: 514-954-2258 **Cuisine:** French
Average Dinner for 2: $100 **Closed:** Sunday

Café de Paris, Ritz-Carlton Hotel
1228 Sherbrooke St. W., Montréal, PQ, H3G 1H6
Ph: 514-842-4212 Fax: 514-842-4907 **Cuisine:** Light French
Average Dinner for 2: $70

Chez La Mère Michel
1209 Guy St., Montréal, PQ, H3H 2K5
Ph: 514-934-0473 Fax: 514-939-0709 **Cuisine:** Classic French
Owner: Micheline Delbuguet **Average Dinner for 2:** $90
Closed: Sunday

Le Latini
1130 Jeanne-Mance, Montréal, PQ, H2Z 1L7
Ph: 514-861-3166 Fax: 514-861-8294 **Cuisine:** Italian
Average Dinner for 2:: $100 **Closed:** Holidays

Le Passe-Partout *page 262
3857 Blvd. Décarie, Montréal, PQ, H4A 3J6
Ph: 514-487-7750 Fax: 514-487-5673 **Cuisine:** French
Owners: James MacGuire & Suzanne Baron-Lafrenière
Average Dinner for 2: $70 **Closed:** Sunday, Monday

Le Piment Rouge *page 262
1170 Peel St., Montréal, PQ, H3B 4P2
Ph: 514-866-7816 Fax: 514-866-1575 **Cuisine:** Szechuan
Owners: Chuck & Hazel Mah **Average Dinner for 2:** $70

Les Chenets
2075 la Rue Bishop, Montréal, PQ, H3G 2E8
Ph: 514-844-1842 Fax: 514-844-0552 **Cuisine:** Classical French
Average Dinner for 2: $100 **Closed:** Holidays

Restaurant Le Marée *page 263
404 Place Jacques Cartier, Montréal, PQ, H2Y 3B2
Ph: 514-861-9794 Fax: 514-861-3944 **Cuisine:** French
Owner: Alfred Grilli **Average Dinner for 2:** $85
Closed: Christmas, New Years

Restaurant Les Halles *page 263
1450 Crescent St., Montréal, PQ, H3G 2R6
Ph: 514-844-2328 Fax: 514-849-1294 **Cuisine:** Modern French
Average Dinner for 2: $65 **Closed:** Sunday

NORTH HATLEY

Auberge Hatley *page 264
325 Virgin Hill Rd., North Hatley, PQ, J0B 2C0
Ph: 819-842-2451 Fax: 819-842-2907 **Cuisine:** Classical French
Owners: Liliane & Robert Gagnon **Average Dinner for 2:** $70
Closed: November 15 - 30

QUEBEC CITY

La Maison Serge Bruyère
1200 Rue St. Jean, Québec City, PQ, G1R 1S8
Ph: 418-694-0618 Fax: 418-694-2120 **Cuisine:** French
Owners: Jean-Francois & Henriette Barre
Average Dinner for 2: $95

Le Champlain Dining Room, Château Frontenac *page 264
1 Rue des Carrières, Québec City, PQ, G1R 4P5
Ph: 418-692-3861 Fax: 418-692-4353 **Cuisine:** French
Average Dinner for 2: $80

STE. ADELE

L' Eau à la Bouche
3003 Boul. St. Adèle, Ste. Adèle, PQ, JOR 1L0
Ph: 514-229-2991 Fax: 514-229-7573 **Cuisine:** French/Regional
Owners: P. Audette & A. Desjardins **Average Dinner for 2:** $80

STE. DOROTHEE-LAVAL

Le Mitoyen *page 265
652 Place Publique, Ste. Dorothée-Laval, PQ, H7X 1G1
Ph: 450-689-2977 Fax: 450-689-0385 **Cuisine:** French
Owner: Richard Bastien **Average Dinner for 2:** $75
Closed: Monday

STE. MARGUERITE DU LAC MASSON

Bistro à Champlain
75 Chemin Masson, Ste. Marguerite du Lac Masson, PQ, JOT 1L0
Ph: 514-228-4988 Fax: 514-228-4893 **Cuisine:** Classical French
Owner: Champlain Charest **Average Dinner for 2:** $100
Closed: Changes Seasonally

STE. ROSE-LAVAL

La Maison Chavignole
3 Avenue des Terraces, Ste. Rose-Laval, PQ, H7L 2C4
Ph: 514-628-0161 Fax: 514-628-7876 **Cuisine:** Classical French
Average Dinner for 2: $100 **Closed:** Holidays

MEXICO

DISTRITO FEDERAL

MEXICO CITY

Antiguo San Angel Inn
Diego Rivera 50, Mexico City, DF, 01060
Ph: 011-525-6162222 Fax: 011-525-6160977 **Cuisine:** Mexican
Average Dinner for 2: $50 **Closed:** Holidays

Champs Elysées
Paseo de La Reforma 316, Mexico City, DF, 06600
Ph: 011-525-5140450 Fax: 011-525/208-2302 **Cuisine:** French
Owners: Paquita & Francois Avernin **Average Dinner for 2:** $100
Closed: Sunday

Estoril *page 265
Alejandro Dumas 24 Polanco, Mexico City, DF, CP 11560
Ph: 011-525-2803414 Fax: 011-525-2809311
Cuisine: French/Mexican **Owner:** Rosa Margarita Martin-Miche
Average Dinner for 2: $55 **Closed:** Sunday, Holidays

Fouquet's de Paris
Mariano Escobedo 700, Mexico City, DF, 11590
Ph: 011-525-2032121 Fax: 011-525-2506723 **Cuisine:** French
Average Dinner for 2: $50

La Cava *page 267
Avenida Insurgentes Sur 2465, Mexico City, DF, 01000
Ph: 011-525-6162201 Fax: 011-525-5503801 **Cuisine:** International
Owner: Jordi Escofet **Average Dinner for 2:** $55

La Hacienda de los Morales
Vasqez de Mella 525, Mexico City, DF, 11510
Ph: 011-525-2814703 Fax: **Cuisine:** Mexican/Continental
Average Dinner for 2: $60 **Closed:** Holidays

St. Honoré *page 268
341 Presidente Masarick, Mexico City, DF, 11560
Ph: 011-525-2811065 Fax: 011-525-2814048 **Cuisine:** Continental
Average Dinner for 2: $70 **Closed:** Holidays

Suntory
14 Torres Adalid, Mexico City, DF, 03100
Ph: 011-525-5369432 Fax: 011-525-5430031 **Cuisine:** Japanese
Owner: Yoko Kase **Average Dinner for 2:** $70 **Closed:** Holidays

GUANAJUATO

SAN MIGUEL DE ALLENDE

Casa de Sierra Nevada *page 268
Hospicio 35, San Miguel de Allende, GT, 37700
Ph: 011-524-6520415 Fax: 011-524-1522337 **Cuisine:** International
Average Dinner for 2: $45

Villa Jacaranda *page 269
Aldama 53, San Miguel de Allende, GTO, 37700
Ph: 011-524-6521015 Fax: 011-524-1520883
Cuisine: International/Mexican
Owner: Don Fenton **Average Dinner for 2:** $55

GUERRERO

ACAPULCO

Casanova *page 269
Av. Escencia Las Brisas 5256, Acapulco, GO,
Ph: 011-527-4846815 Fax: 011-527-4840035 **Cuisine:** Italian
Owner: Arturo Cordova **Average Dinner for 2:** $100

Madeiras
Carretera Escenica #33 Bis, Acapulco, GO, 39880
Ph: 011-527-4846921 **Cuisine:** Regional
Average Dinner for 2: $80 **Closed:** Holidays

JALISCO

GUADALAJARA

Aquellos Tiempos, Camino Real Hotel
Avenue Vallarta 5005, Guadalajara, JA, 45040
Ph: 011-527-1218000 Fax: 011-527-1214444
Cuisine: Mexican/International
Average Dinner for 2: $74 **Closed:** Sunday

MORELOS

CUERNAVACA

Las Mañanitas *page 270
Richardo Linares #107, Cuernavaca, Morelos,
Ph: 011-527-3141466 Fax: 011-527-3183672
Cuisine: Mexican/International
Owners: Margot Krause & Ruben Cerda
Average Dinner for 2: $60

OAXACA CENTRO

OAXACA

El Asador Vasco *page 270
Portal de Flores 11 Centro, Oaxaca Centro, Oaxaca, 68000
Ph: 011-529-5144755 **Cuisine:** Mexican/Basque Spanish
Owners: The Ugartechea Brothers **Average Dinner for 2:** $35

QUINTANA ROO

CANCUN

Blue Bayou
Hyatt Cancun Caribe Blvd., Cancun, QR, 840829
Ph: 011-529-8830044 Fax: 011-529-8831514 **Cuisine:** Cajun
Average Dinner for 2: $60

La Joya, Fiesta Americana Coral Beach Hotel
Fiesta Americana Coral Beach, Cancun, QR, 832900
Ph: 011-529-8832900 **Cuisine:** Mexican/International
Average Dinner for 2: $80 **Closed:** Monday

More information on our DiRōNA Award Restaurants

The Crow's Nest
HOTEL CAPTAIN COOK

The premier restaurant in Anchorage offers new American cuisine featuring fresh seafood. The extensive wine list has more than 10,000 bottles from around the world. The dining room allows you to savor your meal as you enjoy the panoramic view of Cook Inlet and the Chugach Mountains. The cozy cocktail lounge boasts Anchorage's best martini, and we also serve an elegant Sunday Brunch.

Owner: Hotel Captain Cook   Chef: Patrick Hoogerhyde

4th at K St., Anchorage, AK, 99501
PH: 907.276.6000 FAX: 907.343.2211
Website:www.captaincook.com

Simon & Seafort's

Simon & Seafort's is proud to celebrate its 20th anniversary serving American favorites to Alaska. The elegant, turn-of-the-century styled dining room overlooks the Alaskan Range and the beautiful Mt. Susitna. We are famous for hand-picked prime rib, the freshest of Alaskan seafood and the largest selection of malt whiskies in the state. Try our hand-shaken Scratch Margarita in the Grand Saloon and watch the sun set over the waters of Cook Inlet.

Owner: Restaurants Unlimited Inc.   Chef: Tom Hommes

Specialties
Rock Salt Roasted Prime Ribs of Beef
Fresh Caught Alaskan Fish and Seafood

420 L Street, Anchorage AK 99501
PH: 907.274.3502 FAX: 907.274.2487

The Pump House

The most unique restaurant in Alaska has been serving up Fairbanks hospitality for more than 20 years. A truly Alaskan restaurant and National Historic Site with turn-of-the-century antiques. Enjoy the outdoor dining deck or the interior Gold Rush theme, situated on the bank of the Chena River. The menu features fresh Alaskan seafood, wild game and alder-smoked specialties.

Chef: Doug Palmer

Specialties
Halibut Florentine
Caribou Stew

796 Chena Pump Rd.,Fairbanks, AK, 99709
PH: 907.479.8452 FAX: 907.479.8432
Email:pumphse@polarnet.com
Website:www2.polarnet.com/~pumphse

Alouette's

Serene elegance describes the atmosphere in West Little Rock's Alouette's. Three dining rooms, each with a distinctive European-style décor, provide subtle nuances of ambience, perfect for a romantic anniversary celebration or a more casual reunion of friends. Rooms may also be reserved for large parties or professional programs. Chef Denis Seyer hails from Lorraine, France, and the cuisine is classical French complemented by a good wine list.

Owner and Chef: Denis Seyer

Specialties
Lobster Bisque • Fresh Crabcakes
Seabass with Lobster Bearnaise

11401 N Rodney Parham, Little Rock AK 72212
PH: 501.225.4152 FAX: 501.221.7920
Website: www.alouettes.com

The Latilla

The Latilla is The Boulders' fine dining restaurant featuring distinctive American cuisine that combines health consciousness with intense regional flavors and a colourful presentation. Under the direction of Chef Mary Nearn, the Latilla has earned the Award of Excellence from *Wine Spectator* and 'America's Most Romantic Restaurant' from *Dining by Candlelight*. Guests dine in rustic elegance under latilla (meaning 'little sticks') ceilings with views of a cascading waterfall off massive boulder formations.

Chef: Mary Nearn

Specialties

Bourbon Molasses Glazed Quail
Italian Cowboy Veal Chop
Crisp Peppered Range Chicken

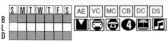

34631 N. Tom Darlington Dr.,
Carefree AZ 85377
PH: 602.488.9009 FAX: 602.488.4118

Chaparral

The best influences of Italy, France, Spain, Mexico and the Great Southwest are woven together to create the exciting tapestry of flavors of the new Chaparral. Featuring a warm decor, our popular Scottsdale landmark sparks your evening with innovative preparations and palate-pleasing inspirations. Chaparral offers wonderful sunset views of Camelback mountain, an award-winning wine list, and the spectacular setting of Marriott's Camelback Inn. Celebrate culinary ecstasy at the new Chaparral.

Owner: Marriott International   Chef: Gary Scherer

Specialties

Cazuela of Shrimp, Scallops, Mussels and Lobster
Chef David's Sharing Platter

5402 E. Lincoln Dr., Scottsdale AZ 85253
PH: 602.948.1700 FAX: 602.905.7843
Website: www.camelbackinn.com

Mary Elaine's
THE PHOENICIAN

The Phoenician's Mary Elaine's restaurant in Scottsdale offers diners a unique mix of European elegance and international culinary influences set against the charming backdrop of the desert southwest. The French-American cuisine of award-winning chef George Mahaffey is grounded in classic culinary techniques, yet is contemporary and innovative. Distinctive cuisine, an impressive wine list and soft jazz combine for a memorable experience.

Owner: The Phoenician Scottsdale   Chef: George Mahaffey

6000 E Camelback Road, Scottsdale, AZ, 85251
PH: 602.941.8200 FAX: 602.947.4311

L'Auberge de Sedona

Overlooking the quiet beauty of Oak Creek, the charming L'Auberge Restaurant has an enchanting air. The glow of candlelight and fragrance of flowers enhances the mood while considerate service attends to every need. A sumptuous lunch and dinner menu is created weekly by our chefs and prepared using only the freshest of ingredients. The menu presents a superb and varied repertoire of French delights.

Chef: Mark May

Specialties
Lobster with Squash, Spinach and Mussel-Saffron Vinaigrette
Foie Gras with Parma Ham and Caramelized Melon

301 L'Auberge Lane, Sedona, AZ, 86336
PH: 520.282.1661 FAX: 520.282.2885

Anthony's in the Catalinas

With breathtaking views of the Santa Catalina Mountains, Anthony's offers a unique dining experience. Elegant tables with light pink linens, fresh flowers and Villeroy and Boch china combine to provide an intimate setting to foster romances or friendships. The impeccable service and outstanding food is sure to impress friends as well as business associates. *Wine Spectator's* Grand Award winning wine list ensures a great selection of wines which are housed in our underground wine cellar.

Owners: Anthony and Brooke Martino

Specialties
Lamb Wellington
Fresh Fish

6440 N Campbell Ave., Tucson, AZ, 85718
PH: 520.299.1771 FAX: 520.299.6635
Email:abmartino@aol.com

Ventana Room
LOEWS VENTANA CANYON RESORT

Take in the panoramic views of Tucson or the canyon waterfall while enjoying an exquisite meal at The Ventana Room. Ranked top in the southwest by *Conde Nast Traveler* magazine readers and the *Zagat Survey*, the restaurant is renowned for its new American cuisine created by Chef Jeffrey Russell and attentive service overseen by maître d' Todd Orlich. The Ventana Room offers an extensive wine list and two tasting menus in additon to its seasonal à la carte menu. A harpist plays nightly.

Chef: Jeffrey Russell

Specialties
Escargot with Shiitake Mushrooms
Grilled Buffalo Tenderloin

7000 N. Resort Dr., Tucson, AZ, 85750
PH: 520.299.2020 FAX: 520.299.6832
Website:www.ventanaroom.com

The Perfect Setting for a Great Meal.

Whether you're in the mood for formal or casual dining, you're sure to enjoy restaurants where the American Express® Card is welcome. With the Card, dining couldn't be more pleasurable or more convenient.

Cards

Trader Vic's

A Bay Area institution for romantic dining since 1934, Trader Vic's features tropical ambience with island-style cuisine and world famous drinks. Home of the original Mai Tai, Trader Vic's offers prime meats, fowl, and daily fish specials cooked to preference: steamed, grilled or barbequed from wood-fired ovens. In Emeryville, overlooking the beautiful Emeryville Marina on San Francisco Bay.

Chef: Jerome R.W. Laugenie

Specialties

Fresh Fish
Meat and Fowl Slow Cooked in Wood-Fired Ovens

9 Anchor Dr., Emeryville CA 94608
PH: 510.653.3400 FAX: 510.653.9384

The Lark Creek Inn

Ensconced in the redwoods with a creek-side dining patio, the Lark Creek Inn is only 15 minutes north of the Golden Gate Bridge. Chef Ogden's daily changing menu offers farm-fresh American fare capitalizing on the bounty of locally produced raw materials. The updated, lightened conceptions are served with pride and skill. The carefully composed wine list includes more than 200 selections.

Owners: Bradley Ogden & Michael Dellar   Chef: Bradley Ogden

Specialties

Gorgonzola Soufflé with Wild Watercress Salad
Seared Halibut Filet with Tempura Prawns
Applewood Smoked Pork Loin Chop with Plum Compote
Grilled King Salmon Filet with Corn and Maui Onions

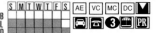

234 Magnolia Ave., Larkspur, CA, 94939
PH: 415.924.7766 FAX: 415.924.7117

Wente Vineyards Restaurant

Wente Vineyards is truly a unique dining destination. Where else could a discriminating diner savor superlative wines, dine in an award-winning restaurant, play on a Greg Norman designed golf course and enjoy a summer night's entertainment by world renowned performers? Executive chef Kimball Jones' award-winning menu reflects a spirit of innovation and features regional American dishes. All recipes express the distinctive Wente style and are created with only the best and freshest seasonal ingredients.

Chef: Kimball Jones

Specialties
Seasonal Menu, Changes Daily

5050 Arroyo Rd., Livermore, CA, 94550
PH: 925.456.2400 FAX: 925.456.2401

Auberge Du Soleil

A hillside of olive trees and a mosaic of vineyards was the setting that inspired Claude Rouas to open this magnificient restaurant in 1981. The cuisine features the full splendor of the region's flavors and colors, enhanced by a selection of 500 California wines. The country cottages built in 1985 welcome you with luxuriously calm and romantic rooms and suites, each with fireplace and private terrace. Nearby, enjoy wineries, cycling, hot air ballooning and browsing for antiques.

Owners: Claude Rouas and Bob Harmon   Chef: Andrew Sutton

Specialties
Tempura Ahi
Salmon Sashimi

180 Rutherford Hill Rd., Rutherford, CA, 94573
PH: 800.348.5406 FAX: 707.963.8764

Biba

Biba Caggiano, acclaimed cookbook author and star of the national cooking show Biba's Italian Kitchen, aired on The Learning Channel, owns and operates Biba. Biba serves exceptional classic Italian cuisine. Service is refined but friendly, ensuring a smooth and pleasurable dining experience.

Owner: Biba Caggiano   Chef: Don Brown

Specialties

Homemade Pasta, Homemade Gnocchi
Risotto, Braised Rabbit and Duck

S	M	T	W	T	F	S
B						
L						
D						

AE VC MC 🍴

🚗🕿❷

2801 Capitol Ave., Sacramento, CA, 95816
PH: 916.455.2422 FAX: 916.455.0542

Acquerello

Named the second-best Italian restaurant in the country by *Wine Spectator*, Acquerello remains in a class by itself, the only truly white tablecloth restaurant in San Francisco. Acquerello's innovative food is presented with the same flawless attention to detail found at top French houses.

Owners: G. Paterlini & S. Gresham   Chef: Suzette Gresham

Specialties

Braised Artichoke Torte with Saffron Mayonnaise
Golden Seared Salmon in White Vermouth and Dill
Ridged Pasta with Foie Gras and Black Truffles

S	M	T	W	T	F	S
B						
L						
D						

AE VC MC DC DS

🍴🚗🕿❹ PR

1722 Sacramento St.,
San Francisco CA 94109
PH: 415.567.5432 FAX: 415.567.6432
Website:www.acquerello.com

Aqua

Aqua is situated in the heart of San Francisco's financial district. Owner Charles Condy and Chef Michael Mina have joined forces to redefine seafood dining and to pay elegant tribute to the flavors of the sea. Chef Mina's intensely flavorful and creative seafood cooking has earned him a reputation as one of the nation's most respected chefs. In 1997, Mina received the James Beard Foundation's Rising Star Chef of the Year Award.

Owner: Charles Condy   Chef: Michael Mina

Specialties

Tartare of Ahi Tuna, Sesame Oil Infused with
Scotch Bonnet Chilies
Parfait of Russian Osetra Caviar

S	M	T	W	T	F	S	AE	VC	MC	DC
B										
L										
D										

252 California St., San Francisco CA 94111
PH: 415.956.9662 FAX: 415.956.5229

Carnelian Room

In a city known for its fine dining and beautiful views, one experience combines it all: the Carnelian Room, located in the heart of the financial district. Dine in a setting reminiscent of an English Manor: warmth and elegance enhanced by master works of 18th and 19th-century art. Savor one of the most breathtaking panoramas on earth: the magnificent sweep of sea and sky, bridges and bay, city and hills that is the San Francisco Bay area.

Chef: Ron Garrido

Specialties

Northern California Products
Menu Changes Seasonally

S	M	T	W	T	F	S	AE	VC	MC	CB	DC	DS
B												
L												
D												

555 California St. 52nd Fl.
San Francisco, CA, 94104
PH: 415.433.7500 Toll Free: 1.888.275.0928

Fournou's Ovens
RENAISSANCE STANFORD COURT HOTEL

Dine in one of San Francisco's best restaurants, located in the Renaissance Stanford Court Hotel atop historic Nob Hill. Enjoy a Mediterranean-themed setting with a menu that emphasizes seasonal specialties. Fournou's Ovens is named for its visual focal point, the massive 54-square-foot European style roasting ovens. For eight consecutive years, our wine list has been chosen as a Grand Award Winner by *Wine Spectator.* Champagne brunch on Saturday and Sunday.

Owner: Renaissance Stanford Court Hotel　　Chef: Thomas Hanson

Specialties
Rack of Lamb
Roast Duck

905 California St., San Francisco, CA, 94108
PH: 415.989.1910 FAX: 415.986.8195

Harris' Restaurant

Harris' Restaurant has been serving San Francisco's finest aged beef since 1984. Harris' is the creation of Ann Lee Harris, who grew up on a ranch in West Texas and has deep roots in the cattle industry. The richly appointed dining rooms feature overstuffed leather booths, mahogany panelled walls, warm murals by local artists, brass fixtures and elegant Victorian details. Ask any San Franciscan about the city's best steak, and they're certain to tell you about Harris'.

Owners: Ann Lee Harris and Goetz Boje　　Chef: Michael Buhagiar

Specialties
Midwestern Dry-Aged Beef

2100 Van Ness Ave., San Francisco, CA, 94109
PH: 415.673.1888 FAX: 415.673.8817

Le Central

The place to see and be seen: an informal, unpretentious bistro brasserie offering the same unique friendly ambience and heart-warming food since 1974. Classic bistro style dishes are all expertly prepared by chefs John and Paul Tamphanich. A chalkboard offers daily specials.

Owners: Paul & John Tamphanich,　　　Chef: John Tamphanich
Michel Bonnet

Specialties
Fresh Celery Remoulade
Leeks Vinaigrette
Cassoulet

S	M	T	W	T	F	S		AE	VC	MC	CB	DC	DS

B
L
D

453 Bush St., San Francisco, CA, 94108
PH: 415.391.2233 FAX: 415.391.3615

Masa's

Since 1983, Masa's reputation, established by founding chef Masataka Kobayashi, continues to soar under chef Chad Callahan. Callahan elevates French cuisine to a new level with the freshest ingredients, classic sauces and elegant presentations. Masa's is famous for its seafood and game specialities, featured on the seasonally changing menu. Masa's wine-by-the-glass program enables guests to taste a variety of vintages throughout their meals.

Chef: Chad Callahan

Specialties
Roasted Langoustines with Petit Pois
Boudin of Fresh Lobster, Shrimp and Scallops
Foie Gras Sautéed with Madeira Truffle Sauce
Médallions of Fallow Deer with Caramelized Apples

S	M	T	W	T	F	S		AE	VC	MC	CB	DC	J	DS

B
L
D

648 Bush St., San Francisco CA 94108
PH: 415.989.7154 FAX: 415.989.3141

North Beach Restaurant

No trip to San Francisco would be complete without a visit to North Beach Restaurant. North Beach vows to serve the finest Tuscan cuisine. We make our own pasta, cure our own prosciutto, and use the best meats and freshest fish available. North Beach's dining room and unique private function rooms provide a relaxed, Italian galleria-inspired ambience. *Wine Spectator* award-winning cellar.

Owner: Lorenzo Petroni   Chef: Bruno Orsi

Specialties
Twenty Different Antipasti
Thirty Different Pastas
Fifty Different Main Courses

1512 Stockton St., San Francisco CA 94133
PH: 415.392.1700 FAX: 415.392.0230
Website:www.citysearch.com/sfo/nbeachrest

Stars

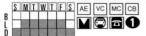

Jeremiah Tower's landmark San Francisco restaurant is a large noisy dining room filled with the city's elité, as well as local and visiting celebrities. Opened in 1984, Stars is still one of the few restaurants that has it all: great food, professional service, and an exciting "see and be seen" atmosphere. Stars is a regular haunt for patrons of the arts. The city's opera, ballet and symphony are mere blocks from the restaurant. The menu offers the finest ingredients with seemingly simple yet innovative preparations and presentations.

Specialties
Menu Changes Daily
Heavenly Desserts

555 Golden Gate Ave, San Francisco, CA, 94102
PH: 415.861.7827 FAX: 415.554.0351

Tommy Toy's

HAUTE CUISINE CHINOISE

This elegant restaurant, located in the heart of San Francisco's financial district, is world-famous for its combination of Chinese and French flavors. Enjoy fine dining at its best in a re-creation of China's Empress Dowager's reading room. A recipient of Mobil's Four-Star Award for Excellence and inducted into *Nation's Restaurant News* Hall of Fame in 1991, this is a "must" when visiting San Francisco.

Specialties

Whole Maine Lobster in Peppercorn Sauce
Peking Duck Carved at the Table

655 Montgomery St., San Francisco, CA, 94111
PH: 415.397.4888 FAX: 415.397.0469

Emile's

Celebrating its 25th Anniversary, Emile's has won award after award displaying our continuous dedication to perfectly prepared cuisine and impeccable service. Coupled with excellent service and cuisine, the enchanting interior is one of the most beautiful in the Silicon Valley. The varied menu features many delicious options based on classical French cuisine. You are certain to enjoy the elegance Emile has maintained for 25 years.

Owner and Chef: Emile Mooser

Specialties

Napoleon of House Cured Gravlax
Roasted Rack of New Zealand Lamb
Grilled Salmon in a Pistachio Nut Crust
Grand Marnier Soufflé

545 South Second St., San Jose, CA, 95112
PH: 408.289.1960 FAX: 408.998.1245
Website:www.Emiles.com

Paolo's

Since 1958, Paolo's has remained a favorite of Silicon Valley locals and visitors alike. Second-generation owner Carolyn Allen maintains her family's commitment to their heritage through the unique art and traditions of regional Italian cuisine, and to acquiring the finest local and imported ingredients. Paolo's style is as fashionable and contemporary today as it was 40 years ago. *Wine Spectator* Award of Excellence recipient.

Owner and Chef: Carolyn Allen   Chef: Mark Hopper

Specialties

Ahi Tuna Carpaccio
Gnocchi with White Truffles and Fontina Val d'Aosta
Roasted Squab with Savoy Cabbage, Apple & Pancetta
Slow Baked Salmon with Potato-Fennel Sofritto, Basil Broth

#150 - 333 W. San Carlos St.,
San Jose, CA, 95110
PH: 408.294.2558 FAX: 408.294.2595
Website:www.paolosrestaurant.com

Le Mouton Noir

Contrary to what its name implies, Le Mouton Noir is certainly not the "black sheep" of Saratoga's famous restaurant row. Located in a 140-year-old Victorian building decorated with Laura Ashley prints, colorful sprays of flowers and tones of pink and dusty rose, this dining establishment has the cheerfulness of a country home. Now featuring chef Kirk Bruderer from The French Laundry in Yountville, CA, the progressive and innovative food is contemporary French-inspired California cuisine. The à la minute preparation technique captures the full flavor of the freshest products available.

Chef: Kirk Bruderer

Specialties

Roasted Rack of Prime Lamb
Duck à la Mouton Noir

14560 Big Basin Way, Saratoga, CA, 95070
PH: 408.867.7017 FAX: 408.867.5048
Website:www.lemoutonnoir.com

The Plumed Horse

Located in the quaint village of Saratoga, The Plumed Horse offers guests a welcome retreat with a panoramic view of redwoods and the Santa Cruz Mountains. The proximity to Silicon Valley, the San Jose Convention Center and the San Jose airport makes the restaurant a convenient meeting place for people who have tight schedules but insist on the very best. Since 1987, winner of the prestigious *Wine Spectator* Grand Award.

Owners: Pache Family   Chef: Patrick Farjas

Specialties

Seasonal Country Fare
French Cuisine

14555 Big Basin Way, Saratoga CA 95070
PH: 408.867.4711 FAX:408.867.6919
Website:www.plumedhorse.com

S	M	T	W	T	F	S		AE	VC	MC	CB	DC	J	

B
L
D

Hasting's Grill

The critically acclaimed Hasting's Grill is renowned for an innovative menu that draws on the best influence of California and Pacific Rim cuisine. Polished brass, mahogany paneling and etched glass create an elegant, yet informal club-like setting. Attentive personal service and an extensive wine list enhance the superb dining experience. Located in the heart of the Hilton Anaheim's entertainment and dining "district", the restaurant counts former President and Mrs. Bush among its celebrity patrons.

Owner: Hilton Hotel   Chef: Fred Mensinga

Specialties

Lobster Tail and Japanese Wheat Noodles
Sautéed Tiger Prawns
Lamb Tenderloin and Lobster
Grilled Fillet of Ostrich

777 Convention Way, Anaheim, CA, 92802
PH: 714.740.4422

S	M	T	W	T	F	S		AE	VC	MC	CB	DC	DS

B
L
D

JW's Steakhouse

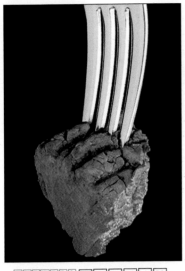

JW's Steakhouse is proud to offer the finest selection of premium well-aged cuts of beef, chops, fresh seafood and a well chosen wine list served in the classic style of great American steakhouse. Join us for a great steakhouse dinner, where the atmosphere is casually elegant and the servers are friendly and knowledgeable.

Owner: Anaheim Marriott   Chef: Jens Lauritzen

Specialties

**Homemade Soups and Breads
Angus Beef, Lamb, Chicken and Pork
Dessert Soufflés**

700 W. Convention Way, Anaheim, CA, 92802
PH: 714.750.8000 FAX: 714.750.9100

Mr. Stox

Located conveniently near Disneyland and the Anaheim Convention Center, Mr. Stox has been operated by the Marshall family since 1977. The early mission-style exterior belies the small elegant dining rooms and cozy fireplace inside. The menu features Colorado lamb, veal, prime steaks and a wide choice of fresh fish. Mr. Stox is noted for its home baked gourmet breads, fresh pasta and exquisite desserts. The award winning wine list offers over 900 selections.

Owners: Chick and Ron Marshall   Chef: Scott Michael Raczek

Specialties

**Maryland Crab Cakes
USDA. Prime Steaks
Home-Baked Breads and Pastries**

1105 E. Katella Ave., Anaheim, CA, 92805
PH: 714.634.2994 FAX: 714.634.0561
Website:www.mrstox.com

Thee White House

Thee White House Restaurant occupies a lovely turn-of-the-century home built in 1909, and features award-winning Northern Italian cuisine served in eight romantically decorated dining areas. The wine list offers nearly 200 wine selections. The restaurant is ideal for groups large and small, for business meetings and special occasions. The Anaheim Convention Center, hotels, Edison Field and the Arrowhead Pond are all nearby.

Owner: Bruno Serato   Chef: David Libby

Specialties

Chicken Breast Baked in Parchment with a Julienne of Leeks, Shiitake and Broken Garlic
Gnocchi in Gorgonzola Sauce
Housemade Ravioli Filled with Lobster, Basil and Prosciutto

887 S. Anaheim Blvd., Anaheim CA 92805
PH: 714.772.1381 FAX: 714.772.7062
Website: www.imenu.com/theewhitehouse

The Grill on the Alley

When Angelenos are in search of grill fare in a truly American setting, one restaurant stands above the rest: The Grill. Modelled after the renowned grills of New York and San Francisco, the Grill's founders, Dick Shapiro, Bob Spivak and Mike Weinstock, along with executive chef John Sola, have continued the legend of these great restaurants. The Grill offers an extensive selection of fresh food, impeccable service and a comfortable atmosphere with a sophisticated big city spirit.

Owner: Grill Concepts, Inc.   Chef: John Sola

Specialties
Prime New York Steak
The Grill Cobb Salad

9560 Dayton Way, Beverly Hills, CA, 90210
PH: 310.276.0615 FAX: 310.276.0284
Website:www.thegrill.com

La Vie en Rose

La Vie en Rose is a charming reproduction of a Normandy farmhouse located in the heart of Orange County. Proprietor Louis Laulhere immigrated to America with family recipes from Gascony and Provence. The restaurant boasts one of the finest wine lists in the country. The French name means "life is rosy" and that's exactly how an evening here will make you feel.

Owner: Louis Laulhere

Specialties

Roasted Rack of Lamb
Sauteed Duck Breast

240 S. State College Blvd., Brea, CA, 92821
PH: 714.529.8333 FAX: 714.529.2751
Email:lavnrose@earthlink.net

S	M	T	W	T	F	S	AE	VC	MC
B									
L									
D									

Saddle Peak Lodge

From its simple beginnings as a waystop and general store in the early 1900s, the rustic yet wonderfully elegant Saddle Peak Lodge is recognized today as one of America's premier dining experiences. Hidden in the Santa Monica Mountains between Malibu and the San Fernando Valley, the restaurant is famous for its extensive game menu. The well-balanced fare also includes a wide selection of exquisitely prepared fish, poultry and meat.

Owner: Ann Graham Ehringer   **Chef: Alex Scrimgeour**

Specialties

Fresh Seafood
Wild Game

419 Cold Canyon Rd., Calabasas, CA, 91302
PH: 818.222.3888 FAX: 818.222.1054

S	M	T	W	T	F	S	AE	VC	MC	DC	DS
B											
L											
D											

Sunday Brunch 11-2 pm

The Cellar

The Cellar is located in the original cellars of the historic California Hotel, built in 1922. The restaurant is a cosy, romantic wine grotto complete with stone walls, pillars, wine casks and ceiling beams. The cuisine is classical French with updated, lighter sauces. The wine list is a winner of *Wine Spectator's* Grand Award, and a connoisseur's dream, with more than 1200 selections of vintage wines from 15 countries.

Owner: Ernest Zingg   Chef: David Kesler

Specialties
Silky Lobster Bisque with a Dash of Armagnac
Grilled Veal Chop with Apples, Walnuts and Calvados

305 N. Harbor Blvd., Fullerton, CA, 92832
PH: 714.525.5682 FAX: 714.525.3853
Email:thecellar@msn.com
Website:www.imenu.com/thecellar

S	M	T	W	T	F	S
B						
L						
D						

AE VC MC CB DC J DS

Chanteclair

Nestled in the heart of Irvine, this charming French restaurant epitomizes warmth and hospitality. Chanteclair's innovative country French cuisine is tantalizing to the eye as well as the palate. A selection from Chanteclair's award-winning wine list provides the finishing touch to any meal, and the attentive staff are well-versed in the subtle touches of fine dining. Private dining rooms are available for social or professional entertaining. If outdoor dining is preferred, reserve a table on the patio - a favorite for the lunch hour.

Owner: John Kookootsedes   Chef: Joe Flores

Specialties
Swordfish with Sundried Tomato Risotto
Bricka for Two

18912 MacArthur Blvd., Irvine, CA, 92612
PH: 949.752.8001 FAX: 949.955.1394

S	M	T	W	T	F	S
B						
L						
D						

AE VC MC CB DC ER J DS

George's at the Cove

Legendary, adventurous, acclaimed from coast to coast, George's at the Cove Fine Dining, Ocean Terrace and Bar offers three tiers of breathtaking ocean view dining overlooking the famous La Jolla cove. Contemporary California cuisine, emphasizing fresh seafood with an award-winning wine list, is creatively prepared in a comfortably elegant setting downstairs. Upstairs, both the Ocean Terrace and Bar offer more casual bistro fare. *Wine Spectator* Award Winner.

Owner: George Hauer   Chef: Scott Meskan

Specialties

Seared Rare Ahi Tuna
Maine Diver Scallops
Marinated Rack of Lamb

1250 Prospect St., La Jolla CA 92037
PH: 619.454.4244 FAX: 619.454.5458
Website: www.george'satthecove.com

The Marine Room
LA JOLLA BEACH & TENNIS CLUB
SEA LODGE HOTEL

The Marine Room is a tradition of sophisticated dining that has flourished for more than half a century on the sands of La Jolla Shores. Its atmosphere is elegantly warm and inviting, with the drama of exhilarating ocean vistas. Graceful service and soft music complement a superb wine list and continental style menus created by award-winning executive chef Bernard Guillas. Live entertainment and dancing nightly. Spectacular brunch buffet featured Sundays.

Owner: La Jolla Beach & Tennis Club, Inc.   Chef: Bernard Guillas

Specialties

Ahi Tuna Tiger-Eye with Spicy Peanut Sauce
Lobster Bisque

2000 Spindrift Dr., La Jolla, CA, 92037
PH: 619.459.7222 FAX: 619.551.4673
Website:www.marineroom.com

Bernard's
REGAL BILTMORE HOTEL

Bernard's award-winning continental cuisine features an epicurean selection of grilled seafood and meats in an elegant wood-panelled setting. Only minutes away from the Music Center, Bernard's offers the perfect location for pre-theater dining or a romantic evening getaway for two.

Owner: Regal Biltmore Hotel   Chef: Roger Pigozzi

Specialties
Tiger Prawns
Oven Roasted Rack of Domestic Lamb

S	M	T	W	T	F	S	AE	VC	MC	DC	J	DS
B												
L												
D												

506 S. Grand Ave., Los Angeles, CA, 90071
PH: 213.612.1580 FAX: 213.612.1628
Website:www.thebiltmore.com

Gardens Restaurant
FOUR SEASONS HOTEL AT BEVERLY HILLS

Gardens, the newly renovated dining room at the Four Seasons Hotel, presents a theatrical Florentine-inspired decor throughout the restaurant and 22-seat private dining salon. For year round outdoor dining, the garden terrace provides the perfect setting for lunches, Sunday brunch and romantic dinners. Focusing on contemporary California cuisine, Executive chef Carrie Nahabedian showcases her individual style of Mediterranean cooking in her seasonal menus.

Owner: Four Seasons Hotel   Chef: Carrie Nahabedian

Specialties
Pavé of Pacific Salmon
Violet Mustard Crusted Rack of Meadow Lamb

300 South Doheny Dr., Los Angeles, CA, 90048
PH: 310.273.2222 FAX: 310.859.3824

Le Petit Chateau

Trendy restaurants come and go; few stand the test of time. Le Petit Chateau is one of those few, serving classic French country cooking for thirty-four years. The quaint castle on Lankershim, near Universal Studios, is a landmark in the San Fernando Valley. Le Petit Chateau is easily accessible from all freeways, and is 15 minutes from downtown Los Angeles in the heart of the entertainment industry.

Owners: Andrew & Christiane Higgs   Chef: Herbert Solis

Specialties

Long Island Duck with Bing Cherry Sauce
Roast Rack of Lamb Bougetière
Escargots • Sweetbreads

	S	M	T	W	T	F	S
B							
L							
D							

AE VC MC CB DC DS ▼🚗☎②🏨 PR

4615 Lankershim Blvd., N. Hollywood CA 91602
PH: 818.769.1812 FAX: 818.769.3431

Cafe Del Rey

This is one restaurant where the food is as spectacular as the view. Known for his stunning food presentation, Chef Katsuo Nagasawa skillfully blends classic French, Mediterranean and Pacific Rim cuisines for his seasonal menu. A celebrated wine cellar, cozy fireplace lounge and exceptional service further enhance the Cafe Del Rey dining experience. The inviting waterfront garden room can accommodate up to 50 people.

Chef: Katsuo Nagasawa

Specialties

Panfried Seafood Tower: Halibut, Shrimp, Lobster
Kung Pao Thai Shellfish Sausage

	S	M	T	W	T	F	S
B							
L							
D							

AE VC MC DC DS ▼🚗☎①PR

4451 Admiralty Way, Marina del Rey, CA, 90292
PH: 310.823.6395 FAX: 310.821.3734
Website: www.calcafe.com/marinadelrey

The Pavilion

In a community renowned for its casual grace, Four Seasons Hotel Newport Beach has become the pre-eminent example of gracious hospitality. Enjoy the finest dining experience in Newport Beach at Pavilion. Pavilion offers Californian cuisine with Mediterranean influences. Our Chef's daily prix fixe menu is known as the best value in town. Recognized as one of the most important restaurants in Orange County, Pavilion should not be missed.

Owners: Four Seasons Hotel   Chef: Mark Kropczynski

Specialties

**Pacific Seabass Broiled under Fresh Herb Crust
Pepper Crusted Lamb with Port Wine Reduction**

690 Newport Ctr Dr., Newport Beach CA 92660
PH: 949.760.4920 FAX: 949.760.8073

The Ritz

Traditional, classic elegance is the hallmark of The Ritz, evident from the moment you arrive at its impressive canopied entrance. Whether you're power dining in the Escoffier Room or eating *al fresco* in the new garden, our national reputation for service is reflected in our attention to every detail. The menu features ample portions of fresh seasonal fare and an ever-changing repertoire of specials and desserts, as well as an award-winning wine list.

Owner: Hans Prager   Chef: Lupe Camarena

Specialties

**Those Ritz Eggs • The Carousel
Carved Châteaubriand • Whole Imported Dover Sole**

880 Newport Center Dr.,
Newport Beach CA 92660
PH: 949.720.1800 FAX: 949.720.8753

LG's Prime Steakhouse

Whether they are seated around the fire pit on the patio at LG's in Palm Springs or dining at LG's original historic adobe landmark in Palm Desert, guests know they're in for award-winning meals. All steaks are aged, prime only, custom cut on premises and served sizzling. Specialties include LG's 'Gold Strike 49er' and the 'Jewel in the Crown', both prime porterhouse steaks; six other cuts of prime steaks and a caesar salad made tableside are not to be missed.

Owners: Leon & Gail Greenberg

Specialties
USDA Prime Only Steaks
Rack of Lamb, Chicken, Fresh Fish & Seafood

74-225 Hwy. 111, Palm Desert CA 92260
PH: 760.779.9799 FAX: 760.779.1979

Mille Fleurs

Located in the heart of an historic village, Mille Fleurs offers elegant haute cuisine in a gracious and welcoming environment. Chef Martin Woesle creates new menus daily, offering only ingredients which reflect the season and inspire his culinary artistry. Owner Bertrand lends his charismatic charm, as he hosts guests in his newly remodeled dining room, a cozy collection of intimate dining areas with two fireplaces. An award-winning wine list adds to the experience.

Owner: Bertrand Hug   Chef: Martin Woesle

Specialties
Seasonal Menu, Changes Daily
Chino's Farm Fresh Vegetables

6009 Paseo Delicias, Rancho Santa Fe CA 92067
PH: 619.756.3085 FAX: 619.756.9945
Website:www.millefleurs.com

El Bizcocho
RANCHO BERNARDO INN

Top rated by *Zagat* for food, service and decor, the El Bizcocho restaurant located in the Rancho Bernardo Inn serves classical French cuisine and seasonal specialties in an elegant and unpretentious atmosphere. Home to one of California's most extensive wine lists, the El Bizcocho was selected by *Gourmet* magazine as one of San Diego's best restaurants. Serving dinner nightly and Sunday Brunch, El Bizcocho is Southern California's highest rated resort restaurant.

Owners: JC Resorts   Chef: Tom Dowling

Specialties
Lobster Bisque
Grilled Chateaubriand for Two

17550 Bernardo Oaks Dr.,
San Diego, CA, 92128
PH: 619.675.8550 FAX: 619.675.8443
Website:www.jcresorts.com

Grant Grill
THE U.S. GRANT

Award-winning Grant Grill, located in the heart of San Diego, has been a downtown favorite since 1910. We specialize in French, Mediterranean and California grill cuisine that will enlighten your culinary senses. Breakfast, lunch and dinner are served daily, with brunch on the weekends. Also, enjoy the beauty of San Diego at our Sidewalk Café.

Chef: Celeste Dunne

Specialties
Mock Turtle Soup
Lobster Bisque
Rack of Lamb

326 Broadway, San Diego, CA, 92101
PH: 619.239.6806 FAX: 619.239.9517

Star of the Sea

Star of the Sea creates magical moments with innovative, uncompromising coastal cuisine and caring, stylish service. Chef Jonathan Pflueger's style reflects his passion for maintaining the integrity of individual flavors and textures. By using only the day's freshest seafood and ingredients at their peak flavor, Chef Pflueger embraces the French concept of *cuisine actuelle*. The result is his own coastal cuisine, unique to the San Diego region.

Chef: Jonathan Pflueger

Specialties

Tian of Lobster
Pepper and Ginger Studded Ahi Tuna Loin

1360 Harbor Dr. at Ash, San Diego CA
PH: 619.232.7408 FAX: 619.232.1877
Website: www.gofishanthonys.com

Downey's

When John Downey opened his namesake restaurant in 1982, the concept was simple: serve the very best food available, and serve it in a comfortable, unintimidating setting where it would be easy to drop in for an exquisite dinner. The idea worked well. It worked so well, that seventeen years later that same tenet still applies, and it has not gone unnoticed. Over the years, food critics have consistently awarded Downey's top honors for fine dining.

Owners: Liz and John Downey   Chef: John Downey

Specialties

Lobster Ragout with Flageolets, Tomato and Smoked Bacon
Fresh Raspberry Milles-Feuille

1305 State St., Santa Barbara, CA, 93101
PH: 805.966.5006

72 Market Street
Oyster Bar and Grill

Just steps from the beach in Venice, 72 Market Street Oyster Bar and Grill is known for its gourmet food and its glamorous atmosphere. The vision of celebrity owners Tony Bill and Dudley Moore, 72 Market Street caters to celebrities, local artists and connoisseurs from all over the world. Renowned chef Roland Gibert's delectable specials include meat and seafood delicacies.

Owners: Tony Bill and Dudley Moore   Chef: Roland Gibert

Specialties

Bouillabaise • Fresh Oysters
Roasted Rack of Lamb

72 Market St., Venice CA 90291
PH: 310.392.8720 FAX: 310.392.8665
Website:www.72marketst.com

The Covey

The Covey offers extraordinary culinary inventiveness and exquisite Euro-Californian cuisine. Renowned chef Bob Williamson presents an à la carte menu featuring the freshest local ingredients complemented by an award-winning wine list, highlighting the best of Monterey County and rare California wines. Enjoy the casual elegant ambience of The Covey while overlooking a sparkling lake with a fountain and charming footbridge, flourishing gardens and the graceful rolling hills of Carmel.

Owner: Quail Lodge   Chef: Bob Williamson

Specialties

Sesame Crusted Ahi • Pan-Roasted Sea Bass
Wild Mushroom Gratin

8205 Valley Greens Drive, Carmel CA 93923
PH: 831.624.1581 FAX: 831.624.3726

The French Poodle

The French Poodle in Carmel has established itself as a citadel of classic French cuisine on the Monterey Peninsula. The original Escoffier-inspired menu, as conceived by Richard Zoellin, has changed little over the past 30 years, and it is this legendary consistency which gives real comfort to those who seek culinary perfection.

Owner and Chef: Richard Zoellin

Specialties

Shelled Dungeness Crablegs with Champagne Sauce and Caviar
Grilled Breast of Duck in Aged Port Sauce

N.W. Corner of Junipero at 5th Ave.,
Carmel, CA, 93921
PH: 831.624.8643 FAX: 831.375-8643

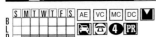

Pacific's Edge

HIGHLANDS INN

A glass-walled restaurant with spectacular ocean vistas. Chef Cal Stamenov's menu draws from the bounty of the region, changing with the offerings of the season. A special prix fixe dinner menu presents the chef's latest innovations each evening. Recipient of *Wine Spectator*'s Grand Award, Pacific's Edge has been described by numerous critics as the best restaurant on the California coast.

Chef: Cal Stamenov

Specialties

Fresh Oysters
Rack of Lamb

Highway 1, Carmel, CA, 93921
PH: 831.624.3801 FAX: 831.626.1574

Raffaello

Remo d'Agliano imports a hint of Florentine art and ambiance to picturesque Carmel at Raffaello. Bevelled glass etched with *fleurs-de-lis* highlights the decor. Fresh flowers decorate the reception room table and the small dining room; the menu and decor reflect Remo's youth and apprenticeship at his family's restaurant in Florence. Formal training at the Culinary Academy in Paris broadened his style, adding a touch of French flair to his Italian repertoire.

Owner and Chef: Remo d'Agliano

Specialties
Homemade Pasta
Veal Piedmontese

Mission St. between Ocean & 7th,
Carmel, CA, 93921
PH: 408.624.1541 FAX: 408.624.9411

S M T W T F S | AE | VC | MC | CB | DC
B L D

Fresh Cream Restaurant

Stunning views and elegant decor set the mood for romantic dinners, special occasions or after theatre desserts. The cuisine, classic French with a California accent, is presented with imagination and flair. Widely acclaimed as one of the Central Coast's finest restaurants, Fresh Cream has been receiving critical praise for its award-winning cuisine for 18 years.

Owner: Steven Chesney   Chef: Gregory Lizza

Specialties
Rack of Lamb Dijonnaise
Roast Boned Duck in Black Currant Sauce
Holland Dover Sole Meuniere

99 Pacific Street, Heritage Harbor, Ste. 100C,
Monterey, CA, 93940
PH: 831.375.9798 FAX: 831.375.2283

S M T W T F | AE | VC | MC | CB | DC | DS
B L D

Sardine Factory

Celebrating its 30th anniversary, the Sardine Factory continues to reflect the excellence that has made it world famous. The unique dining areas, trend-setting entrées of fresh seafood and prime beef, spectacular service and award-winning wine list offer the perfect combination for people who truly love great food and wine. A "must stop" for leaders in business, sports, entertainment and government. A *Wine Spectator* Grand Award winner since 1982.

Owners: Ted Balestreri and Bert Cutino

Specialties
Seared Monterey Bay Prawns
Baked Abalone & Oyster Rockefeller
"Cannery Row" Cioppino
USDA Prime Beef

701 Wave St., Monterey, CA, 93940
PH: 831.373.3775 FAX: 831.373.4241
Website:www.sardinefactory.com

S M T W T F S   AE VC MC CB DC DS
B
L
D

Club XIX

Club XIX at The Lodge at Pebble Beach celebrates a lighter approach to gourmet French cuisine with two prix-fixe meals each evening - one always vegetarian. A cozy, bricked patio, warmed by romantic fireplaces, affords a stunning view of Carmel Bay and the 18th green of Pebble Beach Golf Links.

Owners: Pebble Beach Co.   Chef: Lisa Magadini

Specialties
Seabass Ratatouille Crust with Sundried Tomato Jus
Maine Lobster and Salsafy En Tartelette

17 Mile Drive, Pebble Beach, CA, 93953
PH: 831.625.8519 FAX: 831.622.8746

S M T W T F S   AE VC MC CB DC J DS
B
L
D

E P O Q U E
B Y   G I A N N I   V E R S A C E

ROSENTHAL HOTEL & RESTAURANT SERVICE

Gianni Versace: His artistic creatio
shaped haute couture and the world
the stage in a way rarely matched by ot
ers. Internationally his name stands f
pure luxury — for the ingenious inte
mingling of classic and avant — garde

Exclusively for Rosenthal, Gian
Versace created two elegant and decora
tive tableware designs: "Barocco" a
"Medusa". Their brilliant colors, hi
quality ornamentation and sophisticat
detail create an aesthetic experience
complement any culinary offering.

The shape is Epoque,
the design is Medusa,
by Gianni Versace

Rosenthal, U.S.A., Ltd., Commercial Division • 355 Michele Place Carlstadt, N.J. 07072 • Tel: 201.804.8000 • Fax: 201.804.9300

The Restaurant at the Little Nell Hotel

Enjoy the acclaimed cuisine of Executive Chef Keith Luce at Aspen's Little Nell Restaurant. Chef Luce was recognized with the James Beard Rising Star Award in 1997. The Restaurant sits beneath the majestic Aspen Mountain and takes full advantage of breathtaking views. At night, the room is elegant, with soft lighting and gracious service. One of Aspen's premier restaurants, The Little Nell continues to be a favorite among travellers and locals alike.

Chef: Keith Luce

Specialties
Huckleberry Braised Beef Short Ribs
Herb Steamed Lake Trout with White Truffle Emulsion

675 E. Durant Ave., Aspen, CO, 81611
PH: 970.920.6330 FAX: 970.920.6328

S	M	T	W	T	F	S	AE	VC	MC	DC	DS

B
L
D

Syzygy

The alignment of heavenly bodies finds its perfect earthly counterpart in this unparalleled Aspen restaurant featuring exquisite New American cuisine prepared by chef Martin Oswald. A selection of 600 excellent wines and the region's only Master Sommelier await your discriminating palate. Live jazz and the intimate decor add to the inviting ambiance. Open nightly with a bar menu in effect until midnight.

Owner: Walt Harris   Chef: Martin Oswald

Specialties
Seared Ahi Tuna
Elk Tenderloin

520 E Hyman Ave., Aspen, CO, 81611
PH: 970.925.3700 FAX: 970.925.5593

S	M	T	W	T	F	S	AE	VC	MC	CB	DC	DS

B
L
D

Flagstaff House Restaurant

Located in the middle of a park overlooking Boulder, this 26-year-old restaurant offers enthralling views from either the outdoor dining deck or from inside through massive floor to ceiling windows. The menu features more than 40 items and changes nightly. The impressive wine cellar, with over 28,000 bottles and 1500 selections, has earned a Grand Award from *Wine Spectator* since 1982. This award-winner presents fresh seafood, Colorado game and desserts too tempting to resist.

Owners: Don, Mark & Scott Monette   Chef: Mark Monette

Specialties
**Fresh Seafood, Beef and Lamb
Colorado Game**

1138 Flagstaff Rd., Boulder, CO, 80302
PH: 303.442.4640 FAX: 303.442.8924
Website:www.flagstaffhouse.com

The Broker

Enjoy dining in a 90-year-old bank vault. Offering nostalgia and romantic dining served with the flavor of banking at the turn of the century. Featuring our famous complimentary shrimp bowl as an appetizer followed by traditional American entrées served with pride. Several private dining rooms for groups, plus the largest wine selection in Denver. A Colorado tradition since 1972.

Owners: Jerry Fritzler & Ed Novak   Chef: Jeff French

Specialties
**Filet Wellington • Rocky Mountain Trout
Prime Rib of Beef**

821 17th at Champa, Denver CO 80202
PH: 303.292.5065 FAX: 303.292.2652
Website:www.brokerrestaurant.com

Cliff Young's

Cliff Young's is Denver's tradition in five-star dining, and, since 1984, a premier dining establishment located in a century-old Victorian structure. Considered the crown jewel of Seventeenth Avenue Nouvelle Row, the restaurant features continental cuisine served in grand style with soft lighting and lavishly appointed dining rooms. The impeccable service makes dining here an indulgence. An award-winning wine list of 300 labels is enhanced by live piano and complimentary valet parking.

Owner: J. Stewart Jackson   Chef: Roberto C. Ravara

Specialties
Colorado Rack of Lamb
Peppered Tuna Charred Rare

706 East 17th Avenue,
Denver, CO, 80203 - 1405
PH: 303.831.8900 FAX: 303.831.0360

S	M	T	W	T	F	S
B						
L						
D						

AE | VC | MC | DC | DS

Tante Louise

A one-of-a-kind restaurant reminiscent of a French country bungalow, Tante Louise has served contemporary French cuisine with warm hospitality and quiet elegance for more than 25 years. Glowing fireplaces, stained glass windows and hardwood floors accent intimate dining rooms which are ideal for quiet romance or private business. Tante Louise has consistently earned AAA Four Diamond recognition and the *Wine Spectator* Award of Excellence.

Owner: Corky Douglass   Chef: Michael Degenhart

Specialties
Prosciutto Wrapped Rabbit Loin
Grilled Veal Chop

4900 E. Colfax Ave., Denver CO 80220
PH: 303.355.4488 FAX: 303.321.6312
Website:www.tantelouise.com

S	M	T	W	T	F	S
B						
L						
D						

AE | VC | MC | CB | DC | DS

Ludwig's
SONNENALP RESORT

Located in the Sonnenalp Resort's Bavaria Haus across from Vail Interfaith Chapel. Ludwig's cozy decor, handpainted ceilings, and terrace overlooking Gore Creek make for a truly inviting setting. We feature an innovative international cuisine accompanied by an award-winning wine list and served in royal style. Ludwig's also presents On Stage with Opera and Broadway performances. Open daily for dinner during the winter season only.

Owner: Johannes Fassler   Chef: Mark Berger

Specialties
Butternut Squash and Maine Lobster Bisque
Seared Veal Medallions with Melted Hudson Valley Foie Gras

20 Vail Rd., Vail, CO, 81657
PH: 970.476.5656 FAX: 970.476.8066
Closed in the summer

The Wildflower

A surprising and colorful ambience greets you amidst baskets of cascading flowers and large windows. The Wildflower is a treasure of delightful cuisine, expertly created by chef Thomas Gay, along with a splendid array of fine wines that will indulge the most discerning palate.

Chef: Thomas Gay

Specialties
Maine Lobster Ravioli with Fried Leeks, Tomato Concasse
and Fresh Chives
Grilled Colorado Lamb T-Bone with Gnocchi, Butternut
Squash and Sage-Brown Butter

174 E. Gore Creek Dr., Vail CO 81657
PH: 970.476.5011 FAX: 970.476.7425
Website:www.lodgeatvail.com

Cavey's

Cavey's is actually two restaurants in one building: an elegant French restaurant on the lower level, and a more casual northern Italian restaurant upstairs, offering jazz piano on weekends. Both are furnished with art and antiques, and, in the French restaurant, fabric wall coverings and a profusion of fresh flowers. Both have garnered critical acclaim and have been awarded *Wine Spectator's* Best of Award of Excellence.

Owner and Chef: Stephen Cavagnaro

Specialties

**Roast Quail with Chestnut Tagliatelle
Seared Foie Gras and Truffled Potato Ravioli
Day Boat Local Cod with Little Neck Clams
Grilled Chicken with House Italian Sausage**

45 E. Center St., Manchester CT 06033
PH: 860.643.2751 FAX: 860.649.0344

Columbus Inn

Columbus Inn is the flagship restaurant of the 1492 Hospitality Group. A beautiful and historic stone building provides the setting for a great dining experience. A talented and exacting kitchen, uncommonly good service and an outstanding selection of wines, beers and liquors contribute to our continued popularity. A lighted fireplace in every dining room in cold weather and a magnificent two-tiered stone patio in warmer months create an ambience for every season.

Owner: Davis Sezna   **Chef: Dave Peterson**

Specialties

**Certified Angus Beef • Calypso Seared Halibut
Yellowtail Snapper Roasted on a Cedar Plank**

2216 Pennsylvania, Wilmington DE 19806
PH: 302.571.1492 FAX: 302.571.1111

701 Restaurant

701 Restaurant overlooks the cascading fountains of the US Naval Memorial, and features international cuisine in a supper club setting. The interior is divided by a series of fluid curves in materials as rich and eclectic as etched glass held within chrome panels, polished walnut, granite, and layered torn silk paper. Well-spaced tables and comfortable chairs create an atmosphere of intimacy. There is nightly entertainment and a vodka, caviar and champagne lounge tucked behind the piano.

Owner: Ashok Bajaj   Chef: Trent Conry

Specialties
International Cuisine
Tuna Tartare

701 Pennsylvania Ave. N.W.,
Washington, DC, 20004
PH: 202.393.0701 FAX: 202.393.6439

1789 Restaurant

Tucked away on one of Georgetown's quiet residential streets, 1789 feels like an elegant country inn. Beyond the curbside valet of the two-story Federal townhouse, the setting is refined yet cozy, with Limoges and crystal-clad tables before a blazing fire. Chef Ris Lacoste's seasonal American menu has charmed critics and connoisseurs alike. Every bit as tempting are the fresh breads and desserts by pastry chef Terri Horn.

Owners: Stuart Davidson and John Laytham   Chef: Ris Lacoste

Specialties
Grilled Macadamia-Crusted Shrimp
Maryland Crab Cakes with Leek Vinaigrette
Roasted Rack of American Lamb with Creamy Feta Potatoes
Pine Nut-Crusted Chicken on Mashed Potatoes

1226 36th St. N.W., Washington, DC, 20007
PH: 202.965.1789 FAX: 202.337.1541
Website:www.clydes.com

The Bombay Club

The Bombay Club emulates characteristics of the old clubs of India. The elegant environment with pale pastels, ceiling fans and a profusion of greenery is designed to create a warm and inviting gathering place for relaxation and regeneration. The cuisine is the finest of India, utilizing only the best quality ingredients to create a harmony of subtle flavor and taste. The sophisticated cuisine is enhanced by refined service, an elegant atmosphere and live piano music.

Owner: Ashok Bajaj   Chef: Mahipal Negi

Specialties
Regional Indian Cuisine
Tandoori Salmon, Green Chili Chicken

815 Connecticut Ave. N.W., Washington, DC, 20006
PH: 202.659.3727 FAX: 202.659.5012

Galileo

Galileo has been praised by *Wine Spectator* as one of the 10 best Italian restaurants in America today. Chef Roberto Donna's innovative cuisine emphasizes the flavors of his native Piedmont region of Italy. Winner of *Wine Spectator*'s 1998 Grand Award of Excellence, Galileo boasts a selection of over 1,000 French, American and Italian vintages, specializing in Piedmontese wines to complement the menu. Choose from the main dining room, two private wine cellars, seasonal dining al fresco on the terrace, or the popular chef's table.

Owner and Chef: Roberto Donna

Specialties
White Truffle Risotto
Agnolotti of Beef with a Barolo Wine Sauce

1110 21st St. N.W., Washington, DC, 20036
PH: 202.293.7191 FAX: 202.331.9364
Website:www.robertodonna.com

i Ricchi

With its authentic Italian country cooking, i Ricchi has been awarded the Insegna Del Ristorante Italiano, designating the best Italian restaurants in the world. Designed to resemble the original Villa Ricchi near Florence, with warm earth tones and terra cotta floors, i Ricchi's focal point is an open kitchen with a wood burning oven. Beef grilled over live embers, deceptively simple pastas and risottos, freshly baked Tuscan bread and homemade desserts are highlights.

Owners: Christianne Russo Ricchi   Chef: Christianne Russo Ricchi and Francesco Ricchi

Specialties
Tuscan Grilled Meats
Homemade Pastas

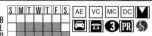

1220 19th St. N.W., Washington, DC, 20036
Tel: 202.835.0459 FAX: 202.872.1220

Melrose

Executive Chef Brian McBride's innovative American cuisine features flavors from around the world. He uses the freshest (and often rarest) ingredients available with an emphasis on seafood. From the outside terrace with its antique water fountain and herbal flower garden to the beautiful dining room bathed in sunlight or candle light, Melrose is a feast for the eyes as well as the appetite. Sunday brunch. Afternoon tea. Saturday evening dinner and dancing.

Chef: Brian McBride

Specialties
Thai Calamari with Lemon Grass, Shallots and Mint
Shrimp Ravioli with Sweet Corn and Cracked Black Pepper
Melrose Crabcakes with Grilled Asparagus

24th at M Street N.W., Washington, DC 20037
PH: 202.955.3899 FAX: 202.408.6118

Morrison-Clark Restaurant

The Morrison-Clark Historic Inn and Restaurant replicates a fashionable turn-of-the-century Victorian home and drawing room. Featuring full-length gilded mirrors circa 1864, tasteful chinoiserie and marble fireplaces. The Morrison-Clark has earned its place among Washington's best restaurants; Chef Susan McCreight-Lindeborg's new American cuisine with southern and regional influences concentrates on big flavors and changes with the seasons. Wines and spirits are carefully chosen to match the cuisine.

Chef: Susan McCreight-Lindeborg

Specialties
**Southern Style Rabbit
Softshell Crabs**

Massachusetts Ave. & 11th St. N.W.
Washington, DC, 20001
PH: 202.898.1200 FAX: 202.289.8576

The Prime Rib

With its black and gold lacquered good looks, an elegant atmosphere of perpetual twilight and piano music in the bar, it is no wonder that The Prime Rib in Washington has consistently been voted the best restaurant in the city by readers of *Washingtonian* magazine. Scores pay tribute to its succulent steaks, prime ribs and jumbo lump crab entrées. A wonderful selection of California wines is available.

Owner: C.P. (Buzz) BeLer   Chef: Santiago Cisneras

THE PRIME RIB ®
The Civilized Steakhouse

Specialties
**Fresh Chesapeake Bay Seafood
Aged Prime Beef**

2020 K St. N.W., Washington, DC, 20006
PH: 202.466.8811 FAX: 202.466.2010
Website:www.theprimerib.com

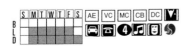

Sam & Harry's

Sam & Harry's, voted 'Best Steak' in Washington, is a classic American steakhouse offering exceptional food, fine wine, great cigars and personalized service. The menu features a variety of prime-aged steaks, a veal T-bone, fresh grilled fish and fresh Maine lobster tails, all in generous portions. Colorful jazz paintings, animated jazz sculptures, a visible wine cellar and intimate private dining rooms create a romantic and clubby atmosphere.

Owners: Michael Steinberg & Larry Work　　　Chef: Ed Hansen

Specialties
Signature Bone-in Strip Steak
Fresh Maine Lobster

1200 19th St. NW, Washington DC 20036
PH: 202.296.4333 FAX: 202.785.1070

S	M	T	W	T	F	S
B						
L						
D						

AE VC MC CB DC DS

Vidalia

Jeffrey and Sallie Buben have owned and operated Vidalia since 1993. Featuring new American cuisine with a southern accent, Vidalia opened to acclaim in downtown Washington and has earned countless accolades ever since, including five James Beard Award nominations and "Best Restaurant" in *Bon Appetit, Gourmet, The Washington Post* and *Washingtonian.*

Owners: Jeffrey & Sallie Buben　　　Chef: Jeffrey Buben

Specialties
Shrimp & Grits with Swiss Chard & Caramelized Onions
Lobster & Vidalia Onion Tart
Pan-Roasted Cornmeal Crusted Shenandoah Trout
with Lump Crabmeat

1990 M St. NW, Washington DC 20036
PH: 202.659.1990

S	M	T	W	T	F	S
B						
L						
D						

AE VC MC DC

Very Distinguished.
Very Accommodating.

Restaurants that have received the prestigious DiRoNA Award of excellence from Distinguished Restaurants of North America are known for their attention to every detail. That includes elegant decor. Exceptional cuisine. Attentive service. And a commitment to accommodating their customers' every preference, including whether they choose to smoke or not. That's why more and more distinguished restaurants are displaying the symbol of The Accommodation Program. Wherever you see it—whether you're a non-smoker or a smoker—you'll find a very accommodating atmosphere. For free information about accommodation, please call 1-800-335-8444.

**NON-SMOKERS
AND SMOKERS
WELCOME**

Elephant Walk

Elephant Walk restaurant overlooks the sugar white beaches and the emerald green waters of the Gulf of Mexico. Elepant Walk offers the finest in steaks, chops, veal and seafood. Known for its impeccable service, exotic cuisine, and atmosphere of subdued elegance, it is an unforgettable experience. Join us in the Governor's Attic, nestled above the restaurant, for cigars, cognacs, ice cream drinks, entertainment and mouthwatering desserts.

Owner: Sandestin Resort

Specialties
Grouper Elizabeth
Rack of Lamb

9300 Hwy. 98 W., Destin FL 32541
PH: 850.267.4800 FAX: 850.267.6120
Website:www. sandestin.com

Marina Café

From the moment you enter Marina Café, you'll notice something special: an impeccable wait staff pays attention to details, service and you, and beautiful Destin Harbor is visible from every table. Our chef creates a new menu daily so each ingredient is at its peak of freshness. Every dish is an unequaled taste experience, from gourmet pizza baked in our wood burning oven to elegant culinary masterpieces. Winner of *Wine Spectator's* Award of Excellence.

Owner: James Altamura

Specialties
Seafood
Continental Cuisine

404 Highway 98 East, Destin, FL, 32540
PH: 850.837.7960 FAX: 850.837.3047
Website:www.marinacafe.com

La Cena Ristorante

Fresh pasta is the word at La Cena. Chef/Owner Jerry Moran's pasta laboratory produces laminated *taglitelle* as well as filled *cappelletti* and other pasta specialties. A huge menu features 21 veal chop or *scalloppine* dishes, and local fresh fish preparations. The glassed-in, temperature controlled wine cellar offers over 275 selections of Italian wine. Signature breads and *grissini* complement the tables. Quiet, adult dining is the norm.

LA CENA RISTORANTE
ITALIAN CONTINENTAL CUISINE

Owner and Chef: Jerry Moran

Specialties
Cappelletti Emiliana
Tagliatelle Cavalieri
Ellie Fish
Loin Veal Chop Boscaiola

6271 St. Augustine Rd., Ste. 7
Jacksonville, FL, 23317
PH: 904.737.5350 FAX: 904.733.7980

Maison & Jardin Restaurant

This grand Mediterranean villa sprawls on five acres of beautifully landscaped grounds dense with magnificent oaks and flowering plants. Inside, you are surrounded by exquisite antiques and Austrian crystal chandeliers and served with the attention to detail you would find in an elegantly appointed home. The ambiance is as eclectic and interesting as the menu. Contemporary classic French dishes are adapted to Florida produce and style. The wine cellar features more than 1,200 selections.

Owners: Bill and Judy Beuret   Chef: Hans Spirig

Specialties
Grilled Elk Medallions and Duck Confit
Duo of Ostrich and Quail Served over Cous Cous

430 S. Wymore Rd.,
Altamonte Springs, FL, 32714
PH: 407.862.4410 FAX: 407.862.0557
Website:www.maison-jardin.com

Ruth's Chris Steak House

This is the steak serious steaklovers rave about! Ruth's Chris Steak House specializes in corn-fed, Midwestern USDA Prime beef. Strips, filets, ribeyes, T-bones and porterhouse steaks are aged to exacting standards, broiled to perfection and served sizzling. An award-winning wine list features premium wines by the glass. The service is attentive, knowledgeable and friendly, and the traditional steak house and setting exquisite.

Owner: Ruth Fertel   Chef: Tenny Flynn

Specialties

USDA Prime Steaks
Seared Ahi Tuna with Spicy Mustard Sauce
Gulf Shrimp with Creole Remoulade Sauce
Creole Crème Brûlée

999 Douglas Ave., Altamonte Springs FL
PH: 407.682.6444 FAX: 407.682.7055
Website:www.ruthschris.com

Peter Scott's

Recipient of the Five Star Diamond Award from the American Academy of Hospitality Sciences in 1996, 1997 and 1998, the *Wine Spectator's* Award of Excellence in 1995, 1996 and 1997, the Four Diamond award from the AAA in 1995, 1996,1997 and 1998. Cited as one of America's top ten restaurants by the *Zagat Survey*.

Specialties

Rack of Lamb
Dover Sole

1811 W State Rd. 434, Longwood, FL, 32750
PH: 407.834.4477 FAX: 407.834.2414

Atlantis

The legend isn't lost after all. At Atlantis in the Renaissance Orlando Resort, we have not lost the art of fine dining. We offer the finest fresh seafood in an elegant, intimate atmosphere, served by gracious and accommodating staff and complemented by an extensive wine list. Perhaps these are the reasons that Atlantis has become legendary. Atlantis is located directly across from Sea World. Dinner is served from 6 to 10 p.m. Reservations are suggested.

Chef: Pam Dubilier

Specialties
Fresh Seafood

6677 Sea Harbor Drive, Orlando, FL, 32821
PH: 407.351.5555 FAX: 407.363.9247
Website:www.renaissancehotels.com

Christini's Ristorante Italiano

Discover the art of exceptional dining at Christini's. By combining the flavors of Italy with world class charm, Christini's has achieved national acclaim. Frosted glass, Italian art and strolling musicians grace the elegantly casual dining room where guests celebrate special occasions and relax in an atmosphere of warmth and graciousness. Special touches such as long-stemmed roses for ladies exemplify old-world charm and elegance. Through insistence on style and elegance, Chris Christini sets standards unheard of in the industry.

Owner: Chris Christini   **Chef: Ralph Oliver**

Specialties
Veal Chops
Homemade Pastas

7600 Dr. Phillips Blvd., Orlando, FL, 32819
PH: 407.345.8770 FAX: 407.345.8700
Website:www.christinis.com

Dux at the Peabody Orlando

Experience traditional American cuisine with the flavors of the world in an intimate setting. Chef de Cuisine Scott Hoyland invites you to try his tasting menu or à la carte items featuring award winning cuisine complemented by Dux's extensive wine cellar and sinfully delicious desserts. Dux at The Peabody Orlando is the only Mobil Four-Star, AAA Four-Diamond restaurant in Central Florida. Truly an unforgettable evening.

Chef: Scott Hoyland

Specialties
Kadaif Wrapped Spiny Lobster and Peekytoe Crab
Taro Crusted Fillet of Black Grouper

9801 International Dr., Orlando, FL, 32819
PH: 407.345.4550 FAX: 407.363.1505
Website:www.peabody-orlando.com

Haifeng

Savor the secrets of the Far East. At Haifeng in the Renaissance Orlando Resort, we go far to please you, with authentic cuisine from China, Japan, and Korea. The service is invariably impeccable and gracious, amid an atmosphere of understated, soothing oriental elegance. Perhaps these are the secrets of our success. Haifeng is located directly across from Sea World. Dinner is served from 6 to 10 p.m. Reservations are suggested.

Chef: Eric Tran

Specialties
Authentic Asian Cuisine

6677 Sea Harbor Drive, Orlando, FL, 32821
PH: 407.351.5555 FAX: 407.363.9247
Website:www.renaissancehotels.com

La Coquina
HYATT REGENCY GRAND CYPRESS

La Coquina restaurant, located in the award-winnning Hyatt Regency Grand Cypress, features sensational new-world cuisine in a luxurious lakeside setting. With a picturesque view of 21-acre Lake Windsong, La Coquina also features piano entertainment for your dining pleasure. La Coquina's one-of-a-kind Sunday Champagne Brunch should not be missed! The chef invites you into his kitchen to experience culinary delights prepared especially for you.

Chef: Kenneth Juran

Specialties
Seared Loin of Tuna Wrapped in Proscuitto
Lobster Ravioli with Avocado and Citrus Beurre Blanc
Herb Roasted Rack of Lamb with Asparagus Salsa
Smoked Salmon and Crisp Straw Potatoes

1 Grand Cypress Blvd., Orlando, FL, 32836
PH: 407.239.1234 FAX: 407.239.3800

Manuel's on the 28th

Located on the 28th floor of the Nations Bank Center in downtown Orlando, Manuel's on the 28th offers a dining experience rarely found in Central Florida. Manuel's food is exquisite, the service is first rate and the ambiance is elegant. Manuel's is an award-winning experience, having earned the prestigious DiRoNA Award, Florida Trend's Golden Spoon Awards and a Four Diamond Award from AAA.

Owner: Manny Garcia　　　　　　　　Chef: Todd Baggett

Specialties
Filo Wrapped Loin of Lamb
Green Curry and Ginger Crusted Yellowfin
Oak Grilled Black Angus Filet and Shrimp
Fire Roasted "Woodsman" Poulet

390 North Orange Ave.
Orlando, FL, 32801
PH: 407.246.6580 FAX: 407.246.6575

The Colony Dining Room

Enjoy the South's most breathtaking sunset view. Nestled on a pristine Gulf of Mexico beach, The Colony Dining Room is the centrepiece of the world-famous Colony Beach & Tennis Resort. Guests delight in the gracious service of an efficient, personable staff serving the freshest seafoods and meats available. The Colony is home to the Stone Crab, Seafood & Wine Festival each October, where celebrity chefs gather to celebrate the beginning of the Florida stone crab season.

Owners: M. Klauber, K. & M. Moulton   Chef: Daniel T. Jackson

Specialties

Crispy Fried Lobster Tail with Sweet Potato Fries
Pan Roasted American Snapper

1620 Gulf of Mexico Dr.,
Longboat Key, FL 34228
PH: 941.383.5558 FAX: 941.387.0250
Website:www.colonybeachresort.com

Lafite

Lafite, at the Registry Resort in Naples, is southwest Florida's most exclusive restaurant and is rapidly gaining national acclaim for its superb continental cuisine and outstanding international wines. Savor the specialty creations of chef Wilhelm Gahabka amidst the delicious aromas and elegant decor of our intimate dining areas.

Owner: The Registry Resort   Chef: Wilhelm Gahabka

Specialties

Sautéed Almond Coated Fillet of Dover Sole
Slow Roasted Oriental Spiced Duckling
with Candied Plum Wine Tamarind Sauce

475 Seagate Dr., Naples, FL, 34103
PH: 941.597.3232 FAX: 941.597.7168

Restaurant on the Bay by Marie-Michelle

With her charming flowered outdoor terrace, Marie-Michelle brings a little corner of the French Riviera to the heart of Naples. Overlooking Venetian Bay you will discover the cuisine, the ambiance and the *joie de vivre* of the South of France. The restaurant offers a rare combination of stunning views and superb French cuisine. There's nothing else quite like it!

Owner: Marie-Michelle Rey

Specialties

Classic French Onion Soup Baked with Gruyere Cheese
Norwegian Salmon Baked with Jumbo Shrimp and Topped with a Whole Grain Mustard Glaze

4236 Gulfshore Blvd. N., Naples, FL, 34103
PH: 941.263.0900 FAX: 941.263.0850

Café L'Europe

For twenty-five years, Café L'Europe has proven to be among Sarasota's most remarkable dining establishments. Café L'Europe has a reputation for providing outstanding cuisine with unwavering attention to service. In this tradition, Café L'Europe introduces New European Cuisine™. New European Cuisine™ is an innovation of diverse but classic food combinations matched in subtle balance to formulate a singular gourmet experience. Award-winning Café L'Europe offers the innovative New European Cuisine™ for lunch and dinner seven days a week.

Owner: Titus Letschert   Chef: Jeffrey Trefry

Specialties

Chilled Galacian Marinated Shrimp
Petite Osso Bucco

431 St. Armands Circle, Sarasota, FL, 34236
PH: 941.388.4415 FAX: 941.388.2362
Website:www.neweuropeancuisine.com

Michael's on East

Sarasota's most celebrated restaurant dazzles guests with a fabulous new look and inspired continental menus. The vibrant, swirling decor creates the ambience of a 1930s private dining club. What hasn't changed is the restaurant's commitment to impeccable service and inspired cuisine from this recipient of eight consecutive Golden Spoon awards as one of Florida's Top 20 restaurants. Visit EastSide, Michael's stylish new lounge with its Tapas-style menu.

Owners: Michael Klauber & Philip Mancini   Chef: Keith Doherty

Specialties

Grilled Black Angus Filet with Wild Mushroom Ragôut
Seared Chilean Sea Bass with Roasted Garlic-Lemon Cream
Crispy Roast Duckling with Fall Chutney

1212 East Ave. S., Sarasota FL 34239
PH: 941.366.0007 FAX: 941.955.1945

S M T W T F S   AE VC MC DC
B
L
D

Armani's
HYATT REGENCY WESTSHORE

On top of the Hyatt Regency Westshore overlooking Old Tampa Bay, sits Armani's, the embodiment of a beautiful, tranquil place to dine. A rich harvest of northern Italian offerings and an extravagant antipasto bar await your contemplation. The chef and his staff prepare traditional entrées with a variety of poultry, beef, seafood and veal, the house specialty.

Chef: Massimo Patano

Specialties
Antipasto Bar
Veal Scaloppine

6200 Courtney Campbell Cswy.
Tampa, Fl, 33607
PH: 813.281.9165 FAX: 813.281.9168

S M T W T F S   AE VC MC CB DC ER J
B
L
D

Bern's Steak House

Since its humble beginnings in 1956, Bern's Steak House has been driven by an obsession for quality and the pursuit of perfection by Bern Laxer, resulting in an exceptional steakhouse with an impressive reputation. From our own organically grown vegetables, to the hand-sorted coffee beans roasted fresh daily, to a service staff trained for over a year before they serve you, every effort has been made to ensure the most memorable evening when you dine at Bern's.

Owner: David Laxer

Specialties

Steak Tartare Bern
Escargot
Aged USDA Prime Beef
Chilled Indonesian Chicken Curry

1208 S. Howard Ave.,Tampa, FL, 33606
PH: 813.251.2421 FAX: 813.251.5001

Chef Allen's Restaurant

Allen Susser was among the first chefs to introduce a perfected interpretation of modern American cooking to Florida. His New World cuisine features local fresh fish, tropical fruits and Latin root vegetables. Susser won the James Beard Foundation's Best Chef, Southeast Region award in 1994, and is one of the country's most accomplished chefs. His magic is performed in full view from a glassed in kitchen. His staff delivers caring service, and the wine list is one of the best in the Southeast.

Owner: Allen Susser   Chef: Tim Andriola

Specialties

Bahamian Lobster and Crab Cakes with Tropical Fruit Chutney
Rock Shrimp Hash with Roast Corn and Mango Ketchup

19088 N.E. 29th Ave., Aventura, FL, 33180
PH: 305.935.2900 FAX: 305.935.9062

Restaurant St. Michel

HOTEL PLACE ST. MICHEL

Join us at the Restaurant St. Michel. Complete dinners and light suppers that trail into the night are our specialty. St. Michel provides a romantic setting with impeccable service and assures its patrons of a high level of creativity in the kitchen, which features an eclectic mix of international cuisines. The wine list consists of carefully chosen domestic and imported selections.

Owner: Stuart Bornstein　　　　　　Chef: Jack Miranda

Specialties
**Pasta and Fresh Local Fish
Game and Prime Aged Meats**

162 Alcazar Ave., Coral Gables, FL, 33134
PH: 305.444.1666 FAX: 305.529.0074
Website:www.restaurantstmichel.com

Ristorante La Bussola

Ristorante La Bussola offers some of the best Italian cuisine available in Florida. *Esquire* says the food is imaginative, the service flawless and Ristorante La Bussola is "easily the most beautiful dining room in Coral Gables." Private banquet rooms and off premise catering are available.

Owner: Elizabeth Giordano and　　　Chef: Aldo Vespero
　　　　Tino Ponticorvo

Specialties
**Ossobucco Milanese
Mango Cheesecake**

264 Giralda Ave., Coral Gables, FL, 33134
PH: 305.445.8783 FAX: 305.441.6435

Burt & Jacks

Burt & Jacks is the award winning restaurant collaboration of actor Burt Reynolds and restaurateur Jack Jackson. The dramatic Mediterranean villa overlooks the spectacular water view of Port Everglades with cruise ships and yachts from all over the world. The menu features prime steaks, chops, and fresh seafood, including jumbo live Maine lobsters. The extensive wine list, combined with an intimate cocktail lounge featuring live piano music and an outside patio, provide the perfect setting for a special occasion.

Owners: Jack Jackson and Burt Reynolds   Chef: Kevin Hyotte

Specialties
Prime Steaks and Chops
Jumbo Live Maine Lobsters

Berth 23, Port Everglades,
Ft. Lauderdale, FL, 33316
PH: 954.522.5225 FAX: 954.522.2048

Eduardo de San Angel

Ignore all other versions of Mexican food, because the Pria family serve the real thing: classic Mexican cuisine fit for an emperor. An artistic and flavorful array of authentic chiles, herbs and spices raise meat, seafood and poultry dishes to Aztec heavens.

Specialties
Gourmet Mexicano

2822 E. Commercial Blvd.,
Ft. Lauderdale FL 33308
PH: 954.772.4731 FAX: 954.772.0794

Il Tartufo on Las Olas

Il Tartufo on Las Olas is one of the most elegant restaurants in south Florida. The charming courtyard has two magnificent hundred-year-old banyan trees and tiny white lights twinkling everywhere. It's like dining under a star-spangled sky. The dining room is a blend of rich forest greens, mahogany, cozy leather booths and beautifully appointed tables. The cuisine is innovative northern Italian, and there is live entertainment nightly. Il Tartufo is a 1998 *Wine Spectator* award winner.

Owner: Gianni Minervini   Chef: Massimo Pisati

Specialties

Black Peppercorn Fettucine with Smoked Duck Breast
Almond Crusted Yellowtail Snapper
Veal Scaloppine

2400 Las Olas Blvd., Ft. Lauderdale FL 33301
PH: 954.767.9190 FAX: 954.767.9821
Website:www.iltartufo.com

Sheffield's

MARRIOTT'S HARBOR BEACH RESORT

The Harbor Beach Resort's signature restaurant promises a memorable meal enhanced by this warm glow of mellow wood and good company. Our award-winning modern continental cuisine, which includes 'Sheffield's Wellington', a pan-seared Certified Angus Beef filet with Mushroom Duxelle, and our unforgettable desserts are all served with impeccable English charm.

Chef: Mark Henry

Specialties

'Sheffield's Wellington'
Rack of Lamb Provençal
Dover Sole Meuniere

3030 Holiday Drive, Ft. Lauderdale, FL, 33316
PH: 954.525.4000 FAX: 954.847.4775

Café L'Europe

Frederick J. Krantz, food editor for *Palm Beach Illustrated Magazine* describes Café L'Europe in the January '99 issue: "The restaurant is a jewel, maintained with great care and affection. Since it opened 18 years ago, it has achieved a benchmark of quality that other high end restaurants find difficulty in even approaching. Throughout the years, the restaurant's owners - Lidia and Norbert Goldner - have sustained this standard, making Café L'Europe the prime destination for both local and visiting epicures."

Owners: Lidia & Norbert Göldner   Chef: Norbert Göldner

Specialties
Caviar & Champagne Bar
Pan Seared Sesame Crusted Tuna

331 S. County Rd., Palm Beach FL 33480
PH: 561.655.4020 FAX: 561.659.6619
Website:www.cafeleurope.com

Cafe Chardonnay

Cafe Chardonnay serves the finest in American cuisine, featuring an eclectic array of lunch and dinner specials. Owners Frank and Gigi Eucalitto offer an award-winning wine list and a prix fixe culinary tour featuring cuisine and wines that capture the essence of wineries from around the world. Cafe Chardonnay's dining room is uniquely south Florida; colorful yet elegant. Desserts are a must.

Owners: Frank and Gigi Eucalitto   Chef: Frank Eucalitto

Specialties
Macadamia Crusted Yellow Tail Snapper
Rosemary Crusted Rack of Lamb

Closed Some Holidays

4533 PGA Blvd., Palm Beach Gardens, FL, 33418
PH: 561.627.2662 FAX: 561.627.3413
Website:www.cafechardonnay.com

Capriccio

Elegant atmosphere with fine Italian dining accompanied by live entertainment nightly. We provide 4-star cuisine served by an accomplished staff. Your host, Gianpiero Cangelosi, completes the evening with song. Our lavish lounge is highlighted with a 7-foot chandelier and finely decorated with antiques. Our lounge delights the crowds on weekends with music for dining and dancing. We offer smoking and non-smoking areas.

Owner: Gianpiero Cangelosi   **Chef: Diego Cruz**

Specialties

**Lumache e Polenta • Gnocchi alla Vodka
Costata di Vitello ai Funghi
Tilapia di Simenza**

2424 North University Dr.,
Pembroke Pines FL 33024
PH: 954.432.7001 FAX: 954.423.7560

Darrel and Oliver's Café Maxx

With Executive Chef Oliver Saucy fusing talent and flavor in his dynamic exhibition-style kitchen, and partner Darrel Broek presiding over the attractive, high-energy dining room, Café Maxx presents innovative regional Florida cuisine that is consistently delicious and dazzling on the plate. Since the partners purchased the restaurant in 1988, it has reigned supreme as one of South Florida's top eateries, and continues to collect the industry's highest awards.

Owner: Darrel Broek   **Chef: Oliver Saucy**

Specialties

**Sweet Onion Crusted Snapper with Madeira Sauce
Grilled Shrimp Brochette with Banana Lime Sauce**

2601 E. Atlantic Blvd.,
Pompano Beach, FL, 33062
PH: 954.782.0606 FAX: 954.782.0648
Website:www.cafemaxx.com

Marker 88 Restaurant

A serene tropical setting, with dockside views of spectacular sunsets and Florida Bay, welcomes you to a waterfront paradise with a unique Florida Keys ambience. Specializing in fresh, native seafood, prepared to order with a touch of the Caribbean. We also serve classical continental cuisine, and our full bar has an extensive wine list. The *New York Times* rated Marker 88 the best restaurant in the Florida Keys.

Owner: André Mueller   Chef: Wes Brage

Specialties

Florida Bay Stone Crab Claws
Key West Pink Shrimp Milanese
Filet Mignon Bearnaise
Rack of Lamb Provençal

Mile Marker 88, Plantation Key, between
Islamorada and Key Largo, FL 33036
PH: 305.852.9315 FAX: 305.852.9069

S	M	T	W	T	F	S		AE	VC	MC	CB	DC		DS

B
L
D

103 West

Atlanta's most glamorous restaurant features continental cuisine with French influences. This Mobil Four-Star posh palace offers luxurious details, impeccable service and the promise of memorable evenings. 103 West has facilities available for business and social private events.

Owner: Pano Karatassos   Chef: Gary Donlick

Specialties

Yellow Fin Tuna
Whole Dover Sole

103 W Paces Ferry Rd., Atlanta, GA, 30305
PH: 404.233.5993 FAX: 404.240.6619

S	M	T	W	T	F	S		AE	VC	MC	CB	DC	J	DS

B
L
D

1848 House

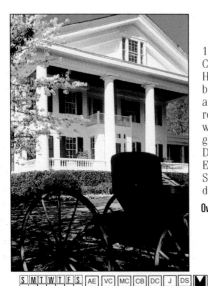

1848 House is a plantation home on a former Civil War battle site listed on the National Historic Register. Dinner and Sunday jazz brunch are served, and space is available at any time for private functions. Authentically restored with eleven private rooms, seven with fireplaces, for two to 125 people and groups of up to 400. Winner of the AAA Four Diamond Award, *Wine Spectator* Award of Excellence and *Atlanta* Magazine's Best Southern Cuisine. Twenty minutes from downtown Atlanta.

Owner: Bill Dunaway   Chef: Tom M^C Eachern

Specialties
Charleston She Crab Soup
Bourbon-Braised Pork Tenderloin

780 South Cobb Dr., Marietta, GA, 30060
PH: 770.428.1848 FAX: 770.427.5886
Website:www.1848house.com

Bone's Restaurant

This internationally acclaimed restaurant is a Buckhead "in" spot for many of Atlanta's movers and shakers. Bone's has long been established as a "must visit" when in the city. Its clubby atmosphere, award-winning food and 10,000-bottle wine cellar have made Bone's not only the place for steak and seafood but also the place to be seen. The walls are covered with photographs of Atlanta landmarks and caricatures of local personalities. Eight private dining rooms.

Owners: Susan DeRose & Richard Lewis   Chef: Gregory Gammage

Specialties
Prime Beef
Live Maine Lobster
Lamb Chops

3130 Piedmont Rd., Atlanta, GA, 30305
Ph: 404.237.2663 FAX: 404.233.5704

Chops

The Tiffany of Atlanta steak houses, Chops is a classic, yet state-of-the-art restaurant consistently ranked one of the top 10 steak houses in the country. Chops offers the best USDA Prime aged beef and seafood available - all served with attentive style. This is power dining at its optimum. The second level lobster bar is an exciting addition to Atlanta's dining scene, featuring crab and lobsters prepared in a variety of delectable styles.

Owner: Pano Karatassos

Specialties
Porterhouse Steak
Yellowfin Tuna

70 W Paces Ferry Rd., Atlanta, GA, 30305
PH: 404.262.2675 FAX: 404.240.6645

The Dining Room
THE RITZ-CARLTON BUCKHEAD

The Dining Room at The Ritz-Carlton, Buckhead reflects a grand residential atmosphere, with silk upholstered seating at tables surrounded by museum quality art on mahogany panelled walls. Internationally acclaimed chef Joel Antunes presents progressive French-Mediterranean, Thai influenced cuisine. To complete the experience, service by a professional waiting staff is impeccable. The restaurant has won numerous awards, including the coveted Mobil five-star award and the AAA Five-Diamond award.

Chef: Joel Antunes

Specialties
Roast Lobster
Duck Filet in Thai Sauce

3434 Peachtree Rd. N.E., Atlanta, GA, 30326
PH: 404.237.2700 FAX: 404.262.2888
Closed all holidays and Sundays

La Grotta Ristorante Italiano

Located in a beautiful in-town setting overlooking a terrace and gardens, La Grotta has earned a national reputation for serving outstanding northern and regional Italian cuisine. A local favorite for 20 years, La Grotta has earned numerous awards, including three *Gourmet* Reader's Choice Awards, five AAA Diamond Awards and has been voted best of Atlanta for 15 years. The European-trained staff provides friendly, knowledgeable service. Extensive wine list.

Owners: Sergio Favalli & Antonio Abizanda   Chef: Antonio Abizanda

Specialties
Homemade Pasta, Fresh Seafood, Filet and Veal

S	M	T	W	T	F	S	AE	VC	MC	CB	DC	J	DS

B
L
D

2637 Peachtree Rd., Atlanta, GA, 30305
PH: 404.231.1368 FAX: 404.231.1274
Website:www.la-grotta.com

Nikolai's Roof
ATLANTA HILTON AND TOWERS

Atlantans have made Nikolai's Roof their restaurant of choice for special occasions. Try it just once and chances are it will become your restaurant of choice too. The cuisine features classic French and authentic Russian specialties, and the setting is absolutely stunning. The elegant decor is the perfect accompaniment to the exquisite dishes and dramatic view of the Atlanta skyline.

Chef: Johannes Klapdohr

Specialties
Piroshki
Infused Vodka

S	M	T	W	T	F	S	AE	VC	MC	CB	DC	DS

B
L
D

255 Courtland St. NE, Atlanta, GA, 30303
PH: 404.221.6362 FAX: 404.221.6811

Pano's & Paul's

This Atlanta institution is known as the city's standard for luxury dining. The restaurant is a winner of Mobil 4-Stars, *Gourmet's* choice for Atlanta's best, and is in *Nation's Restaurant News* Fine Dining Hall of Fame. The cuisine is creative American and continental, the ambiance is clubby but elegant, and the service is considered tops in the country. Pano's & Paul's has been voted Atlanta's best fine dining restaurant by the *Zagat Survey* and *Atlanta* Magazine.

Owner: Pano Karatassos   Chef: Peter Kaiser

Specialties
Jumbo Cold-Water Lobster
American Rack of Lamb

1232 W Paces Ferry Rd., Atlanta, GA, 30327
PH: 404.261.3662 FAX: 404.261.4512

S	M	T	W	T	F	S	AE	VC	MC	CB	DC	J

B
L
D

DS ▼ 🚗 ☎ ❷

Pricci

A contemporary and outrageous, yet entirely authentic Italian restaurant featuring a creative menu, dramatic and fun interior, and beautiful new private dining rooms. The atmosphere is casually chic, and the service is excellent. Pricci features light, unpretentious, flavorful food in a fabulous setting.

Owner: Pano Karatassos

Specialties
Cold-Water Lobster
Osso Bucco

500 Pharr Rd., Atlanta, GA, 30305
PH: 404.237.2941 FAX: 404.261.0058

S	M	T	W	T	F	S	AE	VC	MC	CB	DC	J

B
L
D

DS ▼ 🚗 ☎ ❸ PR

Veni Vidi Vici

Hearty and flavorful Italian food is served with style in this chic Midtown restaurant. Antipasti Piccoli, wood-burning rotisserie roasted meals and hand made pastas are the menu highlights. There is dining on the terrace during the summer season, and the service is excellent. Traditional bocci ball courts complete the uniquely Italian experience.

Owner: Pano Karatassos

Specialties
Linguini Alle Vongole
Roasted Suckling Pig

41 14th St., Atlanta, GA, 30309
PH: 404.875.8424 FAX: 404.875.6533

Elizabeth on 37th

This elegant turn-of-the-century Southern mansion is the setting for chef Elizabeth Terry's stunning new regional cooking based on traditional recipes. The seasonal menu makes use of the bounty of fresh local seafood and produce, highlighted with herbs from her own gardens. The personable and efficient staff is pleased to continue the time-honored tradition of Southern hospitality, serving fine food, spirits, and perfectly matched wine from the carefully chosen wine list.

Chef: Elizabeth Terry

Specialties
Coastal Grouper Celeste
Spicy Savannah Red Rice with Georgia Shrimp

105 E. 37th St., Savannah GA 31401
PH: 912.236.5547 FAX: 912.232.1095
Email:e37@ix.netcom.com

WHAT BETTER PLACE FOR THE WORLD'S FINEST COFFEE THAN IN NORTH AMERICA'S FINEST RESTAURANTS?

Pescatore, Metropolitan, Camlin Hotel, El Gaucho. All known for imaginative menus. Extraordinary food. And, Viaggio™ coffee. That's right, Viaggio: the exclusive new coffee line considered the finest in the world by true coffee connoisseurs. Next time you dine out, enjoy the rich, distinctive flavors of new Viaggio. After all, top restaurateurs have discovered its exceptional qualities. Isn't it time you did too?

VIAGGIO ™

DISCOVER THE WORLD'S FINEST COFFEES.

Beverly's
COEUR D'ALENE RESORT

Beverly's blends personal, professional service with a comfortable environment, a dynamic menu and spectacular views of Lake Coeur d' Alene to create a unique dining experience. Beverly's menu features a varied assortment of fresh northwest products and organically grown foods to create a taste for any palate. As a complement to any meal, add a bottle of wine from the Resort's wine cellar, honored among the best in the world with the prestigious *Wine Spectator* Grand Award.

Specialties
Firecracker Prawns with Angel Hair Pasta
BC Salmon with Beluga Lentils

PO Box 7200, 115 Front St.
Coeur d'Alene, ID, 83814
PH: 208.765.4000 FAX: 208.664.7276
Website:www.cdaresort.com

S	M	T	W	T	F	S	AE	VC	MC	DC	DS
B											
L											
D											

Le Titi De Paris

Chef and proprietor Pierre Pollin's innovative French cuisine is highlighted in a flower-bedecked tranquil setting. An award-winning wine list with over 850 selections is available to complement seasonal game dishes. French delights and regional fare are highlights. Two private dining rooms are available.

Owner: Pierre Pollin **Chef: Michael Maddox**

Specialties
Ostrich Osso Bucco
Crispy Potato Basket with Duck Confit

1015 W. Dundee Rd.
Arlington Heights, IL, 60004
PH: 847.506.0222 FAX: 847.506.0474
Website:www.chicago.sidewalk.com/letitideparis

S	M	T	W	T	F	S	AE	VC	MC	CB	DC	J	DS
B													
L													
D													

Ambria

Deep-toned woods and crystalline etched glass are combined with Art Nouveau architectural touches, like tiny shaded lamps on each table and massive urns of flowers. This 110-seat restaurant, rated four stars in *Chicago Magazine*, is as noted for ambience and style as it is for cuisine. Ambria's renowned chef, Gabino Sotelino, innovates with an approach that relies totally on the freshest ingredients and cooking techniques that enhance food's light, natural flavors.

Owner: Gabino Sotelino   Chef: Anselmo Ruiz

Specialties
**The Freshest Ingredients
Light, Natural Flavors**

2300 N. Lincoln Pk. W., Chicago IL 60614
PH: 773.472.5959 FAX: 773.472.9077

Bistro 110

A lively neighborhood favorite for more than 10 years, Bistro 110 continues the French bistro tradition with an American accent. Known for its fabulous oven-roasted whole garlic served with crusty French bread, Bistro 110 specializes in hearty wood-burning oven-roasted cuisine, flavorful pasta dishes, salads, sandwiches and extraordinary desserts. Every selection can be accompanied by the perfect wine selected from the restaurant's extensive French-American wine list.

Owners: Doug Roth and   Chef: Dominique Tougne
Larry Levy

Specialties
**Wood-Roasted Mushrooms with Garlic and Thyme
Oven-Roasted Half Chicken with Rosemary and Thyme
Wood Roasted Maine Sea Scallops**

110 E. Pearson, Chicago IL 60611
PH: 312.266.3110 FAX: 312.266.3116

Coco Pazzo

Coco Pazzo features authentic regional Italian cuisine focusing on Tuscan specialities. This elegantly casual setting is housed in a converted loft building with wood beam ceilings, Australian cypress floors, brick walls and large bay windows. Blue velvet drapes and theatrical lighting enhance the ambience, and customers can see beyond the 80-foot antique bar into the open kitchen with a ceramic-tiled wood-fired oven.

Owner: Pino Luongo   Chef: Tony Priolo

Specialties

Calamari al Forno
Rigatoni alla Buttera
Foccaccia Robiolo
Bistecca alla Fiorentina

300 W. Hubbard, Chicago IL 60610
PH: 312.836.0900 FAX: 312.836.0257

Everest

Situated on the 40th floor of the Chicago stock exchange, in the heart of the city's downtown financial district, Everest is a luxuriously elegant restaurant featuring the personalized cuisine of Jean Joho. Service strikes a perfect balance of warm hospitality and polished professionalism. The prestigious wine list features one of the finest collections of Alsace wines in the world.

Owner and Chef: Jean Joho

Specialties

Foie Gras Terrine and Marinated Figs
Roasted Maine Lobster in Gewurztraminer Butter & Ginger
Filet of Halibut Wrapped and Roasted in Potato
Poached Tenderloin of Beef, Pot au Feu Style

440 S. Lasalle St., Chicago IL 60605
PH: 312.663.8920 FAX: 312.663.8802

Gordon

The classy Gordon, chosen in 1998 by *Bon Appetit* as one of America's "Tried and True" restaurants, is chic in both menu and decor. The internationally-inspired cooking is prepared by the brilliant Don Yamauchi, and many of the restaurant's dishes are enhanced by the flavors of the vegetables and herbs grown in the owner's organic garden. All entrées are served in half portions to create your own tasting menu. Piano nightly; jazz trio Saturdays.

Owner: Gordon Sinclair　　　　　　　Chef: Don Yamauchi

Specialties
**The Original Artichoke Fritters
Roasted New Zealand Venison
Sautéed Alaskan Halibut
Chef's Five-Course Tasting Menu**

500 N. Clark St., Chicago IL 60610
PH: 312.467.9780 FAX: 312.467.1671
Website:www.gordonrestaurant.com

La Strada Ristorante

Located in the heart of Chicago's theatre district, La Strada has served authentic, inspired Italian cuisine for the past 17 years, to locals and vistors alike. We feature fettuccini with lobster, rack of lamb, Dover sole, zabaglione and crème brûlée. La Strada has an extensive Italian, French and Californian wine list, and offers pre-theatre and children's menus.

Owner: Michael Mormando　　　　　　Chef: Marc Rosen

Specialties
**Veal Chops
Seafood**

155 N. Michigan Ave., Chicago, IL 60601
PH: 312.565.2200 FAX: 312.565.2216
Website:www.lastradaristorante.com

Spiaggia

Spiaggia features a spectacular view of Lake Michigan and authentic Italian cuisine by James Beard Award-winning Chef Paul Bartolotta. Vibrant scents and haunting flavors are the signatures of his cuisine, and his menus are a celebration of simplicity and seasonality. The name Spiaggia, meaning 'beach' in Italian, is inspired by the breathtaking view. Tables are tiered and floor-to-ceiling windows offer splendid viewing to accompany the unsurpassed cuisine. Every detail has been orchestrated to create the ultimate dining experience.

Owner: Levy Restaurants   Chef: Paul Bartolotta

Specialties
**Ricotta Ravioli with Sweet Tuscan Pecorino Cheese
Filet of Salmon with Asparagus, Basil & White Wine Sauce**

980 N. Michigan Ave., Chicago IL 60611
PH: 312.280.2750 FAX: 312.943.8560

S	M	T	W	T	F	S		AE	VC	MC	CB	DC	DS

B
L
D

Vivere

Chicago's Vivere: eye-alluring, comforting, and romantic, offering genuine Italian food with one of the best wine lists in the country. The Vivere experience features a contemporary Italian menu and a longtime *Wine Spectator* Grand Award-winning wine list, complemented by breathtaking Jordan Mozer design. The restaurant's polished, warm service and the Capitanini family's rare hospitality separate Vivere from the fray.

Owners: Capitanini Family   Chef: Marcello Gallegos

Specialties
**Tortine di Funghi Misti
Agnolotti di Fagiano • Quaglie alla Griglia
Petto d'Anatra con Salsa d'Aceto Balsamico**

71 W. Monroe St, Chicago IL 60603
PH: 312.332.4040 FAX: 312.332.2656

S	M	T	W	T	F	S		AE	VC	MC	CB	DC	J	DS

B
L
D

Carlos'

For 15 years, residents of Chicago's North Shore communities have come to Carlos' for celebrations that call for a memorable meal. They come for distinguished service all the more notable for its cordiality and lack of pomp. Carlos' customers come for the beautifully presented, stylish and satisfying cuisine. They come for the *Wine Spectator*'s Grand Award winning wine list. Most of all, though, people come to see Carlos and Debbie Nieto, a personable and dedicated couple.

Owners: Carlos & Debbie Nieto   **Chef: Alan Wolf**

Specialties
Roasted Australian Rack of Lamb
Chilean Sea Bass with Middle Eastern Vegetable Couscous

429 Temple Av., Highland Park IL 60035
PH: 847.432.0770 FAX: 847.432.2047

Café 36

The owners of Café 36, Reinhard Barthel Sr. and Jr. are impressing critics with exceptional cuisine and outstanding service in their charming and comfortable French-style restaurant. Named one of America's top restaurants by *Zagat* and acclaimed by the *Chicago Tribune* and the *Chicago Sun Times,* Café 36 maintains high standards to ensure a memorable experience with each visit. An extensive wine list awaits your consideration, and main courses range from the exotic ostrich to pasta and poussin.

Chef: Reinhard Bartel

Specialties
Medallions of Ostrich and Kangaroo Sautéed
with Wild Mushrooms

36 S La Grange Rd., La Grange, IL, 60525
PH: 708.354.5722 FAX: 708.354.5042

Le Vichyssois

A French country inn featuring fresh fish, veal with mushrooms, and duck. With home-made desserts and an extensive wine list, Le Vichyssois is a charming, casual French restaurant with white tablecloths and fresh flowers on each table. Classical music plays in the background.

Owners: Bernard and Priscilla Cretier   Chef: Bernard Cretier

Specialties
Salmon en Croute
Dover Sole

220 W. Rt. 120, Lakemoor, IL, 60050
PH: 815.385.8221 FAX: 815.385.8223

Carlucci

Traditional Tuscan cooking favoring simple earthy ingredients rather than the usual heavy sauces. Meals are prepared authentically: meat, fish and poultry are baked in a wood-burning oven, roasted on a spit, or grilled. The restaurant, which has the feeling of a Tuscan country estate, is highlighted by a skilled and friendly staff. Our restaurant offers a variety of private dining and meeting rooms that cater to all of your needs. Conveniently located near O'Hare Airport.

Owners: Joe & Charlie Carlucci   Chef: Luigi Negroni

Specialties
Cappellacci di Agnello con Sugo di Arrosto
Composizione de Pesce Milano Marittima

6111 N. River Rd., Rosemont IL 60018
PH: 847.518.0990 FAX: 847.518.0999
Website:www.carluccirestaurant.com

The Glass Chimney

The Glass Chimney was established in 1976 in a converted house in Carmel, Indiana, a suburb north of Indianapolis. Operated from the beginning by Dieter G. Puska, Austrian-born and European-trained chef/owner, the atmosphere is warm and elegant Viennese style. Our 300-plus wine list, extensive selection of cognac, port and single malt scotches, all available in our mahogany lounge will please the connoisseur. For cigar lovers we have a humidor in our bar, stocked with a variety of fine cigars.

Owner and Chef: Dieter G. Puska

Specialties

Black Angus Steak • Seafood
Provimi Veal • Domestic Lamb

12901 Old Meridian St., Carmel IN 46032
PH: 317.844.0921 FAX: 317.574.1360

The Restaurant at the Canterbury

Nestled in the heart of downtown Indianapolis, The Restaurant at the Canterbury is located just off the lobby of the historic Canterbury Hotel. A long-standing reputation promises a memorable dining experience. The intimate ambiance and unobtrusive, professional staff are sure to exceed the expectations of the most discriminating guest. The Restaurant features American and continental cuisine expertly prepared by renowned chef Volker Rudolph. Winemaker Dinner nightly.

Owners: The Canterbury Hotel   Chef: Volker Rudolph

Specialties
Lobster and Veal Tivoli
Trio of Rocky Mountain Lamb Chops

123 S Illinois St., Indianapolis, IN, 46225
PH: 317.634.3000 FAX: 317.685.2519

Le Relais

Located in historic Bowman Field, Le Relais is known for its fine French cuisine and romantic Art Deco atmosphere. Now in our 10th year, we would like to invite you to explore our award-winning wine list and put the romance back in your life. Zesty crab cakes and a tender veal chop are two favorites that remain on our seasonal menu year round. Try a savory homemade dessert to complete your dining experience.

Owner: Anthony R. Dike   Chef: Roberta Cattan

Specialties
Shrimp Bisque • Crab Cakes
Veal Chop • Crème Brûlée

2817 Taylorsville Rd., Bowman Field,
Louisville KY 40205
PH: 502.451.9020 FAX: 502.459.3112

Vincenzo's

Located in the heart of downtown Louisville, just one block from the Kentucky Center for the Arts, award-winning Vincenzo's features refined sophistication, attentive tableside preparation, a formidable wine cellar and Chef Agostino's exclusive specialties prepared in one of the country's largest à la carte kitchens. Welcoming local regulars and internationally renowned personalities since 1986, Vincenzo's also offers nine private dining rooms accommodating from six to 250 guests.

Owners: Vincenzo and Agostino Gabriele   Chef: Agostino Gabriele

Specialties
Cappellini Alla Aragosta
Filettini di Vitello Con Funghetti di Bosco

150 S 5th St., Louisville, KY, 40202
PH: 502.580.1350 FAX: 502.580.1355
Catering: 502.580.1371

Lafitte's Landing Restaurant

AT BITTERSWEET PLANTATION

Located in the heart of plantation country, Lafitte's Landing Restaurant is one of the most renowned eateries in South Louisiana. The restaurant is housed in the old Viala Plantation House where the son of pirate Jean Lafitte married Emma Viala in 1825. Lafitte's has won numerous national and international awards, including the DiRoNA Award in 1996, and induction into the Fine Dining Hall of Fame in 1989.

Owner and Chef: John D. Folse, CEC, AAC

Specialties
Cajun and Creole Cuisine

404 Claiborne Ave., Donaldsonville, LA, 70346
PH: 225.473.1232 FAX: 225.473.1161

Bayona

Sitting demurely in the historic French Quarter is a quaint and lovely Creole cottage. Striking Mediterranean cuisine is prepared by chef Susan Spicer, winner of the 1993 James Beard Award, Best Chef - Southeast Region. Expect gracious service in an inviting and sincere climate. This is a favorite with locals and tourists alike, not only for the incredibly good food, but also for the allure of the courtyard, fountain and native flora.

Owner: Regina Keever   Chef: Susan Spicer

Specialties
Grilled Shrimp with Black Bean Cake and Coriander Sauce
Grilled Duck Breast with Pepper Jelly Glaze

430 Dauphine St., New Orleans LA 70112
PH: 504.525.4455 FAX: 504.522.0589
Website:www.bayona.com

Brigtsen's

Brigtsen's offers modern Creole and Acadian cuisine served in a quaint Victorian cottage. Chef Frank Brigtsen was named Best Chef in the Southeast at the 1998 James Beard Awards.

Owners: Frank & Marna Brigtsen   Chef: Frank Brigtsen

Specialties

Butternut Shrimp Bisque
Blackened Tuna with Smoked Corn Sauce & Red Bean Salsa
Roast Duck with Cornbread Dressing & Honey Pecan Gravy
Broiled Gulf Fish with Crabmeat Parmesan Crust

723 Dante St., New Orleans LA 70118
PH: 504.861.7610 FAX: 504.866.7397

S M T W T F S AE VC MC DC
B
L
D

Broussard's

For more than half a century, Broussard's has been one of the French Quarter's most historic restaurants. Chef/owner Günter Preuss was featured on the PBS series *Great Chefs of New Orleans*. Wife Evelyn and son Marc present traditional Creole dishes in an atmosphere of sparkling chandeliers and plush furnishings. A perfect complement to the elegant dining room is the lush courtyard where flowers, fountains and soft lighting create an aura of romance.

Owners: Evelyn & Günter Preuss   Chef: Günter Preuss

Specialties

Creole Cuisine
Fresh Seafood

819 Conti, New Orleans LA 70112
PH: 504.581.3866 FAX: 504.581.3873

S M T W T F S AE VC MC
B
L
D

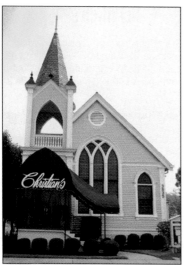

Christian's Restaurant

Consistently recognized by both local and national diners for its culinary imagination, Christian's is located in Mid-City in a quaint, renovated old church. The unique design features stained glass windows, cathedral ceilings and a bar that was once the "crying room." This unusual setting provides a charming atmosphere where New Orleans Creole and classical French cuisine are delicately blended for a truly divine dining experience.

Manager: Donna Le Blanc   **Chef: Michael Patrick McGuire**

Specialties
Smoked Softshell Crab
Bouillabaise Marseillaise

S	M	T	W	T	F	S	AE	VC	MC	CB	DC

B
L
D

3835 Iberville St., New Orleans, LA, 70119
PH: 504.482.4924 FAX: 504.482.6852

Grill Room
WINDSOR COURT HOTEL

The only AAA Five-Diamond and Mobil Five-Star restaurant in Louisiana, the Grill Room is a delight to the eye as well as the palate. The restaurant was voted the number one dining establishment in New Orleans by *Gourmet* in 1998. Executive Chef René Bajeux offers traditional cuisine with French flair.

Owner: Windsor Court Hotel   **Chef: René Bajeux**

Specialties
Fresh Fish and Seafood
Rack of Lamb

S	M	T	W	T	F	S	AE	VC	MC	CB	DC	DS

B
L
D

300 Gravier St., New Orleans, LA, 70130
PH: 504.522.1992 FAX: 504.596.4513

Louis XVI Restaurant Français

Praised as New Orleans' most impressive combination of interior elegance and exterior beauty, Louis XVI features classic French cuisine with many courses prepared tableside by the classically trained wait staff. The restaurant and all its private dining rooms surround a beautiful, lush courtyard. Live musicians entertain nightly.

Owner: Mark Smith III   Chef: Agnes Bellet

Specialties

Rack of Lamb with French Mustard and Mint Sauce
Marinated Beef (Venison Style) with Sweet and Spicy Sauce
Filet of Fish topped with Sautéed Banana and Red Bell Peppers
Chateaubriand in a Puff Pastry Shell with Perigueux Sauce

730 Bienville St., New Orleans, LA, 70130
PH: 504.581.7000 FAX: 504.524.8925
Website:www.louisXVI.com

The White Barn Inn

The White Barn Inn is southern Maine's only AAA Five Diamond dining establishment. It is an authentic, lovingly restored eighteenth century barn embellished with exposed beams and an antique-filled loft. Progressive American cuisine with robust New England overtones woven in make this the award-winner it is. Flickering soft candlelight and affable and professional service unite to form the ideal setting for celebrating life's special occasions.

Owner: Lawrence Bongiorno   Chef: Jonathan Cartwright

Specialties

New England Fish and Seafood
Grilled Beef Tenderloin

37 Beach St., Kennebunkport, ME, 04043
PH: 207.967.2321 FAX: 207.967.1100
Website:www.whitebarninn.com

Hampton's
HARBOR COURT HOTEL

Hampton's is located on Baltimore's fabulous inner harbor, and features contemporary American cuisine in an elegant Edwardian setting. The restaurant was recently awarded a four-star rating by the Baltimore Sun dining guide, four diamonds by AAA and listed among *Conde Nast Traveler's* top fifty American restaurants. Regular monthly Cellarmaster dinners are scheduled.

Specialties
Rack of Lamb
Maryland Seafood

550 Light St., Baltimore, MD, 21202
PH: 410.234.0550 FAX: 410.659.5925
Website:www.harborcourt.com

S	M	T	W	T	F	S	AE	VC	MC	DC	DS
B											
L											
D											

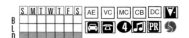

The Prime Rib

At The Prime Rib, the emphasis is on great aged beef and fresh Chesapeake Bay seafood, served in an atmosphere conducive to a romantic rendezvous. In fact, for the past nine years, the local cognoscenti have considered The Prime Rib Baltimore's most romantic restaurant. A showcase list of California wines, starring particularly good Cabernet Sauvignons, and a magnificient cocktail bar makes any visit here one to be relished.

Owner: C.P. (Buzz) BeLer   Chef: Jim Minarik

Specialties
Fresh Chesapeake Seafood
Aged Prime Rib

1101 N. Calvert St., Baltimore, MD, 21202
PH: 410.539.1804 FAX: 410.837.0244
Website:www.theprimerib.com

S	M	T	W	T	F	S	AE	VC	MC	CB	DC
B											
L											
D											

Tragara

"So what if the chef is French? Tragara serves some really delicious Italian food, food of refinement that displays the brilliance of Italian simplicity," says Phyllis Richman of the Washington Post. Tragara is also a winner of the 100 Very Best Restaurants Award from the Washingtonian. Chef Michel Laudiere and Claude and Shelley Amsellem continue the excellence patrons expect. Tragara is also known for its banquet facilities, and the staff takes pleasure in making dining experiences memorable.

Owner: Claude Amsellem **Chef: Michel Laudiere**

Specialties

**Linguine with Lobster, Pesto and Mascarpone Cheese
Agnolotti Stuffed with Spinach and Ricotta Cheese**

4935 Cordell Ave., Bethesda, MD, 20814
PH: 301.951.4935 FAX: 301.951.0401

Stone Manor

Savor the magic of exceptional cuisine, luxurious suites, and eighteenth-century charm in this 114-acre country estate. Outside are gardens, a pond, a stream, rolling farmlands and forest. Inside the majestic eighteen-room farm house are three candlelit dining rooms with fireplaces. The six suites, stylishly furnished with antiques, have tables for "in-suite dining." The Chef's Regional American Cuisine is presented in two *prix fixe* menus with suggested wine packages.

Chef: Charles Zeran

Specialties

**Seared Sea Scallop, Salmon Caviar and Portabella "Sandwich"
Wild Mushroom and Leek Tart with White Truffle Crème Fraîche
Cherry Ale Braised Rabbit with Andouille Sausage**

5820 Carroll Boyer Rd., Middletown, MD, 21769
PH: 301.473.5454 FAX: 301.371.5622
Website:www.stonemanor.com

208 Talbot

Chef owned and operated, 208 Talbot is located in historic St. Michaels, just minutes from the waters of the Chesapeake Bay. The innovative cuisine served in this charming establishment reflects the area's bounty of fresh seafood and produce. The atmosphere is casually elegant, and the excellent food, well-chosen wine list and exceptional service will guarantee a wonderful dining experience. When visiting the area, stay at our waterfront inn, The Oaks.

Owner and Chef: Paul Milne

Specialties

Baked Oysters with a Champagne Sauce
Crispy Soft Shell Crabs with Green Tomato Butter
Sautéed Rockfish with Oyster Cream Sauce

208 N. Talbot St., St.Michaels MD 21663
PH: 410.745.3838
Website: www.208talbot.com

The Inn at Perry Cabin

The Inn at Perry Cabin is a 41-room premier British country house hotel situated on 25 quiet acres along the Miles River. One compelling reason to visit The Inn is to explore the culinary talents of Mark Salter, executive chef. Chef Mark and his team create subtle and imaginative Chesapeake specialties using fresh fish and local produce, mixed with international fare and complemented by an extensive wine list.

Owner: Sir Bernard Ashley　　　　Chef: Mark Salter

Specialties

Honey Glazed Shank of Lamb
Smoked Bluefish • Crab Spring Roll

308 Watkins Lane, St. Michaels MD 21663
PH: 410.745.2200 FAX: 410.745.3348

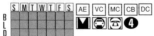

Anthony's Pier 4

The place to go in a city known for its abundance of fresh seafood, Anthony's Pier 4 has been serving fresh seafood for 35 years, in a spectacular setting overlooking Boston Harbor. The restaurant reflects the character and charm of a time-honored classic. Anthony's is also known for prime steaks and chops, and offers over 400 wines from an acclaimed list which has won the *Wine Spectator's* Grand Award of Excellence since 1982.

Owners: Anthony Athanas and Sons

Specialties
New England Fish and Seafood
Aged Prime Steaks and Chops

140 Northern Ave., Boston, MA, 02210
PH: 617.482.6262 FAX: 617.426.2324
Website:www.pier4.com

The Bay Tower

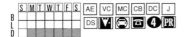

The Bay Tower is Boston's most spectacular and romantic restaurant, with a panoramic view of Boston Harbor from the 33rd floor. We are centrally located in the financial district, next to Faneuil Hall Marketplace and ten minutes from the airport. Chef Kim Lambrechts blends local traditions with global trends, based upon a foundation in the classic French style. Winner of the *Wine Spectator* Award of Excellence.

Chef: Kim Lambrechts

Specialties
Pan-Seared Foie Gras with Parsnip Purée
Sesame-Crusted Yellowfin Tuna
Maine Lobster with Wild Mushroom Ragôut

Sixty State St., Boston, MA 02109
PH: 617.723.1666 FAX: 617.723.7887

Biba

Lydia Shire's impressively creative, eclectic cuisine is always interesting, served in an exotically elegant dining room overlooking the Public Gardens. The downstairs bar is a trendy spot serving some of Boston's best bar food. Lydia has recently opened a second Boston restaurant, Pignoli, a modern interpretation of Italian cuisine with a take-out bakery. Lydia was named Best Chef in the Northeast in 1992, and her partner, Susan Regis, was awarded the same honor in 1998.

Owner: Lydia Shire   Chefs: Lydia Shire & Susan Regis

Specialties

Pot-Roasted Foie Gras with Honey and Clove
Catalan-Style Lobster
Biba's Own Lobster Pizza
Cedar-Planked Club Sirloin with White Burgundy Sauce

272 Boylston St., Boston, MA 02116
PH: 617.426.7878 FAX: 617.426.9253

Café Budapest

Experience European elegance at this world famous award-winning restaurant in the heart of Boston. Bostonians have chosen the Café Budapest as the city's Most Romantic Restaurant since it was established. Enjoy enchanting Hungarian and European delicacies in a charming old world setting.

Owner: Hedda Rev-Kury   Chef: Chris Barton

Specialties

Iced Tart Cherry Soup
Veal Gulyas

90 Exeter St., Boston, MA, 02116
PH: 617.266.1979 FAX: 617.266.1395

The Dining Room
RITZ-CARLTON BOSTON

Since the Ritz-Carlton opened in 1927, the Dining Room has been recognized continually as one of the city's award-winning culinary classics. Under the direction of innovative chef Richard Rayment, the seasonal menus are sophisticated blendings of traditional and contemporary specialties. His tasting menu has become a city favorite. *Food and Wine* magazine has ranked its wine list the best in Boston. From grand occasion dinners to a splendid Sunday brunch, excitement and experimentation are on the menu.

Chef: Richard Rayment

Specialties
**Fig and Proscuitto Risotto with Seared Foie Gras
Lobster, Spinach, and Celery Root Lasagne**

15 Arlington Street, Boston, MA, 02117
PH: 617.536.5700 FAX: 617.536.9340

Galleria Italiana

Old world Italian charms and delicate aromas of savory dishes await those who enter Galleria Italiana. Continuously seeking to recreate the culture and tradition of Italian cuisine in Boston's theatre district, diners can enjoy breakfast, lunch or dinner with service synonymous with Italian traditions. Spotlit tables and marble walls with brightly-coloured paintings and photographs of Italy's Abruzzi region create an inviting atmosphere in which to dine.

Owners: Marisa Iocco & Rita D'Angelo   Chef: Rene Michelena

Specialties
**Veal Tartare with Salsa Tonnato
Gnocchi with White Truffle Essence
Trout Stuffed with Mushrooms and Tarragon
Braised Rabbit with Turnip and Black Truffle Sauce**

177 Tremont St., Boston, MA 02111
PH: 617.423.2092 FAX: 617.423.4436

Grill 23 & Bar

The Commodities Trading Floor of the Old Salada Tea Co. provides the mahogany and brass setting for Grill 23 & Bar. The restaurant was rated Top Bar and Grill, among other top designations, by the 1998 *Zagat* guide. We are recognized nationally for our prime, dry-aged beef, creative seafood dishes, elegant and eclectic wine list and superb service. Restaurant clientèle appreciate our upscale, charming ambience while enjoying grill classics and seafood for business or pleasure.

Owner: Kenneth Himmel   Chef: Jay Murray

Specialties

Maple Pecan Crusted Catfish with Roasted Vegetables
Sage and Mustard Rubbed Tuna with Red Potatoes
Braised Colorado Lamb Shank with Lemon, Dill and Feta

S	M	T	W	T	F	S	AE	VC	MC	CB	DC	J	DS

161 Berkeley St., Boston MA 02116
PH: 617.542.2255 FAX: 617.542.5114
Website: www.grill23.com

Hamersley's Bistro

This lovely, warm restaurant with its old beams and yellow walls is reminiscent of the French countryside. The contemporary French food confirms that impression, with its emphasis on fresh seasonal ingredients and commitment to respect both innovation and tradition. The eclectic wine list reflects the owners passion for food wines. "Best of Boston" winner for 8 years and nationally acclaimed, it is consistently wonderful.

Owners: Gordon & Fiona Hamersley   Chef: Gordon Hamersley

Specialties

Roast Chicken with Garlic, Lemon and Parsley
Crispy Duck Confit
Grilled Mushroom and Garlic Sandwich on Country Bread
Souffléed Lemon Custard

S	M	T	W	T	F	S	AE	VC	MC	CB	DC	DS

553 Tremont St. Boston, MA, 02116
PH: 617.423.2700 FAX: 617.423.7710

Icarus

After nearly twenty years, chef and co-owner Chris Douglass' American regional menu continues to set the standard for fine dining in Boston's exciting South End. Locally grown produce, the finest farm raised meat and poultry and the freshest in New England seafood combine with sumptuous desserts and an award winning wine list to assure a memorable dining experience. Icarus features a lovely two-level dining room appointed in rich woods and mission furniture, highlighted by soft lighting and spacious seating. Live jazz in the bar on Friday nights.

Co-owner and Chef: Chris Douglass

Specialties
Lobster and Chanterelle Risotto
Roast Breast and Sausage of Vermont Pheasant

3 Appleton St., Boston, MA, 02116
PH: 617.426.1790 FAX: 617.426.2150
Website:www.icarusrestaurant.com

S	M	T	W	T	F	S		AE	VC	MC	CB	DC	DS
B							
L							
D							

Julien

LE MERIDIEN HOTEL

Considered by many to be Boston's most exquisite dining room, Julien continues to secure national acclaim for both atmosphere and cuisine. Vaulted gold leaf-edged ceilings and five magnificent chandeliers create an elegantly rich ambiance. The cuisine, under the direction of Chef Alain Rayé, who is previous owner of three one-star Michelin restaurants, is classically French with a modern flair. Piano entertainment nightly.

Chef: Alain Rayé

Specialties
Roasted Rack of Lamb
Sautéed Maine Lobster
Young Rabbit with Crusty Eggplant

250 Franklin St., Boston, MA, 02110
PH: 617.451.1900 FAX: 617.451.0919
Website:www.lemeridian.com

S	M	T	W	T	F	S		AE	VC	MC	DC	DS
B							
L							
D							

L'Espalier

What the French call *la joie de vivre*: excellent food, wine and atmosphere is in essence what you will find at L'Espalier. Recently, the readers of *Gourmet* voted L'Espalier Top Table 1998 for Boston. Chef-Owner Frank McClelland's inventive New England-French cuisine is based on local, fresh ingredients. Located in an historic Back Bay townhouse, L'Espalier is perfect for intimate evenings or a grand celebration.

Owners: Frank & Catherine McClelland   Chef: Frank McClelland

Specialties

Warm Lobster & Sausage Salad Mille-Feuille
Poached Atlantic Halibut in Fall Black Truffles

30 Gloucester St., Boston MA 02115
PH: 617.262.3023 FAX: 617.375.9297

Maison Robert

Maison Robert is located in the stately Historic Old City Hall and offers diners a choice of two restaurants, the elegant Formal Dining Room and Ben's Café. The upper retaurant retains much of the building's original decoration, in a French Second Empire style. The stately and gracious main dining room was formerly the office of the City Treasurer, where dinner is served in the classical French tradition. Six rooms provide private dining spaces.

Owner: Lucien Robert   Chef: Jacky Robert

Specialties

Maine Lobster Cooked in Smoke
Savory and Dessert Soufflés

45 School St., Boston MA 02108
PH: 617.227.3370 FAX: 617.227.5977

Seasons
REGAL BOSTONIAN HOTEL

Earning praise from food and wine critics around the world, Seasons has built its reputation on its seasonally changing menu and extensive all-American wine list. Enjoy the finest new American cuisine from chef Michael Taylor, impeccable service, and a spectacular rooftop view of Faneuil Hall Marketplace.

Owner: Regal International   Chef: Michael Taylor

Specialties
Seared New York State Foie Gras
Forest Mushroom Consommé, Sweet Garlic Flan
Roast Maine Lobster
Tapenade Pesto-Roasted Alaskan Halibut

Regal Bostonian Hotel, Faneuil Hall Marketplace
Boston, MA, 02109
PH: 617.523.4119 FAX: 617.523.2593

Top of the Hub

Located on the 52nd floor of the Prudential Tower in Boston's historic Back Bay, Top of the Hub features outstanding food that delights the eye and satisfies the soul. You and your guests will enjoy impeccable service with a waitstaff that anticipates your every need in a setting that is literally above it all. Featuring live jazz seven nights a week and a late night dinner menu served until midnight, Top of the Hub is the perfect place for an unforgettable affair.

Owner: Select Restaurants   Chef: Dean Moore

Specialties
Hudson Valley Duck Foie Gras & Oxtail Stew
Pan Roasted Monkfish & Fried Calamari
Skillet Roasted Center Cut Pork Chop
Rack & Medallion of Vermont Fallow Deer

800 Boylston St., Boston, MA, 02199
PH: 617.536.1775 FAX: 617.859.8298

Salamander Restaurant

The Boston Globe's Alison Arnett calls Salamander "a four star restaurant in the making," and the restaurant has been listed as a top-ten Boston restaurant by both the *Zagat Survey* and *Gourmet* magazine. The myriad of unique flavor combinations on chef Stan Frankenthaler's Asian inspired menu, combined with the heady aromas of the wood burning hearth, make this a dining experience certain to delight your palate.

Owner and Chef: Stan Frankenthaler

Specialties
**Hoisin Glazed Rotisserie Pork Chop
Pan Fried Lobster with Lemongrass and Ginger**

S M T W T F S | AE | VC | MC | CB | DC | DS

1 Athenaeum St., Cambridge, MA, 02142
PH: 617.225.2121 FAX: 617.494.8871

The Castle

For over 50 years, The Castle has been the epitome of fine dining in Central Massachusetts. Continental cuisine, masterful flambés and elegant service are The Castle's hallmarks. Located on beautiful Lake Sargent, The Castle's outdoor patio and herb gardens provide an enchanting afternoon of dining pleasure. With our award-winning wine list, The Castle offers a fine array of both domestic and foreign wines and after-dinner liqueurs.

Owners: Nicas Family   **Chef: Dr. Stanley Nicas**

Specialties
**Steak au Poivre • Roast Rack of Lamb
Châteaubriand • Game du Jour**

S M T W T F S | AE | VC | MC | CB | DC | DS

1230 Main St., Leicester MA 01524
PH: 508.892.9090 FAX: 508.892.3620
Website:www.castlerestaurant.com

Wheatleigh

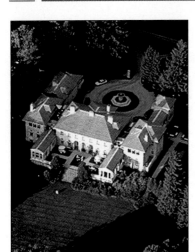

The *New York Times* called the Wheatleigh dining experience "a table fit for a prince." The small luxury hotel with a European flavor is a replica of a sixteenth-century Florentine Palazzo, built in the Berkshires by an American industrialist as a wedding gift for his daughter. The style of cuisine is a contemporary interpretation of classical French food utilizing a large network of local organic farmers.

Chef: Peter Platt

Specialties
Roasted Sweet Dumpling Squash Soup
Black Truffle Encrusted Squab Breast
Pan-Roasted Loin of Wild Axis Venison

Hawthorne Road, Lenox, MA, 01240
PH: 413.637.0610 FAX: 413.637.4507
Website:www.wheatleigh.com

Silks at Stonehedge Inn

Designed in the style of a luxurious English country manor, Stonehedge Inn is nestled in 33 acres of woodlands, overlooking manicured pastures grazed by thoroughbred racehorses. Silks has established an award-winning reputation for its gourmet French provençal cuisine under the direction of chef Jon Mathieson. The wine list has garnered worldwide acclaim and boasts over 1200 vintages from around the world.

Owner: Levent Bozkurt   **Chef: Jon Mathieson**

Specialties
Warm Shrimp Salad
Maine Lobster
Roast Rack of Lamb
Hudson Valley Foie Gras

160 Pawtucket Blvd., Tyngsboro MA 01879
PH: 978.649.4400 FAX: 978.649.9256
Website:www.stonehedgeinn.com

Chillingsworth

An antique cape house, surrounded by six acres of lawns and gardens, is the enchanting setting for this landmark restaurant on Cape Cod. Modern French cuisine with California flair is served in a six course table d'hôte format in the flower-filled, antique-appointed dining rooms of the main house. An airy solarium and brick patio offer casual à la carte luncheons as well as a Bistro dinner menu in the evening. There are several antique-filled guest rooms as well as an eclectic gourmet shop.

Owners: Robert and Pat Rabin   Chef: Robert Rabin

Specialties
Native Seafood, Pheasant, Rabbit, Veal & Lamb
Fresh Native Ingredients
2449 Main St.
PO Box 1819, Brewster, MA, 02631
PH: 508.896.3640 FAX: 508.896.7540
Website:www.chillingsworth.com

S	M	T	W	T	F	S	AE	VC	MC	DC	🍴	🚗

B
L ☎ ④ 🏨 PR ⑨
D

Dan'l Webster Inn

Ideally located between heaven, history and the ocean, the Dan'l Webster Inn is the centerpiece of Cape Cod's most picturesque village. The Inn offers the essence of colonial charm and elegance, with forty-seven beautifully appointed guest rooms, a tavern, and a gift shop on the premises. Fireside dining, or dining in the sun or moonlit Conservatory, are combined with an award-winning wine list, innovative cuisine and outstanding service.

Owners: Catania Family   Chef: Robert Catania

Specialties
Contemporary American Cuisine
Local Seafood

149 Main St., Sandwich, MA, 02563
PH: 508.888.3622 FAX: 508.888.5156
Website:www.danlwebsterinn.com

S	M	T	W	T	F	S	AE	VC	MC	CB	DC

B
L DS 🍴 🚗 ☎ ②
D

The Chanticleer

"One of the 10 Most Romantic Restaurants," according to The Rich and Famous. A *Wine Spectator* Grand Award winner for one of the best wine lists since 1987. This year we are celebrating 30 years of excellence. We specialize in Nantucket weddings and special lunches in our beautiful rose garden.

Owner and Chef: Jean-Charles Berruet

Specialties

**Nantucket Bay Scallops with Truffles
Roasted Lobster Injected with Champagne Butter**

9 New St., Siasconset, MA, 02564
PH: 508.257.6231 FAX: 508.257.4154
Website:www.thechanticleerinn.com

S	M	T	W	T	F	S	AE	VC	MC
B									
L									
D									

Opus One

American cuisine with a continental flair describes Opus One's signature style at lunch, dinner and a wide range of special catered events. The restaurant's interior is an eye-catching blend of deep woods, marble, etched glass and interesting artwork , reflecting the attention to detail evident in the food. The award-winning wine list includes an assortment of current releases as well as a more challenging selection of vintages.

Owner: James C. Kokas and　　　**Chef: Timothy Giznsky**
Edward R. Mandziara

Specialties

**Shrimp Helene
Pastry Cart**

565 E. Larned St., Detroit, MI, 48226
PH: 313.961.7766 FAX: 313.961.9423
Website:www.opus-one.com

S	M	T	W	T	F	S	AE	VC	MC	CB	DC	DS
B												
L												
D												

Ristorante Café Cortina

Since Café Cortina was started in 1976, its reputation as a "True Ristorante" has spread. In today's fast paced environment, this restaurant continues to present the true heart and soul of Italian cooking. The Tonon family, from the Veneto region of Italy known for its earthy polentas, risottos, wild game and beautiful wines, recreate the dishes of their Italian heritage. Formerly an orchard, the grounds are utilized for farming the aromatic herbs and vegetables used in Café Cortina's distinctive cuisine.

Owners: Tonon Family   Chefs: Hoffa and Blinderini

Specialties
Pesce é Carne alla Griglia

30715 W 10 Mile Rd.
Farmington Hills, MI, 48336
PH: 248.474.3033 FAX: 248.474.9064

Golden Mushroom

Celebrating over 25 years of serving Michigan's most discriminating diners, Golden Mushroom offers unparalleled service, distinctive cuisine and a 800-selection wine list. Executive Chef Derin Moore, a member of the US Culinary Olympics Team and a graduate of the famed Culinary Institute of America, carries on the rich tradition of talent and innovation. The restaurant has trained more than 50 chefs and has won more culinary awards than any other Michigan dining establishment.

Owner: Reid L. Ashton   Chef: Derin Moore

Specialties
Porcini & Armagnac injected Veal Chop
Rack of Lamb in Persillade Crust

18100 West Ten Mile Rd.,
Southfield, MI, 48075
PH: 248.559.4230 FAX: 248.559.7312

The Lark

Consistently named Michigan's most romantic restaurant, The Lark was also first place winner in *Gourmet's* Top Table Awards and the best restaurant in America in *Condé Nast Traveler's* reader's poll. A European-style country inn with outdoor tables in season, the Lark's eclectic cuisine ranges from the latest French creations to Maine lobster and steak. An award-winning wine cellar houses 800 selections.

Owners: Jim and Mary Lark   Chef: Marcus Haight

Specialties
Rack of Lamb Genghis Khan
Curried Duck Salad

6430 Farmington Rd. West Bloomfield, MI, 48322
PH: 248.661.4466 FAX: 248.661.8891

D'Amico Cucina

Opened in 1987, D'Amico Cucina serves world-class Italian cuisine with a contemporary accent. The restaurant features an outstanding, Italian-only wine list, along with an extensive selection of rare Italian grappas and other liqueurs. Located downtown in historic Butler Square, D'Amico Cucina has been recognized for its innovative fare, wine list and stunning interior, and has won countless local and national awards.

Chef: J.P. Samuelson

Specialties
Butternut Squash Cappelletti with Pistachio and Sage
Pangrattato Crusted Pork Tenderloin with Soft Polenta

100 N. 6th St., Minneapolis MN 55403
PH: 612.338.2401 FAX: 612.337.5130
Website:www.damico.com

Goodfellow's

Goodfellow's serves award-winning food and wine in a historic Art Deco environment. This premier restaurant has received many accolades, including the DiRoNA Award, AAA Four Diamond and *Wine Spectator* awards. In 1997, Goodfellow's was inducted into *Nation's Restaurant News* Hall of Fame. Goodfellow's has private dining and meeting facilities for groups of 10 to 100. The restaurant is located in the heart of downtown Minneapolis with convenient evening and valet parking.

Owners: John Dayton and Wayne Kostroski Chef: Kevin Cullen

Specialties
Roast Glenwood Pheasant
Wisconsin Veal Chop

S	M	T	W	T	F	S		AE	VC	MC	CB	DC	DS	

B
L
D

40 S. 7th St., Minneapolis, MN, 55402
PH: 612.332.4800 FAX: 612.332.1274

The Rosewood Room
CROWNE PLAZA NORTHSTAR HOTEL

A dining tradition for over 30 years, The Rosewood Room has cultivated a reputation for fine food and excellent service. The menu features classical cuisine and tableside service. Traditional beef and seafood entrées are also offered with innovative style. With selections from around the world, the wine list has great variety and value. A Minneapolis favorite for both business lunches and elegant dinners, The Rosewood Room is the perfect place for your next special occasion.

Owner: Crowne Plaza Northstar Hotel Chef: Virgil Emmert

Specialties
Châteaubriand Prepared Table-side
Rack of Lamb

S	M	T	W	T	F	S		AE	VC	MC	DC	DS	

B
L
D

618 2nd Ave. S, Minneapolis, MN, 55402
PH: 612.338.2288 FAX: 612.673.6194

Vrazel's

Dine under majestic southern oaks as you view the beautiful gardens and the Mississippi Sound. The freshness of local seafood and prime beef come alive as chef Bill Vrazel lends his distinctive touch to French, Italian and Cajun cuisine. To complete your evening of fine dining, relax and enjoy flaming desserts and coffees prepared by our professional wait staff. Vrazel's is a place where relaxation, great food and great service present Mississippi coast cuisine at its best.

Owner and Chef: William Vrazel

Specialties
Fresh Seafood, Beef, Veal and Chicken
Regional Style French, Italian and Cajun Cuisine

3206 West Beach Blvd. Hwy 90, Gulfport, MS, 39501
PH: 228.863.2229 FAX: 228.863.2240
Website:www.gcww.com/vrazels/

Fairbanks Steakhouse

Fairbanks Steakhouse offers customers a premier dining experience with mouth watering certified Black Angus steaks and lobster to gourmet specialty dishes prepared fresh each evening by our staff of award-winning chefs. The 88-seat restaurant offers diners a delight for the eye with Hollywood motion picture memorabilia from the Douglas Fairbanks era, including swashbuckling costumes and crossed swords. A fine wine menu and fully-stocked humidor with premium cigars is available for the most discriminating of tastes.

Owner: Hollywood Casino

Specialties
Crispy Salmon • Coldwater Lobster Tail
Black Angus Steaks • Daiquiri Chicken

1150 Casino Strip Blvd., Robinsonville, MS, 38664
PH: 800.871.0711 FAX: 601.357.7800
Website:www.hollywoodtunica.com

Al's Restaurant

After 72 years of family operation at the same location, Al's is an institution in St. Louis. Instead of a printed menu, the day's available seafoods and meats are presented to you on a silver platter while an amiable table captain describes the preparation of each entrée and suggests suitable accompaniments. Drinks in the riverboat lounge are a delightful interlude.

Owner: Al Barroni

Specialties
Steak Romano
Veal Marsala

1200 N 1st St., St. Louis, MI, 63102
PH: 314.421.6399

Benedetto's

Benedetto's Ristorante is one of St. Louis' premier Italian gourmet restaurants. Located in the heart of West St. Louis County, this formal and intimate restaurant will give you the true definition of European flair. Benedetto Buzzetta's hard work and dedication is evident in every dish that is prepared. Service is refined but friendly, ensuring the ultimate Italian dining experience. Open every night for dinner and lunch Monday through Friday. Banquet rooms are available.

Owner: Benedetto Buzzetta   Chef: Lia Buzzetta

Specialties
Parpadella Paesana
Filetto Ripieno

10411 Clayton Rd., Frontenac, MO, 63131
PH: 314.432.8585 FAX: 314.432.3199

Café de France

When Monique and Marcel Keraval say "meet you in St. Louis," they mean that you can expect to have a memorable time visiting when you experience their formal but friendly restaurant. Fresh seafood, wild game, poultry, lamb and fresh pastries all await you in this undisputed leader.

Owner: Monique & Marcel Keraval Chef: Marcel Keraval

Specialties

Escargot Bouillabaise
Pheasant

410 Olive St., St Louis, MO, 63102
PH: 314.231.2204 FAX: 314.231.0391

S	M	T	W	T	F	S		AE	VC	MC	CB	DC	DS
B													
L													
D													

Dominic's

Dominic's is a comfortable restaurant built through the hard work, dedication and talent of the Galati family. With meticulous attention to detail, they have crafted consistently superior food, superior table-side service and one of St. Louis' most generous wine cellars. There is an open, yet cozy feel to the dining room and the fine Italian food has developed a dedicated following.

Owner and Chef: Giovanni D. Galati

Specialties

Fettuccine Verdi with Shrimps and Sweet Peppers
Veal Chop with Truffles

5101 Wilson Ave., St. Louis, MO, 63110
PH: 314.771.1632 FAX: 314.771.1695

S	M	T	W	T	F	S		AE	VC	MC	DC	DS
B												
L												
D												

G.P. Agostino's

G.P. Agostino's – a St. Louis landmark for over 30 years. Bringing you delicious food, informal elegance and intimate ambience, featuring northern Italian cuisine, an extensive wine list and a dessert cart. G.P. Agostino's has three private dining rooms, balcony seating and a full bar. Recipient of the Five Star Diamond Award and the *Mobil* Excellence Award.

Chef: Paul Gabriel

Specialties

Gamberi Galiano • Châteaubriand Casanova
Farfalline Pescatore • Costoletta Siciliano

15846 Manchester Rd., Ellisville MO 63011
PH: 314.391.5480 FAX: 314.391.3892

Seventh Inn

Experience distinguished continental dining in elegant, relaxed surroundings at The Seventh Inn Restaurant. The glow of candlelight and the fragrance of flowers enhance the mood while professional servers attend to your every need. The menu presents a superb and varied repertoire featuring more than 150 entrées created daily and prepared using only the freshest and best of ingredients.

Owner: Else Barth   Chef: Chris Urbané

Specialties
Fresh Seafood
Aged Beef

100 Seven Trails Dr., St. Louis, MO, 63011
PH: 314.227.6686 FAX: 314.227.6595

The Grill
RITZ-CARLTON, ST LOUIS

The Grill in the Ritz-Carlton offers superb American cuisine served in a beautiful traditional dining room. The Grill is an AAA four diamond award winner and recipient of the DiRoNA Award. The menu highlights American regional fare, and entrées are priced $18.00 and up. Open for lunch Monday through Friday and dinner seven nights a week.

Owner: The Ritz-Carlton   Chef: Richard Poye

Specialties
Roasted Rack of Lamb
Regional American Cuisine

100 Carondelet Plaza, Clayton, MO, 63105
PH: 314.863.6300 FAX: 314.719.1428

Tony's

Tony's has been chosen as the best Italian restaurant in the U.S. by *Conde Nast Traveler* magazine. It is the restaurant in St. Louis by which all others are measured. Italian cuisine, fresh seafood, prime steaks and house-made desserts round out the many excellent attributes of this perennial winner.

Owner: Vincent J. Bommarito   Chef: Vincent P. Bommarito

Specialties
Great Wine Cellar
Tableside Service

410 Market St., St Louis, MO, 63102
PH: 314.231.7007 FAX: 314.231.4740

Gallatin Gateway Inn

Just outside Bozeman, Montana lies one of the grand railroad hotels of the Rocky Mountain west, the perfect setting for a romantic getaway, family vacation, conference or retreat. Listed on the national register of historic places, the Gallatin Gateway Inn is a full-service hotel offering accommodations with an historic flair. Known regionally for its creative American cuisine, the inn is a popular choice for weddings, holidays and local special events.

Chef: Scottie Burton

Specialties

Locally Raised Beef and Bison
Grilled Venison Loin with Whole Grain Mustard Pecan Crust
Stuffed Maple-Roasted Buttercup Squash

Hwy 191, 76405 Gallatin Rd., Bozeman MT 59715
PH/FAX: 406.763.4672
Website:www.gallatingatewayinn.com

Llewellyn's

HARVEYS RESORT HOTEL & CASINO

Contemporary international cuisine complemented by impeccable service and panoramic views of Lake Tahoe provide a magical and exceptionally memorable dining experience. Guests who return again and again have voted Llewellyn's lake view, wine list and a fabulous Sunday Brunch as the best of Tahoe. Named in honor of the late Llewellyn Gross, who with husband Harvey founded Harveys in 1944, the restaurant is on the 19th floor of the hotel, overlooking Lake Tahoe.

Owner: Harveys Resort Hotel & Casino

Specialties

Abalone
Whole Dover Sole

U.S. Hwy. 50 & Stateline Ave.
Stateline (Lake Tahoe) NV, 89449
PH: 702.588.2411

André's

Tucked away from the bright lights of the Strip, André's is located in a quiet residential neighborhood just one block east of Las Vegas Blvd. Chef André converted the home into a country French restaurant with a warm, inviting atmosphere. With exquisite classic French cuisine, superior service and a wine list with over 1000 labels, André's continues to be voted Top French Restaurant in the *Zagat* survey year after year.

Owner and Chef: André Rochat

Specialties

Grilled Ahi Tuna Medallions with Sauce Escabeche
Grilled Vegetable Sausage with Balck Bean Sauce
Oven Roasted Rack of Lamb with Flageolet Bean Purée

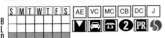

401 S. 6th St.. Las Vegas NV 89101
PH: 702.385.5016 FAX: 702.384.8574
Website:www.andresfrenchrest.com

Fiore

Recognized for excellence in the culinary arts and service, the Rio Suite Hotel and Casino presents fine dining at its best, Fiore Restaurant and Grille. Fiore celebrates culinary delights from the south of France to the northern coast of Italy. Its subtle elegance is enhanced by an unbelievable wine list and a serene cigar terrace overlooking the Rio's beautiful Ipanema pools.

Chef: Gervais Henric

Specialties

Wood-Fired Filet of Beef with Fromage des Pyrenées
and Merlot Sauce
Wild Mushroom Ravioli with Truffle Shavings and Essence

3700 W. Flamingo Rd., Las Vegas NV 89103
PH: 702.252.7702 FAX: 702.247.7932

Michael's

Tucked away in the heart of the Las Vegas Strip in the Barbary Coast Hotel and Casino, Michael's is the premier gourmet restaurant in a city acclaimed for fine dining. Red velvet and stained glass surround the diner with Victorian elegance, and four-star service rounds out the experience. Connoisseurs will be delighted when ordering tender veal, Maine lobster and Dover sole, flown in daily.

Owner: Michael Gaughan   Chef: Fred Bielak

Specialties
Stone Crab in Season
Dover Sole

3595 Las Vegas Blvd S., Las Vegas, NV, 89109
PH: 702.737.7111
Website:www.barbarycoastcasino.com

Monte Carlo

Gracious ambience, reminiscent of the charm and romance of the Côte D'Azur, awaits in The Desert Inn's signature restaurant, Monte Carlo. Nevada's only AAA Four Diamond restaurant, Monte Carlo is located on the mezzanine level, with its main dining room overlooking lush gardens and a lagoon-style pool. As one of the last gourmet rooms in Las Vegas to offer tableside presentation and flambé items, Monte Carlo offers the ultimate dining experience.

Owner: The Desert Inn Resort   Chef: Francois Meulien

Specialties
Jumbo Sautéed Shrimp with Thai & Indian Curries
Peppered Châteaubriand
Roasted Duck à l'Orange with Vanilla

3145 Las Vegas Blvd. S.,
Las Vegas NV 89109
PH: 702.733.4400 FAX: 702.733.4675

Piero's

Piero's should be on the "must do" list for your next trip to Las Vegas. This award-winning northern Italian restaurant is famous for its osso bucco, seasonal fresh Florida stone crab claws and Maryland crab cakes. Piero's is three blocks from the strip and has been named *Zagat Survey's* top Italian restaurant in Las Vegas, as well as one of the top people-watching places in the city. Look for Piero's on the Food Channel and in *Bon Appetit*.

Owner: Fred Glusman   Chef: Gilbert Fetaz

Specialties
Osso Bucco
Fresh Florida Stone Crab Claws

355 Convention Center Dr., Las Vegas, NV, 89109
PH: 702.369.2305 FAX: 702.735.5699
Website:www.vegas.com

Harrah's Steakhouse

Lunch or dinner at Harrah's Steakhouse is truly the experience of a lifetime. Signature items that will take your breath away, tableside preparation and attention to the smallest details have made Harrah's award-winning Steakhouse one of Reno's best restaurants since 1967. Our commitment to creating an outstanding and elegant dining experience makes Harrah's Steakhouse the perfect place for an intimate dinner or your special celebrations.

Chef: John Frank

Specialties
Creamy Five Onion Soup
Steak Diane

219 N. Center St., Reno, NV, 89501
PH: 775.788.2929

The Bedford Village Inn

A sense of history permeates the imagination in this intimate dining room, with wide pine floor boards covered with antique oriental rugs. The meticulously restored walls once resonated to the labor and laughter of families who resided here centuries before your arrival. The accommodations are as unique as the history that shaped the setting: decidedly small, intentionally quiet. Uncompromising regional fare is prepared by one of the most talented culinary teams in New England.

Owners: Jack and Andrea Carnevale   Chef: Nathan Baldwin

Specialties
Arctic Char with Barley Risotto
Veal Chops

2 Village Inn Lane, Bedford, NH, 03110
PH: 603.472.2001 FAX: 603.472.2379

Ram's Head Inn

Just seven miles from the bustling Atlantic City casinos, beautiful Ram's Head Inn provides a respite for the senses. Decorated with authentic antiques and enhanced by a gracious courtyard, this delightful restaurant offers guests the chance to enjoy relaxed, distinctive American dining in an elegant country atmosphere. Wood-burning fireplaces and soft candlelight enhance this four-diamond restaurant which features traditional American cuisine.

Owner: Harry Knowles   Chef: Luigi Baretto

Specialties
Jumbo Shrimp Stuffed with Lump Crabmeat
Sautéed Medallions of Veal with Peach Brandy Sauce
and Sorbet Garnish

9 W. White Horse Pike, Absecon, NJ, 08201
PH: 609.652.1700 FAX: 609.748.1588
Website:www.ramsheadinn.com

Scheherazade
TRUMP TAJ MAHAL CASINO RESORT

Located in the magnificent Trump Taj Mahal, Scheherazade is a one-of-a-kind dining experience. With its ambiance of elegance and sophistication, Scheherazade is the only restaurant in the world where guests can dine on superb contemporary gourmet cuisine while overlooking a high stakes game of baccarat. Winner of the American Academy's Five Star Diamond award, Scheherazade offers distinctive cuisine prepared with French élan.

Manager: Mark Stadler   Chef: Guy Reinbolt

Specialties
Strudel of Mallard Duck and Porcini Mushrooms
Lamb Chops "Baccarat" • Medallions of Monkfish and Shrimp

S	M	T	W	T	F	S		AE	VC	MC	CB	DC	DS
B													
L													
D													

Weekday hours vary

1000 Boardwalk, Atlantic City, NJ, 08401
PH: 609.449.6840 FAX: 609.449.6842

Beau Rivage Restaurant

The Beau Rivage Restaurant, overlooking Lake Pine and founded by Gerard Gehin, master chef, has been aptly described as the "Paris of the Pinelands." Its offerings of veal and seafood dishes, plus extravagant desserts, make a visit to this lovely country refuge a treat for those who know and enjoy good food. There is a very intriguing wine list for those who enjoy good wines.

Owner and Chef: Gerard Gehin

Specialties
Lobster Bisque Flamed with Crab Meat
Roast Rack of Lamb

S	M	T	W	T	F	S		AE	VC	MC
B										
L										
D										

128 Taunton Blvd., Medford, NJ, 08055
PH: 609.983.1999 FAX: 609.988.1136

Panico's

Established in 1987, Panico's is committed to excellence. Noted for fine wines and innovative Italian cuisine, Panico's was the only Italian restaurant given a rating of Excellent by *New York Times* food critics in 1993. The restaurant has also received top billing in *The Star Ledger* and is lauded by an army of regular guests. Chef Gregg Freda uses only the very best fresh ingredients, and his culinary creations are served by a legion of formally dressed, unobtrusive servers.

Owner: Frank Panico   Chef: Gregg Freda

Specialties
Osso Bucco
Sole Pignolia

103 Church St., New Brunswick, NJ, 08901
PH: 732.545.6100 FAX: 732.545.7346

Diamond's

Diamond's is an award-winning Italian restaurant conveniently located to major centres, in the heart of the Chambersburg Restaurant District of historic Trenton. Diamond's features Prime Dry Aged Steaks and truly authentic Italian cuisine. The extraordinary wine list is recognized by *Wine Spectator* as among the best in the world. Diamond's is owned and operated by Anthony and Thomas Zucchetti, brothers who were born and raised just two doors away from the restaurant.

Owners: Anthony & Thomas Zucchetti

Specialties
Prime Dry Aged Steaks • Fresh Seafood
Milk-Fed Veal • Italian Cuisine

132 Kent St., Trenton NJ 08611
PH: 609.393.1000 FAX: 609.393.1672
Website: www.diamonds.inter.net

Highlawn Pavilion

With its French rotisserie, wood-burning oven and open kitchen, Highlawn Pavilion's cuisine is aptly described as American fare with European flair. The Manhattan skyline, visible from every table, offers scenic dining at its best. "Among the very best overall dining experiences in the East," said Bob Lape in *Crain's New York Business. The Record* asserted there may not be "a more beautiful restaurant in New Jersey....even the water tastes better here."

Owner: Harry Knowles   Chef: Ossama Mickail

Specialties
Grilled Salmon with Saffron Jasmin Rice
Honey Orange Spit Roasted Duck

Eagle Rock Reservation, W. Orange, NJ, 07052
PH: 973.731.3463 FAX: 973.731.0034
Website:www.highlawn.com

The Manor

A gracious manor house set in acres of magnificient formal gardens, The Manor fuses distinctive American cuisine with exacting service and luxuriously romantic ambiance. In 42 years of presenting fine dining, the restaurant has consistently received many of the most coveted awards for culinary excellence and for an exceptional wine list. The manor has been referred to as a "culinary Versailles," and *The New York Times* rated it "Excellent . . the ultimate in four-star luxury food."

Owner: Harry Knowles

Specialties
Poached Halibut Filet and Crispy Shrimp
Porcini-Crusted Veal Medallions

111 Prospect Ave., West Orange, NJ, 07052
PH: 973.731.2360 FAX: 973.731.4838
Website:www.themanorrestaurant.com

Rancher's Club
ALBUQUERQUE HILTON HOTEL

New Mexico's only authentic grill is an experience in dining that no visitor to the Land of Enchantment should miss. Abundant portions of prime beef, poultry and seafood, grilled over a variety of aromatic hardwoods, impart a distinctive taste and flavor. Served in western elegance.

Specialties
Grilled Steak and Seafood

1901 University Blvd. NE,
Albuquerque NM 87107
PH: 505.884.2500 FAX: 505.837.1715

Villa Fontana

Experience excellent northern Italian dining in a restaurant where tradition and sophistication come together to create a unique and charming atmosphere. At Villa Fontana, you will find expertise in service, cuisine and food presentation. The house specialty is dishes prepared with wild mushrooms gathered from local forests. A carefully selected wine list and classical European service will make your dinner a truly memorable occasion.

Owners: Carlo and Siobhan Gislimberti   Chef: Carlo Gislimberti

Specialties
Wild Mushrooms
Wild Game Dishes - Venison

5 Miles North of Taos on Hwy 522,
Taos, NM, 87571
PH: 505.758.5800 FAX: 505.758.0301
Website:www.silverhawk./com/villafontana/taos

There'll be a man overboard
any second now.

The GLENLIVET

AGED 12 YEARS
Pure Single Malt
Scotch Whisky

PRODUCT OF SCOTLAND

The Glenlivet Single Malt.
Once discovered, always treasured.

Those who appreciate quality enjoy it responsibly.

© 1995 Imported by The Glenlivet Distilling Co., N.Y., N.Y. 12 Year Old Single Malt Scotch Whisky. Alc. 40% by Vol. (80 proof). The Glenlivet is a registered trademark.

The River Café

Renowned as one of the world's finest restaurants, The River Café offers exceptional cuisine and one of the most spectacular views in America. From it's home nestled under the Brooklyn Bridge, the restaurant's exemplary wine list perfectly complements chef Rick Laakkonen's American cuisine, whose signature dishes include poached salmon with kaffir lime leaf nage.

Chef: Rick Laakkonen

Specialties
Smoked Duck Foie Gras
Grilled Jumbo Quail

1 Water St., Brooklyn, NY, 11201
PH: 718.522.5200 FAX: 718.875.0037

'21' Club

Founded as a speakeasy in Greenwich Village in the 1920s, '21' moved to its present location on New Year's Eve 1929. Since then, patrons of this landmark restaurant have passed through the wrought-iron gates to enjoy the ambiance and cuisine of this "hangout" for people from entertainment, society, high finance and politics. Don't miss the legendary hidden Wine Cellar with its 10,000 bottles, now a popular private party room for up to 20 guests.

Owners: Orient Express Hotels   Chef: Erik Blanberg

Specialties
Spit Roasted Rack of Lamb
Crisp Black Sea Bass

21 W. 52nd St., New York, NY, 10019
PH: 212.582.7200 FAX: 212.586.5065
Website:www.21club.com

Aquavit

When he opened Aquavit in 1987, Håkan Swahn's self-assigned mission was as simple as it was ambitious - serve the finest Swedish cuisine available. Named for a popular icy neutral spirit (which the restaurant serves in a variety of flavored incarnations), Aquavit showcases the culinary creations of 25-year-old Marcus Samuelsson, who brings a world of influences and a precocious talent to his bustling kitchen.

Owner: Håkan Swahn   Chef: Marcus Samuelsson

Specialties

Gravlax
Smorgasbord Plate
Vegetarian Menu
Eight Course Tasting Menu

13 W. 54th St., New York NY 10019
PH: 212.307.7311 FAX: 212.957.9043
Website:www.aquavit.org

Barbetta

Barbetta, celebrating its 93rd year, is the oldest restaurant in New York still owned by the original founding family. Opened in 1906 by Sebastiano Maioglio, Barbetta is now owned by his daughter Laura. Barbetta serves the cuisine of Piemonte in a spectacular setting decorated with historic 18th-century Piemontese antiques and a verdant summer garden, scented with the blossoms of magnolia, wisteria, jasmine and gardenia.

Owner: Laura Maioglio   Chef: Marius Pavlak

Specialties

Classic Piemontese Dishes, served with
Truffles Hunted by Barbetta's Own Hounds

321 W 46th St., New York, NY, 10036
Ph: 212.246.9171 FAX: 212.246.1279
Website:www.barbettarestaurant.com

Cité

Big city atmosphere pervades this stunning steak house in New York's Time & Life building. At night, the crowd comes for the pre-theatre menu, and oenophiles flow in after 8:00 for the all-you-can-quaff $59.50 Wine Dinner prix fixe. Art Deco grillwork and architectural embellishments that once graced Paris's Au Bon Marche department store give Cité and Cité Grill an atmosphere of informal elegance. Cité is located in the theatre district, close to Radio City Music Hall.

Owner: Alan Stillman   **Chef: David Amorelli**

Specialties
Crabcake with Caponata
Rack of Lamb

W. 51st Street (between 6th & 7th Avenues)
New York, NY, 10020
PH: 212.956.7100 FAX: 212.956.7157

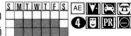

La Caravelle

La Caravelle has reigned as one of Manhattan's finest French restaurants since 1960. The elegant hand-painted murals by Jean Pagès represent charming Parisian street scenes. La Caravelle's graceful setting is the ideal backdrop for chef Renaud's brilliant integration of classical and contemporary French cuisine. Private dining is also available for parties of up to 30 people. Guests receive excellent care under the watchful eye of owners André and Rita Jammet.

Owners: André & Rita Jammet   **Chef: Cyril Renaud**

Specialties
House Smoked Salmon
Crispy Roast Duck with Cranberries
Pike Quenelles with Lobster Sauce

33 W. 55th St., New York, NY 10019
PH: 212.586.4252 FAX: 212.956.8269
Website:www.lacaravellerestaurant.com

Manhattan Ocean Club

A classic seafood restaurant in the heart of midtown Manhattan. "In this city by the sea, shockingly few restaurants specialize in American seafood. Fortunately we have the Manhattan Ocean Club," writes *The New York Times*. "Polished and swimmingly wonderful, this Midtowner is one of the best seafood retaurants in town and many think it is the best," says *Zagat* 1995. This two-tiered restaurant features a broad open staircase reminiscent of the between-decks access of a cruise ship.

Owner: Alan Stillman   Chef: Jonathan Parker

Specialties

**Shellfish Bouquet • Red Snapper in Moroccan Spices
White Chocolate Mousse in Bittersweet Chocolate Bag**

W. 58th St. btwn 5th & 6th Aves.,
New York, NY, 10019
PH: 212.371.7777
Website:www.manhattanoceanclub.com

S M T W T F S | AE | VC | MC | CB | DC | J | DS
B
L   ▼ 🚗 ☎ ③ PR 💲
D

Palio

From the ground level bar with its explosive wrap-around mural by Sandro Chia to the elegant second floor dining room, you will be dazzled by Palio's decor as well as the delectable creations from its kitchens. The ambiance here is unmatched anywhere else. The dining room is splendid, with high ceilings, trellised woodwork and sunflower bouquets. The diverse menu is sure to bring satisfaction to the most discriminating patron.

Owner: Maria Pia Hellrigl   Chef: Claudia Crociani

Specialties
Variety of Homemade Italian Pastas

151 W. 51st St., New York, NY, 10019
PH: 212.245.4850 FAX: 212.397.7814

S M T W T F S | AE | VC | MC | CB | DC | J | DS
B
L   ▼ 🚗 ☎ ④ 🍴 PR
D

Park Avenue Cafe

"A class act . . . Chef David Burke takes creative cooking a step beyond other American chefs with innovative techniques and whimsical presentations," says the *Zagat Survey*. Burke is *Chef* magazine's Chef of the Year, while Richard Leach has won the James Beard Award as Pastry Chef of the Year. Try the Chef's private "Kitchen Table", or celebrate a special occasion in The Park Avenue Café Townhouse next door.

Owner: Alan Stillman   Chef: David Burke

Specialties
Swordfish Chop • Pastrami Salmon
Mustard Crusted Tuna Teriyaki

63rd St. and Park Avenue,
New York, NY, 10021
PH: 212.644.1900 FAX: 212.688.0373

S	M	T	W	T	F	S	AE	VC	MC	CB	DC	J	DS

B
L
D

The Post House

According to *Wine Spectator*, The Post House is one of the ten best steakhouses in America. *Zagat Survey* also bestows lavish praise: "You'll feel like you're in the age of robber barons in this classy, civilized East Side steakhouse that's a grand place to sign deals over wonderful slabs of steak and lobsters that could eat New York, accompanied by fine wines; one of the few steakhouses where women feel welcome." Few can resist pastry chef Meredith Frederick's sumptuous desserts; her Cappuccino Custard has been featured in *Chocolatier* magazine.

Owner: Alan Stillman   Chef: Andres Tzul

Specialties
Sirloin Steaks
Seafood

East 63rd St.(between Park and
Madison Aves.), New York, NY, 10021
PH: 212.935.2888

S	M	T	W	T	F	S	AE	VC	MC	CB	DC	J

B
L
D

Restaurant Raphael

An oasis in midtown Manhattan, opposite the MOMA, Restaurant Raphael provides a château-like feeling in a charming townhouse with gardens and a fireplace. For the past 21 years, we have served contemporary French cuisine in a setting perfect for romance or business. Our flavorful and colorful dishes are complemented by a well-chosen wine list and topped off with scrumptious desserts, thus satisfying the total culinary experience.

Owners: Mira & Raphael Edery

Specialties

Roasted Foie Gras with Pineapple Tomato Jam
Charred Yellowfin Tuna with Baby Spinach

33 West 54th St., New York NY 10019
PH: 212.582.8993

San Domenico

This year, San Domenico NY celebrates its 10th Anniversary. The overall philosophy of San Domenico NY is to present the tastes of modern Italy to the American dining public. Chef Odette Fada creates contemporary versions of historic recipes, extraordinary dishes bursting with flavor and clarity. San Domenico NY also brings the style and ambiance of modern Italy to New York and continues to set the standard for modern Italian cuisine in the U.S.

Owner: Tony May   Chef: Odette Fada

Specialties

Soft Egg-Filled Raviolo with Truffle Butter
Jumbo Shrimp with Cannellini Beans and Rosemary
Roasted Quails Filled with Sausage

240 Central Park South, New York, NY, 10019
PH: 212.265.5959 FAX: 212.397.0844
Website:www.tonymay.com

Smith & Wollensky

"A steakhouse to end all arguments," says *The New York Times*. The restaurant features an enormous selection of meats and seafood, as well as generous desserts. The 100,000-bottle wine cellar adds to the appeal, and ". . . slabs of prime meat, hash browns, creamed spinach and an award-winning wine cellar get high marks year after year," says the *Zagat Survey*. Customers can purchase Smith & Wollensky's steak sauce and even the famous dry-aged-on-premises steaks. Visit our locations in Miami Beach, Chicago, New Orleans, Las Vegas and Washington D.C.

Owner: Alan Stillman　　　　　　Chef: Victor Chavez

Specialties
S&W Famous Split Pea Soup
Filet Mignon

49th St. at 3rd Ave., New York, NY, 10022
PH: 212.753.1530

S	M	T	W	T	F	S	AE	VC	MC	CB	DC	J	DS
B													
L													
D													

Sparks Steak House

An all-American, robust outpost which is everything a popular steak house should be. The rosy dry aged steaks with charred edge crusts are perfection. Jumbo lobster, fresh fish, veal and lamb chops, plus fresh vegetables cooked to order, are the order of the day. The wine list is a consistent *Wine Spectator* Grand Award winner.

Owner: Pat and Mike Cetta

Specialties
Steak and Lobsters

210 E 46th St., New York, NY, 10017
PH: 212.687.4855 FAX: 212.557.7409

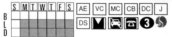

S	M	T	W	T	F	S	AE	VC	MC	CB	DC	J
B												
L												
D												

Piccolo

Piccolo was given the number-one rating in 1996 and 1997 by the *Zagat* survey, and was rated the top Italian restaurant in 1998. The decor is elegant and romantic. Owner-manager Dean Phillippis greets you with a genuine, warm and gracious welcome. The waitstaff is knowledgeable, attentive and courteous. The wine list is extensive, the desserts are homemade. Piccolo's sister restaurant, Mazzi, serves eclectic American cuisine in a charming century-old farmhouse.

Owner: Dean Phillippis   Chef: Angel Vanegas

Specialties

Pan-Seared Diver Scallops with Truffle Oil
Mustard Aniseed Roasted Double Cut Pork Chops
Slow-Roasted Long Island Duck with Cassis Sauce

215 Wall St., Huntington NY 11743
PH: 516.424.5592 FAX: 516.421.5555

Il Fiorentino

The Bruni family arrived from Florence, Italy, in 1989 to recreate a Tuscan restaurant similar to their own in the Tuscan hills. Chef Giancarlo Bruni prepares all his dishes to order using only the freshest ingredients. His wonderful garden produces Mediterranean herbs essential to his cooking. The menu changes each season and is set up in the typical Italian style. All desserts are house made from scratch, and the wine list is strictly Italian, representing all regions of Italy.

Owners: Sandra & Giancarlo Bruni   Chef: Giancarlo Bruni

Specialties
Veal Chops with Truffles
Grilled Spicy Pheasant
Pasta with Walnuts and Gorgonzola
Black Rice Risotto

8485 E. Transit Rd., E. Amherst NY 14051
PH: 716.625.4250 FAX: 716.689.0476
Website:www.nvo.com/ilfiorentino

Friends Lake Inn

Friends Lake Inn is an elegant restaurant and country inn in the foothills of the Adirondacks. Enjoy acclaimed New American cuisine, personable service, and a *Grand Award*-winning wine collection in our candlelit dining room, complete with its original 19th-century tin ceiling and chestnut woodwork. Host a private soirée in our intimate wine cellar dining room. We are located minutes from I-87, just over an hour north of Albany and one hour south of Lake Placid.

Chef: Timothy Stephenson

Specialties
**Sautéed Scallops and Lobster Crepe
Roasted Venison Loin with Red Currant Sauce
Grilled Muscovy Duck Breast**

S	M	T	W	T	F	S	AE	VC	MC	CB	DC

B
L
D

963 Friends Lake Rd., Chestertown NY 12817
PH: 518.494.4751 FAX: 518.494.4616
Website: www.friendslake.com

Pierce's 1894 Restaurant

Any business still in the hands of its founding family after four generations is a rarity in our culture, but that is the case with Pierce's. The founder's great-grandchildren are actively involved in the day-to-day operation, and are very aware of their responsibilities for maintaining the restaurant's reputation for excellence in quality, value and service. Winner of prestigious awards from *Wine Spectator* and AAA.

Owner: C. Joseph Pierce, II   **Chef: David Schlefen**

Specialties
**Roasted Classic Châteaubriand For Two
Roasted Rack of New Zealand Lamb**

S	M	T	W	T	F	S	AE	VC	MC	DS

B
L
D

228 Oakwood Ave., Elmira Heights, NY, 14903
PH: 607.734.2022 FAX: 607.734.2024

The Rio

Housed in a fetching Victorian home, The Rio opened its doors as a restaurant in 1949. The timeless design and tasteful appointments are a setting for a seasonal menu dashed with contemporary flair. For patrons who just want a little "taste of The Rio," the restaurant offers a three-course dinner served Monday to Friday from 5:00 pm to 6:30 pm.

Chef: Stephen Burgoon

Specialties

Rack of Lamb
Fresh Seafood Specialties

282 Alexander St., Rochester NY 14607
PH: 716.473.2806 FAX: 716.473.2809

Tavern at Sterup Square

Sterup Square has an international European atmosphere. We offer casual dining in the Tavern and Torchlit Terrace, or fine dining in our Van Rensselaer Room. Although the rooms have different menus and service, the cuisine is prepared by the same chef and culinary staff. Our complex also includes the Rathskeller Room and the Europa Ballroom for special parties, an award-winning bakery and a gourmet deli.

Owner: Peter N. Matzen   Chef: Larry Schepici

Specialties

Pistachio Encrusted Rack of Lamb • Wild Game
Black Angus Beef • Fresh Fish and Lobster

2113 NY 7, Troy NY 12180
PH: 518. 663.5800 FAX: 518.663.9261
Website:www.sterupsquare.com

23 Page

Enjoy casual, elegant dining in a relaxed, romantic setting, featuring our area's finest organic produce, French cooking techniques and innovative daily specials. We are closed on selected holidays.

Owners: Aletha Roper & Broc Fountain   Chef: Broc Fountain

Specialties

Low-Country Style Crab Cakes
Braised Lamb Shanks with Balsamic Reduction
and Tomato Poivrade

1 Battery Pk. Ave., Asheville NC 28801
PH: 828.252.3685 FAX: 828.252.8102

Horizons

Amid the setting of The Grove Park Inn Resort, Horizons features innovative classic cuisine and spectacular views of the Blue Ridge mountains. A winner of prestigious awards, including AAA Four Diamond, the restaurant has an intimate, elegant environment in the Arts and Crafts style. Chef Bill McBee creates beautifully presented meals showcasing American regional cuisine with European and Asian influences.

Chef: Bill McBee

Specialties

Whole Coffee Bean Smoked Rack of New Zealand Lamb
Apple Florentine with Cinnamon Bourbon Ice Cream
Coffee Presentation and Cordial Cart

290 Macon Ave., Asheville NC 28804
PH: 828.252.2711 FAX: 828.253.7053
Website:www.groveparkinn.com

Charleston Grill

Join us for cocktails, live jazz and wonderful Lowcountry cooking. The complexities of Chef Bob Waggoner's cuisine represent an evolution of his travels throughout the culinary world, including France's top kitchens and Nashville's five-diamond The Wild Boar. Now, Bob is receiving national recognition for bringing Charleston the only Mobil Four-Star restaurant in the state of South Carolina. Come indulge while relaxing in our spectacular dining room, where the atmosphere exudes warmth.

Owner: Orient-Express Hotels   Chef: Robert Waggoner

Specialties

Maine Lobster Tempura over Lemon Grits
McClellanville Lump Crabmeat Cakes
Harvested Scallops with Stuffed Zucchini Blossoms
Sautéed Dorchester County Rabbit Loin

224 King Street, Charleston, SC 29401
PH: 843.577.4522 FAX: 843.724.8405
Website: www.Charleston-place.com

S M T W T F S   AE   VC   MC   CB   DC   DS
B
L
D

Fig Tree Restaurant

You will find Fig Tree is unlike any other restaurant on the San Antonio riverwalk. Our four-tiered terrace, which has a flourishing view, adorns the riverside of the restaurant. Indoors, multi-level dining rooms hold beautiful paintings, chandeliers, and original collections from the Phelps family. Elegant china, crystal, flatware, and fresh flowers create an enchanting atmosphere. Whether for personal entertaining or business dinners, let us treat you to an evening you will never forget.

Owner: Thomas Phelps   Chef: Tan Nguyen

Specialties

Rack of Lamb • Chateaubriand
Duck Breast • Bananas Foster

515 Villita, San Antonio, TX 78205
PH: 210.224.1976 FAX: 210.271.9180

S M T W T F S   AE   VC   MC   DC   DS
B
L
D

Errata and updates
1999 Guide
to Distinguished Restaurants of North America

Page 14: Anthony and Brooke Martino are the owners of Anthony's in the Catalinas
Page 18: Tommy Toy and Alon Yu are the owners of Tommy Toy's
Page 22: the area code for Patina has been changed to 323
Page 23: the area code for Pascal has been changed to 949
Page 24: the area code for Le Vallauris has been changed to 760
Page 26: Steven Chesney is the owner of Fresh Cream
Page 26: Ted Balestreri and Bert Cutino are the owners of Sardine Factory
Page 28: Vail Associates are the owners of Wildflower
Page 33: Nancy Christiansen is the owner of Sign of the Vine
Page 42: Pino Luongo is the owner of CoCo Pazzo
Page 42: Jean Joho is the owner of Everest
Page 55: Malmaison's phone number is (314) 458-4803
Page 56: The Hyatt Regency Hotel is the owner of the Station Grill
Page 56: Else Barth is the owner of Seventh Inn
Page 61: Gila Baruch is the owner of The Box Tree
Page 62: Lidia Matticchio and Felix Bastianich are the owners of Felidia
Page 62: Daniel is located at 60 E. 65th Street

Correction - Wrong picture used for Cavey's pg. 131

=== **Connecticut** === === Manchester ===

Cavey's

Cavey's is actually two restaurants in one building: an elegant French restaurant on the lower level, and a more casual northern Italian restaurant upstairs, offering jazz piano on weekends. Both are furnished with art and antiques, and, in the French restaurant, fabric wall coverings and a profusion of fresh flowers. Both have garnered critical acclaim and have been awarded *Wine Spectator's* Best of Award of Excellence.

Owner and Chef: Stephen Cavagnaro

Specialties
**Roast Quail with Chestnut Tagliatelle
Seared Foie Gras and Truffled Potato Ravioli
Day Boat Local Cod with Little Neck Clams
Grilled Chicken with House Italian Sausage**

45 E. Center St., Manchester CT 06033
PH: 860.643.2751 FAX: 860.649.0344

Due to seasonal menu variations, all prices quoted in this book should be verified before visiting any DiRoNA Award Restaurant.

The LampLighter

The LampLighter Restaurant is a Charlotte tradition synonymous with fine dining. Located in a renovated Mediterranean villa in the historic Dilworth area, The LampLighter offers the perfect setting for any occasion. The only restaurant in Charlotte to win the prestigious DiRoNA Award, The LampLighter features American and continental cuisine unparalleled in the area. Elegantly prepared seafood, beef, chicken, duck and pasta are impeccably served by an expert staff.

Owner: Woody Fox   Chef: John Thompson

Specialties
Aged Filet of Tenderloin
LampLighter Lump Crabcake

1065 E. Morehead St., Charlotte, NC, 28204
PH: 704.372.5343 FAX: 704.372.5354

The Fearrington House

National and regional magazines, including *Gourmet, Travel & Leisure, Food and Wine,* and *Southern Living,* have celebrated the Fearrington House's sophisticated southern cuisine. Candlelight, original art and antiques help to create a warm, intimate atmosphere. The Fearrington House serves a fixed-price menu, which offers a tempting array of selections in several courses.

Owners: The Fitch Family   Chef: Cory Mattson

Specialties
Carolina Crab Cakes with Lemon Mayonnaise
Air-Cured Antelope Carpaccio with Fresh Basil and Tomato
Sautéed Softshell Crayfish with Orange Creole Butter
Hot Chocolate Soufflé

2000 Fearrington Village, Pittsboro, NC, 27312
PH: 919.542.2121 FAX: 919.542.4202
Website:www.fearrington.com

The Angus Barn

In the Angus Barn's wine cellar dining room, you will be surrounded by 1,000 selections of wine as you savor our chef's French country cuisine. Or you may prefer to dine in our original dining rooms in a rustic 'barn' atmosphere and feast on fresh seafood or aged steaks. Our desserts, dressings and sauces are made on the premises and prepared fresh daily. Our staff is well trained in the art of fine dining, and we take great pride in our service.

Owner: Van Eure   Chef: Walter Royal

Specialties
**Certified Angus Beef, Aged In-House
Baby Back Spare Ribs**

9401 Glenwood Ave., Raleigh, NC, 27628
PH: 919.787.3505 FAX: 919.783.5568

Maisonette

Charming and elegant, Maisonette is noted not only for its fine cuisine, but for its flawless service and outstanding wine list. Chef Jean Robert de Cavel prepares contemporary and classic French dishes in a warm and sumptuous setting. This all comes together to create a most extraordinary dining experience. It's no wonder Maisonette is the longest-running five star restaurant in America. Closed Sundays and holidays.

Owners: The Comisar Family   Chef: Jean Robert de Cavel

Specialties
Seasonal Menu, Changes Weekly

114 E. 6th St., Cincinnati, OH, 45202
PH: 513.721.2260 FAX: 513.287.7785
Website:www.maisonette.com

The Palace

The Palace Restaurant has long been the destination for the discriminating gourmet. The understated elegance and grace of The Palace's staff and environs beautifully complement each culinary creation. Featuring regional new American cuisine, The Palace's menu changes seasonally to ensure only the freshest ingredients available grace your table. Make your next special occasion a time to remember at The Palace Restaurant.

Owners: Brothers Property Corp.   Chef: Sean Kagy

Specialties

Seasonal Menu
featuring
Crab Cakes and Crème Brûlée

601 Vine St., Cincinnati OH 45202
PH: 513.381.3000 FAX: 513.381.2659

The Baricelli Inn

The Baricelli Inn is a turn-of-the-century brownstone located in the heart of Cleveland's cultural center. Paul Minnillo's internationally acclaimed restaurant is dedicated to creating fine European and American cuisine. From his larder, he creates a seasonal menu reflecting the freshest regional ingredients available, prepared in a style that is uniquely his. "Simplicity in cooking is a greatly underrated virtue, " Minnillo states, "I love grains, beans, fresh herbs."

Owner and Chef: Paul Minnillo

Specialties

Smoked Capon Ravioli on Goat Cheese Impastata
Porcini Crusted Walleye

2203 Cornell Rd., Cleveland, OH 44106
PH: 216.791.6500 FAX: 216.791.9131

Sammy's

Overlooking the picturesque bridges of the Cuyahoga River for 18 years, Sammy's is the only north east Ohio member of the Fine Dining Hall of Fame. Live jazz filters through the dining room nightly. Chef Hachicho takes pride in creating his contemporary American cuisine with a Mediterranean influence. A selection of 300 excellent wines, as well as courteous and impeccable service, make dining at Sammy's an indulgence. Private rooms and complimentary valet parking make Sammy's the perfect place for your next special occasion.

Owners: Denise Fugo & Ralph Diorio   Chef: Jihad Hachicho

Specialties
Boule de Neige • Seafood Rawbar
Live Jazz

1400 W. 10th St., Cleveland, OH 44113
PH: 216.523.5560 FAX: 216.523.1873

The Refectory

The Refectory is one of only 92 restaurants worldwide to receive *The Wine Spectator's* Grand Award for outstanding wine cellars. A native of Lyon, France, and protegé of Chef Paul Bocuse, Chef de Cuisine Richard Blondin and his staff change the menu with the seasons to highlight nature's best offerings. Four Diamonds - AAA, Five Stars and Best Restaurant - *Columbus Monthly.*

Owner: Kamal Boulos   Chef: Richard Blondin

Specialties
Fresh Seafood • Ohio Lamb
Seasonal Menu

1092 Bethel Road, Columbus, OH, 43220
PH: 614.451.9774 FAX: 614.451.4434
Website:www.refectory.com

L'Auberge

For a dining experience unsurpassed in elegance and sophistication, L'Auberge is the *piece de resistance.* Owners Josef Reif and Dieter Krug have developed an international reputation for fine dining that encompasses excellence in food, wine, service and presentation. The luxurious decor is evident throughout the mansion, in the contemporary bistro with its famous murals, the outside cafe Le Jardin, the private salons, the magnificent wine cellar, or our world renowned L'Auberge restaurant.

Owners: Josef Reif and Dieter Krug

Specialties
Ravioli with Pheasant and Truffles
Faisan d'Ecosse Roti au Foie Gras et Airelles

4120 Far Hills Ave., Dayton, OH, 45429
PH: 937.299.5536 FAX: 937.299.9129

Alberini's

The marriage of fine wines from our extensive wine list and outstanding cuisine consummate the ultimate dining experience. Alberini's atmosphere is sociable and unpretentious, yet maintains a subtle touch of sophistication. Experience a variety of pastas enhanced with fragrant Italian spices, succulent seafoods and choice cuts of fork-tender meats. There is a room for every mood, a menu for every occassion, a wine for every palate, and there's always an Alberini on hand if you need one.

Owners: Alberini Family   Chef: Richard Alberini Jr.

Specialties
Classic Italian Cuisine
Fresh Seafood and Provimi Veal

1201 Youngstown-Warren Rd.,
Niles OH 44446
PH: 330.652.5895 FAX: 330.652.7041

Chanterelle

Intimate, understated and sophisticated, Chanterelle offers the freshest of every season, prepared by Chef Ralf Schmidt with respect and restrained imagination.

Owner and Chef: Ralf Schmidt

Specialties
Seafood
Game

207 E 5th Ave, Ste 109, Eugene, OR, 97401
PH: 541.484.4065
Closed major holidays

Atwater's Restaurant & Bar

With each turn, you see Portland. From our 30th floor vantage point, you can see in every direction. Atwater's cuisine comes from these views: mushrooms from the forest, wild greens hand-picked by a gardener across town, salmon from fresh Northwest waters and pinot noir from the Willamette Valley. Cool jazz is played nightly in the bar. Join us. Taste Portland.

Owner: U.S. Bancorp   Chef: Joe Nouhan

Specialties
Grilled Duck Breast with Quince Sauce
Seared Foie Gras with Apples

111 S.W. 5th Ave., Portland, OR, 97204
PH: 503.275.3600 FAX: 503.275.8587
Website:www.atwaters.com

The Heathman

A rising star of the nineties, chef Philippe Boulot's strengths add to Portland's growing reputation as an international food destination. Striving for freshness, flavor and truthful presentation on every plate, Boulot's French Northwest cuisine is a marriage of traditional French training with contemporary sensibilities, using only the finest seasonal ingredients on the market.

Chef: Philippe Boulot

Specialties

Wild Mushroom and Port Cappuccino with Foie Gras
Braised Leg of Lamb
Coq au Vin à la Bourguignonne
Chocolate Gourmandise

1001 SW Broadway, Portland OR 97205
PH: 503.790.7752 FAX: 503.790.7112
Website:www.heathmanhotel.com

Zefiro Restaurant

Every two weeks, chef Christopher Israel changes his Mediterranean-inspired menu to reflect the seasons and the bounty of the Pacific Northwest. An exciting urban setting, attentive service, a trend setting bar and an extensive wine list complete the Zefiro experience.

Owner and Chef: Christopher Israel

Specialties

Grilled Fish, Fresh Oysters
Risotto and Gnocchi

500 N.W. 21st Ave., Portland, OR
PH: 503.226.3394 FAX: 503.226.4744

Haydn Zug's

The atmosphere and decor of our 18th-century roadhouse is Colonial Williamsburg, with pewter candlesticks and accessories at each table. Seven intimate dining rooms are available to treat the discriminating diner to innovative American cuisine prepared and served by the Lee family. Winner of the 1997 *Wine Spectator* Award of Excellence.

Owners: The Lee Family   Chef: Byron Kehr

Specialties
Grilled Lamb Tenderloin with Dijonnaise Sauce
Maryland Lump Crabcakes, in Season

1987 State St.
East Petersburg (Lancaster), PA, 17520
PH: 717.569.5746 FAX: 717.569.8450

EverMay on-the-Delaware

Nature lovers come to this area every year to bask in its natural beauty. At EverMay on-the-Delaware, you can enjoy a country house hotel set in twenty-five acres of gardens and woodlawn paths. The hotel is listed on the National Register of Historic Places. The restaurant serves contemporary American fare in a conservatory garden room or the more formal Victorian room. It lets the spirit soar.

Owners: William & Danielle Moffly   Chef: William Finnegan

Specialties
Grilled Sea Bass Creole
Roast Loin of Venison
Roasted Moularde Breast on Sautéed Ruby Chard
Grilled Veal with Caramelized Turnip and Fennel Timbale

River Road, Erwinna, Bucks Co. PA 18920
PH: 610.294.9100 FAX: 610.294.8249

Vallozzi's

Our nationally acclaimed menu combines traditional and contemporary Italian dishes that range from market-fresh seafood to thick cut steaks and chops. The restaurant is nestled in the warmth of an Italian villa, with a complete inventory of Italianate and American wines. A winner of the Barilla Pasta National Recipe Contest and *Wine Spectator* Award of Excellence. Be a part of the excitement; be a part of the family.

Owner: Ernie Vallozzi   Chef: Gina Mrdjenovich

Specialties
Maryland Crab Cakes
Prosciutto Wrapped Scallops
Fillet with Jumbo Lump Crab
Cappelletti and Lobster

Rt. 30 East, RD# 12, Box 2
Greensburg, PA, 15601
PH: 724.836.7663 FAX: 724.836.7917

La Bonne Auberge

La Bonne Auberge is a charming, chef-owned, 200-year-old farmhouse serving exquisite food in elegant surroundings since 1972. Renowned for its gracious service and attention to detail, it is both a romantic hideaway and a superb location for special occasions. It is a place for all seasons: cozy fireplaces in winter provide a warm welcome, and cocktails and hors d'oeuvres can be savoured in beautifully landscaped gardens in the spring.

Owner and Chef: Gerard Caronello

Specialties
Carré d'Agneau • Veau Morilles
Filet de Sole Tout Paris

Village 2, New Hope PA 18938
PH: 215.862.2462

Ciboulette
THE BELLEVUE

If you are looking for an exceptional dining experience Ciboulette may be your answer! Located on the Avenue of the Arts in the historic Bellevue building, sample Chef Lim's healthy AAA Four Diamond French cuisine in appetizer-size courses, while sipping a selection from our winecellar, recognized as "one of the most outstanding in the world" by *Wine Spectator*. Exquisite service and a regal French renaissance setting complete this ultimate dining experience.

Owner and Chef: Bruce Lim

Specialties
Daily Five-Course Chef's Degustation Menu
Organic Produce and Free-Range Meats

200 S. Broad St., Philadelphia, PA, 19102
PH: 215.790.1210 FAX: 215.790.1209
Website:www.ciboulette.com

S	M	T	W	T	F	S
B
L
D

AE VC MC

Closed some holidays

The Monte Carlo Living Room

Located in the Society Hill area of Philadelphia, the elegant Monte Carlo Restaurant features blue-ribbon Italian cuisine. Attentive waiters and tableside presentation increase your dining pleasure. A recipient of *Wine Spectator's* Award of Excellence for the past three years, and the only AAA Four Diamond award Italian restaurant in the Delaware Valley since 1992. Upstairs, the club offers listening and dancing enjoyment to top 40, South American and romantic European music.

Owner: Savas Soc. Ent. Ltd.   Chef: Nunzio Petruno

Specialties
Imported and Domestic Fresh Fish
Wild Seasonal Mushrooms

150 South St., Philadelphia, PA, 19147
PH: 215.925.2220 FAX: 215.925.9956

S	M	T	W	T	F	S
B
L
D

AE VC MC CB DC

Ristorante La Buca

La Buca is a below-ground restaurant built around its wine cellar. Giuseppe Giuliani offers an authentic taste of Tuscany, with regional specialties such as ribollita, crespelle alla fiorentina and tagliolini ai porcini. While offering a variety of pasta and meats, La Buca emphasizes freshly grilled seafood. Sole, pompano and langostini are among those served daily. La Buca also offers an extensive wine list, with a focus on Tuscan wines.

Owner and Chef: Giuseppe Giuliani

Specialties
Dover Sole
Regional Tuscan Fare

711 Locust St., Philadelphia, PA, 19106
PH: 215.928.0556 FAX: 215.928.1175

Hyeholde

Hyeholde restaurant is the definition of romance. Located on acres of woodland gardens in a castle with slate roofed towers, Hyeholde is the perfect place to escape from the rigors of everyday life. Inside, small dining rooms are enriched with tapestries, fireplaces, slate floors and bouquets of flowers. An underground tunnel leads to a large stone and glass dining room for private functions. Elegant picnics and Friday garden markets culminate in a feast for all the senses.

Owners: Barbara & Quentin McKenna   Chef: Christopher O'Brien

Specialties
Menu Items Change Seasonally

190 Hyeholde Dr., Pittsburgh, PA, 15108
PH: 412.264.3116 FAX: 412.264.5723

Le Mont

Only one restaurant in Pittsburgh offers world class dining with fabulous views of the entire city. Dishes such as Raspberry Duck and Hunter's Quarry further define Le Mont as the destination for distinguished dining. The wine list has won the coveted *Wine Spectator's* Award of Excellence. Recently awarded the AAA Four Diamond Award, Le Mont continues to offer only the best quality food and service.

Chef: Tom Turner

Specialties
Hunter's Quarry: Rabbit, Quail, Seasonal Game
Rack of New Zealand Lamb

1114 Grandview Ave., Pittsburgh, PA, 15211
PH: 412.431.3100 FAX: 412.431.1204

Dilworthtown Inn

Offering warm hospitality since 1758, the Inn has been meticulously restored to its original Old World elegance. The Inn provides exquisite candlelight dining in the polished simplicity of its many rooms, or weather permitting, à la carte dining in the renovated stables. The *Zagat Survey* describes an "incredible attention to detail" and *Wine Spectator* has awarded high praise to the wine cellar's 800 vintages and 12,000 bottles for almost a decade.

Owner: Jim Barnes & Bob Rafetto   Chef: Dave Gottlieb

Specialties
Potato Crusted Halibut • Breast of Pekin Duck
Pan-Roasted South African Lobster Tail

1390 Old Wilmington Pike
West Chester PA 19382
PH: 610.399.1390

Sea Fare Inn

The Sea Fare Inn, Rhode Island's only five star restaurant, is the perfect setting for any special occasion. Housed in an elegant Victorian mansion in Portsmouth, the restaurant's seven dining rooms can accommodate a group as small as 10 or as large as 250. Ten acres of beautifully landscaped flower gardens and fruit orchards make it a lovely setting for any gathering.

Owners: George & Anna Karousos
Master Chef: George Karousos

Specialties

**Award-Winning Seafood
Service**

3352 E. Main Rd., Portsmouth RI 02871
PH: 401.683.0577 FAX: 401.683.2910
Website:www.seafareinn.com

	S	M	T	W	T	F	S
B							
L							
D							

AE VC MC

1109 South Main Restaurant and Inn

1109 South Main Restaurant and Inn is a plush, restored Bed and Breakfast with a continental gourmet restaurant next door. The two historic mansions sit on two and a half acres of land, and are listed in the National Register. The restaurant opened in 1982, and Peter Ryter, the award-winning Swiss trained owner and chef, has received rave reviews since day one. Three dining rooms offer a choice of decor sure to please everyone.

Owners: Peter and Myrna Ryter   Chef: Peter Ryter

Specialties

**Wild Mushrooms in Puff Pastry
Lump Crabcake with Sweet Red Pepper Coulis**

1109 South Main St., Anderson, SC, 29621
PH: 864.225.1109 FAX: 864.225.3884

	S	M	T	W	T	F	S
B							
L							
D							

AE VC MC CB DC DS

Louis's

Located in one of the few contemporary buildings in the city, Louis's shows that the present is as rich as the past. Known for his "southern food, more sophisticated than traditional," *The New York Times* credited chef Louis Osteen as the "spiritual general of the new Charleston chefs." Osteen's innovative updates of lowcountry mainstays have won him accolades that include *Gourmet's* Great American Chef. The restaurant design, by Adam Tihany, echoes Osteen's style in its subtle use of unusual, natural materials.

Owner: Louis & Marlene Osteen   Chef: Louis Osteen

Specialties

Lowcountry Crab & Lobster Cakes with Grained Mustard
Grilled Pork Porterhouse with Sage Cornbread Dressing
Spiced Salmon with Watermelon & Red Onion Salsa

200 Meeting St., Charleston SC 29401
PH: 843.853.2550 FAX: 843.722.9485

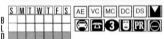

Magnolias

From its prestigious location in Charleston's historic district to its dynamic southern cuisine, Magnolias combines old world charm with contemporary excitement. Chef Donald Barickman is recognized as a pioneer in the creative use of the lowcountry's bounty. Magnolias' main dining room features high ceilings, pine floors, wrought-iron accents and stunning paintings by Taos artist Rod Gobel. *Southern Living* magazine sums it up best: "Magnolias...the city's most celebrated restaurant."

Owner: Thomas Parsell   Chef: Donald Barickman

Specialties

Shellfish over Creamy White Grits with Lobster Butter
Down South Egg Roll

185 E. Bay St., Charleston SC 29401
PH: 843.577.7771 FAX: 843.722.0035
Website:www.magnolias-blossom.com

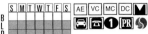

The Troutdale Dining Room

Established in 1976, the Troutdale Dining Room serves leading edge international and American fare, served in cozy dining rooms with fireplaces and candlelight. We have an extensive wine list, and feature more than fifty single malt scotches. We live by our motto "We make everything but the butter."

Owners: Barry & Carol Serber   Chef: Barry Serber

Specialties

Trout • Lamb
Duck • Game

412 6th St., Bristol TN 37620
PH: 423.968.9099

S	M	T	W	T	F	S	AE	VC	MC	DS
B										
L										
D										

The Orangery

Founded in 1971 by Kristopher and Karen Kendrick, The Orangery began as a charming luncheon spot for customers shopping in nearby exclusive boutiques. It has grown into an elegant, full-service restaurant famous for its classic French cuisine, as well as its ever-expanding Nouvelle American menu. The excellence of its diverse menu, combined with an award-winning wine list, has made The Orangery a Knoxville favorite for 27 years.

Owner: Karen Kendrick   Chef: David Wolff

Specialties

Veal Chop with Foie Gras and Port Wine Glaze
Elk with Hedgehog Mushrooms and Chipolte Demi Glace
Grouper with Rice Bean Purée and Roasted Tomato Coulis
Sea Bass with Red Curry Sauce

5412 Kingston Pike, Knoxville TN 37919
PH: 423.588.2964 FAX: 423.588.5499

S	M	T	W	T	F	S	AE	VC	MC	CB	DC
B											
L											
D											

Regas Restaurant

The Regas family has been making memories in Knoxville since 1919. Hand-carved, heavy aged prime and choice beef and the finest fresh seafood flown in daily are among the selections expertly prepared by our renowned Chef Bruce Bogartz. Recently chef Bogartz prepared dinner for the James Beard Foundation in New York. A world class wine cellar offers the perfect complement to our slow roasted Prime Rib or New Zealand Lobster. Freshly baked breads and desserts are prepared daily in our own bake shop. Full banquet and catering services are available.

Chef: Bruce Bogartz

Specialties
Prime Steak • Prime Rib
New Zealand Lobster

318 North Gay St., Knoxville, TN, 37917
PH: 423.637.9288 FAX: 423.546.5031

Chez Philippe
THE PEABODY HOTEL

A classic French approach to combining ingredients from around the world distinguishes Chez Philippe's cuisine as the best in Memphis. Seafood, exotic spices, southern specialties and fine meats by award-winning chef José H. Gutierrez are featured. The setting is opulent, the presentation is classical French and the ambiance is grand. Voted Memphis' best restaurant.

Owner: Betz Enterprises

Specialties
Hushpuppies Stuffed with Shrimp Provencale
Roasted Rack of Lamb with Potpourri of Herbs

149 Union Ave., Memphis, TN, 38103
PH: 901.529.4188 FAX: 901.529.3639
Email:peabody@wspice.com

La Tourelle

Award-winning chef Lynn Kennedy-Tilyou continues the fine dining tradition La Tourelle has established for 21 years. Set in a Queen Anne cottage near Overton Square and recognized for its romantic and intimate atmosphere, La Tourelle serves French cuisine with an emphasis on fresh seafood. Other specialties include rack of lamb, foie gras and game. The menu changes seasonally. La Tourelle recently received an Award of Excellence from *Wine Spectator.*

Owner: Glenn T. Hays   Chef: Lynn Kennedy-Tilyou

Specialties

Seabass with Asparagus Cream
Layered Lobster Salad with Guacamole and Tapenade
Rosemary Rack of Lamb with Garlic Parsley Crust

2146 Monroe Ave., Memphis TN 38104
PH: 901.726.5771 FAX: 901.272.0492

Arthur's

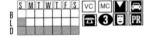

Located in the historic Union Station Hotel, Arthur's 24-foot ceilings, Tiffany stained glass windows, well-spaced tables and candlelight ensure privacy for either romantic or business dinners. A verbal presentation of the menu is recited by our captains each evening. Fresh fish is flown in daily, in addition to other selections including beef, lamb, poultry and wild game. We offer the finest food, beverages and service available.

Owner: Sheila Thrailkill   Chef: Alessandro Bozzato

Specialties

Roast Rack of Colorado Lamb
Fresh Fish Daily

1001 Broadway, Nashville TN 37203
PH: 615.255.1494 FAX: 615.255.1496
Website:http://users.aol.com/arthursin

Mario's

Internationally acclaimed for its overall dining experience, Mario's is celebrating its 34th year. With over 714 selections of the wine list, Mario's has won major restaurant awards including *Wine Spectator's* Award of Excellence. Mario's delicious food, elegant atmosphere and superb service have all contributed to its receiving numerous awards, including the AAA Four Diamond award. Mario's is perfect for both romantic and business dinners, and specializes in northern Italian cuisine.

Owner: Mario Ferrari   Chef: Giovanni Giosa

Specialties
Ossobuco Milanese • Dover Sole ai Pignoli
Tagliatelle Gamberi e Asparagi • Gnocchi all Parigina

2005 Broadway, Nashville TN 37203
PH: 615.327.3232 FAX: 615.321.2675

The Wild Boar

With an exceptional 15,000-bottle wine list and the contemporary French cuisine of Chef Guillaume Burlion, the Wild Boar has established itself as one of America's premier stops for the serious connoisseur. Winner of the *Wine Spectator* Grand Award six years in a row (1993-1998), the DiRoNA Award (1994-1998), and the AAA Five Diamond Award (1996-1998), The Wild Boar pairs global delicacies with wines from Old World Burgundy to California Cabernets.

Owner: Z-1 Corporation   Chef: Guillaume Burlion

Specialties
Potato Crusted Rouget Barbet
Filet Mignon of Texas Antelope
Braised Maplewood Farms Quail

2014 Broadway, Nashville, TN, 37203
PH: 615.329.1313 FAX: 615.329.4930

Café Pacific

This exceptional restaurant, located in the midst of Highland Park Village, the city's most upscale shopping area, is a Dallas institution. Impeccably prepared cuisine and polished service provide a background for many of the city's social and business leaders. Café Pacific, acclaimed by *Zagat* as the number one seafood restaurant in Dallas and winner of *Gourmet's* 1997 Top Tables Award, is the perfect setting for Current American Cuisine.

Owner: Jack Knox   Chef: Brad Albers

Specialties

Short Smoked Salmon
Peppered Steak
Oriental Chicken Salad

24 Highland Park Village, Dallas, TX, 75205
PH: 214.526.1170 FAX: 214.526.0332

The French Room
HOTEL ADOLPHUS

Chef William Koval has distinguished himself at five-star restaurants from New York to Paris. His genius for adapting classic French cooking to contemporary tastes has earned him kudos in *Bon Appetit*, *Travel & Leisure*, *Zagat*, and *Gourmet*, which recently named the French Room one of America's Top Tables and the best restaurant in Dallas/Fort Worth for the second consecutive year. Chef Koval works closely with Maitre d'Hotel Jim Donahue to create a one-of-a-kind dining experience for every guest.

Owner: Hotel Adolphus   Chef: William A. Koval

Specialties

Jumbo Lump Crab Cake
Hot Chocolate Cake

1321 Commerce St., Dallas, TX, 75202
PH: 214.742.8200 FAX: 214.651.3683
Website:www.adolphus.com

Chez Nous

"The owner is the chef, as it should be, and the chef is in the kitchen where he belongs." Classic French cuisine in a delightful, intimate setting with a comprehensive wine list of reasonably priced French and California wines. Located just 20 minutes from downtown Houston in Humble. Open Monday through Saturday at 5:30 p.m.

Owner and Chef: Gerard Brach

Specialties
Fresh Foie Gras, Caramelized Apple and Honey Vinegar
Chartreuse of Pheasant
Alaskan Halibut with Mussels and Scallops
Grand Marnier Chocolate Mousse in Chocolate Bag

S	M	T	W	T	F	S
B						
L						
D						

AE VC MC CB

217 South Ave. G., Humble, TX, 77338
PH: 281.446.6717

DeVille

DeVille is one of the benchmarks of high style cuisine in Houston. The innovative and exotic menu, created by chef Tim Keating, features modern French cuisine, offering diners an extraordinary culinary experience. The award-winning DeVille boasts a first-class menu, extensive wine list and superb service.

Chef: Tim Keating

Specialties
Day Boat Fish Selections
Veal, Lamb and Black Angus Beef

S	M	T	W	T	F	S
B						
L						
D						

AE VC MC DS

1300 Lamar St., Houston, TX, 77010
PH: 713.652.6250 FAX: 713.650.1203
Website:www.fourseasons.com

Empress

One of Houston's best-kept secrets, Empress specializes in fusion cuisine. Scott Chen, chef and owner, has a fresh approach, blending Chinese, French, Asian and contemporary American ideas, using unique ingredients and cooking techniques. A new restaurant, Scott Chen's, will open in the Galleria area (San Felipe at Voss) in early 1999.

Owner and Chef: Scott Chen

Specialties

**Dungeness Crab with Avocado, Tomato & Mango
Filet Mignon with Blackened Pepper Sauce
Jumbo Lump Crabcakes with Creole Mustard Sauce
Scott's Seafood Platter**

5419 - A FM 1960 W., Houston TX 77069
PH: 281.583.8021 FAX: 281.583.8071

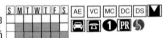

La Reserve

THE OMNI HOTEL

The grandly elegant and sophisticated La Reserve restaurant appeals to the most discriminating diner. Lavish and trend-setting menu selections are the focus for the adventurous palate. Exquisitely prepared international cuisine is served in a dramatic setting of luxurious fabrics, beveled glass and crystal chandeliers. La Reserve, inside the Omni Houston Hotel, touts an incomparable wine list and impeccable service.

Chef: Mercer Moore

Specialties

**Dried Bing Cherry Stuffed African Pheasant Breast
Pan-Seared Texas Seabass with Crisp Potato Scales
Sautéed Atlantic Salmon with Steamed Asparagus**

Four Riverway, Houston TX 77056
PH: 713.871.8181 FAX: 713.871.8116

Maxim's Restaurant and Piano Bar

For 50 years, a legend in fine dining, owner Ronnie Bermann has carried on a tradition while keeping up with the changing times. The chef invites you to savor his traditional favorites as well as newly created dishes. A piano bar, wine cellar and other private dining rooms are available for banquets. Elegant dining with a casual atmosphere. Lunch and dinner Mon.-Fri. with continuous service throughout the afternoon. Saturday dinner only.

Owner: Ronnie Bermann   Chef: Joe Perez

Specialties
Fresh Gulf Seafood/Lobster Bisque
Veal Camille, Rack of Lamb

3755 Richmond, Houston, TX, 77046
PH 713.877.8899 FAX: 713.877.8855
Email:maxims@intergate.com

The Rivoli

One of Houston's premier restaurants for continental dining, The Rivoli boasts a chef and complete staff of European-trained professionals. The restaurant has won awards for both its casual lunches and its dramatic dinners. Sisters Rosalinda and Rosi welcome their guests for intimate gatherings, business meetings and grand celebrations. For large or small parties, several private dining rooms are available, including the wine cellar and garden room.

Owner: Rosa E. Cantu   Chef: Pierre Gutknecht

Specialties
Lobster Monte Carlo
Stuffed Dover Sole

5636 Richmond St., Houston, TX, 77057
PH: 713.789.1900 FAX: 713.266.5265

Rotisserie for Beef and Bird

The glories of Rotisserie for Beef and Bird are well known to Houston gourmets who have long enjoyed the finest in traditional American cooking, prepared under the watchful eye of chef and proprietor Joe Mannke. The menu changes seasonally to utilize products from the forest, the sea and the agricultural bounty of Texas. The Rotisserie for Beef and Bird features one of the finest wine lists in Texas, with more than 900 selections.

Owner and Chef: Joe Mannke

Specialties
Wild Game
Fresh Lobster

2200 Wilcrest, Houston, TX, 77042
PH: 713.977.9524 FAX: 713.977.9568

Tony's Restaurant

For more than three decades, Tony's has been recognized the world over as Houston's ultimate dining experience. Owner Tony Vallone and Executive Chef Bruce McMillan have created an innovative, contemporary menu steeped in classical European traditions guaranteeing an extraordinary dining experience. Professionalism and hospitality are the hallmarks of Tony's elegant service, while quality and freshness are the cuisine's guarantee. The wine cellar boasts an incredible 30,000 bottles of the world's finest wines to perfectly complement any meal.

Owner: Tony Vallone   Chef: Bruce McMillan

Specialties
Warm Lobster and Yukon Gold Potato Salad
Medallions of Beef 'Sorrentino'

1801 Post Oak Blvd., Houston, TX, 77056
PH: 713.622.6778

Riverhorse Cafe

Riverhorse Cafe is located on historic Main Street in Park City. The setting combines the turn of the century charm of the Main Dining Room with the contemporary ambiance of the Atrium Room with its floor to ceiling windows. The Atrium Room also showcases Utah's finest pop and jazz entertainers nightly throughout the winter and on weekends the rest of the year. The Riverhorse Cafe's menu features contemporary American regional cuisine with Pacific Rim influences.

Specialties

Grilled Norwegian Salmon
Utah Rack of Lamb

540 Main St., Park City, UT,
PH: 435.649.3536 FAX: 435.649.2409

Hemingway's

A warm, gracious evening awaits you in a beautifully restored 1860 country home. Dine fireside, in the old world romance of a stone wine cellar, or under a vaulted ceiling. Hand-crafted American cuisine features fresh Atlantic seafoods, Vermont game birds, lamb, steaks, venison and vegetarian specialties. A wine tasting menu is also available. One of the "Top 25 Restaurants in America," according to *Food and Wine*.
Owners: Ted and Linda Fondulas

Specialties

Filet of Atlantic Salmon with Chanterelles
Halibut Maine Lobster with Hand-Rolled Fettuccine
Deconstructed "Reuben" of Quail
Native Pheasant Roasted in Grape Leaves

Route 4, Killington, VT, 05751
PH: 802.422.3886 FAX: 802.422.3468
Website:www.hemingwaysrestaurant.com

The Inn at Sawmill Farm

Not far from the busy sophistication of Boston and New York, The Inn at Sawmill Farm is quietly situated in the village of West Dover. The Inn is noted for its warmth and courtesy, which is extended upon your arrival. The dining room is one of country elegance, where the American-Continental menu and unobtrusive service has earned the Inn a pronounced reputation. A member of Relais & Châteaux and a *Wine Spectator* Grand Award winner.

Owner and Chef: Brill Williams

Specialties

Grilled Loin of Venison in Green Peppercorn Sauce
Breast of Pheasant with Port Reduction

Rt. 100 & Crosstown Rd., W. Dover VT 05356
PH: 802.464.8131 FAX: 802.464.1130

La Bergerie

Located in the heart of colonial old town Alexandria, La Bergerie is decorated with French countryside paintings, richly appointed leather banquettes, and crystal chandeliers. Its charming and intimate atmosphere provides the perfect ambience for any special occasion. Receptions may be held in the Atrium and the two private party rooms. French cuisine with Basque specialties will delight your palate. Just minutes from R. Reagan airport and Washington, D.C.

Owners: Jean and Bernard Campagne　　　Chef: Jean Campagne

Specialties

Basque Duck Confit with Sauteéd Potato
Broiled Assorted Seafood with Tomato, Garlic Sauce
Almond Cake
Raspberries Soufflé

218 North Lee Street, Alexandria, VA, 22314
PH: 703.683.1007 FAX: 703.519.6114

L'Auberge Chez Francois

"a French Country Inn"

A French country inn situated in the verdant rolling hills of Virginia, this gastronomic delight satisfies our secret longings to get away from it all to a peaceful spot where we can be pampered and revived. The restaurant has received national recognition for its fine French-Alsatian cuisine, and the accommodating service and homemade pastries and desserts create a harmony to be cherished.

Owner: Francois Haeringer   Chef: Jacques Haeringer

Specialties
Salmon Soufflé
Choucroute Sweetbreads

332 Springvale Rd., Great Falls, VA, 22066
PH: 703.759.3800

Prince Michel Restaurant

An easy drive from Washington, DC or Richmond, Virginia, Prince Michel Restaurant is located in Virginia's leading winery at Prince Michel Vineyards. Visitors can savor the congenial ambiance and outstanding European-style service as they enjoy chef Alain Lecomte's fine French cuisine and selections from the award-winning wine list. The winery offers wine tours and tastings daily.

Owners: Mr & Mrs Jean Leducq   Chef: Alain Lecomte

Specialties
Foie Gras with Calvados Sauce
Grenadine of Veal with Chanterelles

Route 29 South, HCR 4, Box 77, Leon, VA, 22725
PH: 800.800.WINE FAX: 504.547.3088
Website:www.princemichel.com

Evans Farm Inn
and The Sitting Duck Pub

Enjoy gracious country dining in an 18th-century atmosphere with waitstaff in period costume. Evans Farm Inn is decorated throughout with authentic antiques, primitive cooking utensils and hand-hewn beams. Outside dining and crackling log fires in season. Located on a 24 acre working farm, the outbuildings include an early American log "smoke house" where salmon, trout and other items are smoked. The cuisine is American, with continental specialties and fresh vegetables grown on the farm.

Owner: Ralph B. & Maria S. Evans   Chef: Jumas Kahn

Specialties
Roast Duckling
Chesapeake Bay Crab Cakes

1696 Chain Bridge Rd., McLean, VA, 22101
PH: 703.356.8000 FAX: 703.821.3396

Lemaire
THE JEFFERSON HOTEL

Lemaire, at the historic Jefferson Hotel, is Richmond's only AAA Five Diamond restaurant, and one of only 40 establishments across North America to have received this prestigious award. The 118-seat restaurant is comprised of seven separate and intimate dining rooms. The menu features updated regional southern cuisine, to which Chef Jeffrey Waite adds his own classical European and Contemporary American influences.

Chef: Jeffrey Waite

Specialties
Sautéed Lemaire Lump Crab Cakes
Grilled Venison Tenderloin

The Jefferson Hotel, Franklin and Adams St.
Richmond, VA, 23220 PH: 804.788.8000
Email:sales@jefferson-hotel.com

Tivoli Restaurant

The Tivoli entices you with the finest northern Italian cuisine available in the DC area; we offer our guests award-winning wines, freshly made pastas and daily specials of seafood and game. The sparkling, spacious dining room and personable and attentive service make a meal at Tivoli's a memorable affair. The restaurant is located five minutes from the Kennedy Center and offers a generous pre-theatre dinner menu.

Chef: Klaus Helmin

Specialties
Fresh Pasta
Game and Seafood

1700 N. Moore St., Rosslyn, VA, 22209
PH: 703.524.8900 FAX: 703.524.4971

S M T W T F S AE VC MC CB DC DS
B
L
D

The Dining Room at Ford's Colony

This acclaimed restaurant features the modern American cuisine of chef David Everett. We are located four miles from historic Williamsburg in the 2,500 acre Ford's Colony Resort. The elegant Georgian style dining room features intimate seating and a view of the kitchen or the chef's table. Details are important here: we have an extensive wine list, and fresh local ingredients are mixed with the finest of imports to produce a truly world-class experience.

Owner: Richard J. Ford   Chef: David Everett

Specialties
Yukon Gold Potato Soup and Black Truffles
Day Scallops in Parmesan Crust

240 Ford's Colony Dr., Williamsburg, VA, 23188
PH: 757.258.4107 FAX: 757.258.4168

S M T W T F S AE VC MC
B
L
D

Canlis

For almost 50 years, this independent restaurant has romanced the Pacific Northwest with its local seafood, prime steak and unparalleled wine list. This tradition of excellence continues with recent awards such as the *Wine Spectator* Grand Award, recognition from *Bon Appetit* as one of America's top 10 "Tried and True" restaurants, and top awards from the *Gourmet* Reader's Poll. Canlis has proven that with age, maturity and greatness abound.

Owner: Christopher Canlis   Chef: Greg Atkinson

Specialties
**Pacific King Salmon Grilled with Apples
Hand Cut Steaks from the Copper Grill
Dungeness Crab Legs with Tangy Mustard Sauce
The Canlis Salad**

S	M	T	W	T	F	S	AE	VC	MC	CB	DC	ER	DS

B
L
D

2576 Aurora Ave. N., Seattle, WA, 98109
PH: 206.283.3313 FAX: 206.283.1766
Website:www.canlis.com

Place Pigalle Restaurant

Place Pigalle, tucked in the Pike Place Market, overlooks Elliott Bay and the Olympic Mountains. Seasonal menus reflect the bounty of the Northwest, mingling classical, Mediterranean and Asian influences. The resulting dishes "always have been artful, always entertaining, always fresh...disarmingly successful." A cozy bar specializes in an award-winning wine list, vintage Ports and Madeiras, grappas and eaux-de-vie, and local microbrews. Since 1982, kudos have appeared in *Bon Appétit, Gourmet, Northwest Best Places, Wine Spectator* and the *Zagat Survey.*

Owner: Bill Frank   Chef: Michael Parpart

Specialties
**Fresh Northwest Seafood, Rabbit and Other Game
Crème Brûlée**

S	M	T	W	T	F	S	AE	VC	MC	CB	DC

B
L
D

81 Pike St. Pike Place Market, Seattle, WA, 98101
PH: 206.624.1756
Website:www.savvydiner.com/seattle/placepigalle

Reiner's

Reiner's is distinct among the city's fine restaurants, serving classic continental cuisine with European charm. Intimate and inviting, this small restaurant sets a high standard for personal attention. Banquet menus and other special services are available for corporate or social functions. Conveniently located, Reiner's is within 10 minutes' walking distance from most downtown hotels, and is two blocks south of the Convention Center.

Owner and Chef: Hanspeter Aebersold

Specialties

Seared Duck Foie Gras on Grilled Apple Slices
Veal Tenderloin Bernoise with Homemade Spaetzli
Jaeger Schnitzel • Halibut Cheeks (in season)

1106 8th Ave., Seattle WA 98101
between Spring and Seneca
PH: 206.624.2222 FAX: 206.624.2519

Rover's

Thierry Rautureau (the Chef in the Hat) has a philosophy about cooking: he says, "it starts with freshness and continues with treating all ingredients with attention." Rover's and Rautureau offer Northwest contemporary cuisine with a French accent, and have received both local and national accolades over the last 12 years. Look for Thierry Rautureau's new cookbook, in bookstores in 2001.

Owner and Chef: Thierry Rautureau

Specialties

Five Course Degustation Menu
Five Course Vegetarian Menu
Eight Course Grand Menu

2808 E. Madison St., Seattle WA 98112
PH: 206.325.7442 FAX: 206.325.1092
Website:www.rovers-seattle.com

Main Dining Room
THE GREENBRIER RESORT

The Main Dining Room at The Greenbrier offers an outstanding dining experience. An elegant and enchanting ambiance featuring live violin and piano music complements world-renowned cuisine at this Mobil Five-Star and AAA Five-Diamond resort. A wide selection of fine wines enhances our cuisine prepared to please the most discriminating palates.

Specialties
American • Continental • Classical Cuisine

300 W Main St.
White Sulphur Springs, WV, 24986
PH: 304.536.1110 FAX: 304.536.7854
Website:www.greenbrier.com

The Immigrant Restaurant & Winery
THE AMERICAN CLUB

Secluded in The American Club, the midwest's only AAA Five-Diamond resort hotel, The Immigrant's six dining areas each reflect a different rich European heritage. Enjoy the signature "Tournedoes Immigrant" masterfully prepared by our award-winning chef, Charles Lebar. Sumptuous contemporary cuisine, fine wines and exceptional service create this ultimate dining experience.

Chef: Charles Lebar

Specialties
Sweet Butter Braised Maine Lobster
Oven Roasted Veal Loin with Sweetbreads

444 Highland Dr., Kohler WI, 53044
PH: 920.457.8888 FAX: 920.457.7011

Karl Ratzsch's

A tradition in Milwaukee, Karl Ratzsch's is billed as 'the impressive German restaurant,' and indeed it is! Housed within its walls is a priceless collection of German steins, porcelain and glassware. The top-tier German dishes all vie for your attention and the large selection of fine German wines will keep you pondering for quite a while. The Ratzsch family have owned and run this establishment for three generations...all one can say is that it only improves with age.

Owner: Josef Ratzsch   Chef: John Poulos

Specialties

**Roast Goose Shank • Saubraten
Planked Whitefish • Roast Duck**

320 E. Mason St., Milwaukee WI 53202
PH: 414.276.2720 FAX: 414.276.3534

The Granary

Perched high atop the Gros Venture Butte looking out at the towering Teton Mountains, The Granary is, to say the very least, an unforgettable dining experience. Part of Spring Creek, Wyoming's only year-round AAA Four Diamond resort, The Granary offers superb cuisine and views that elevate fine dining to unprecedented heights, even for a place as awe-inspiring as Jackson Hole.

Owner: Stephen Price   Chef: Robert Corliss

Specialties

**Elk Tenderloin with Black Bay Sauce
Lamb Loin with Garlic Flan**

1800 Spirit Dance Rd.
PO Box 4780, Jackson Hole, WY, 83001
PH: 800.443.6139 FAX: 307.733.1524

The Conservatory

Enjoy the sophisticated atmosphere of The Conservatory Dining Room, featuring regional cuisine with award-winning interpretations of western game and fish. We are a Five-time award winner of the AAA/CAA Four Diamond award. The restaurant highlights art from Canada's Western Lights group, and has Calgary's largest selection of VQA Canadian wines. A culinary experience in The Conservatory is not to be missed when visiting Calgary.

Chef: Doug Ghanam

Specialties
Roast Rack of Alberta Lamb
Spice-Encrusted Alberta Ostrich
Fresh Nova Scotia Lobster

209 4th Ave. SE, Calgary AB T2G 0C6
PH: 403.205.5433 FAX: 403.266.0007

S	M	T	W	T	F	S		AE	VC	MC	DC	ER	J	DS

B
L
D

La Chaumière Restaurant

Calgary's La Chaumière offers creative cuisine in an elegant 65-seat dining room and comfortable patio. The extensive wine list, featuring 450 selections from around the world, is matched by the chef's imaginative menu. Special features include a small private room for business lunches or dinners, a banquet room which can accommodate up to 100 people for special functions, and private dining in the wine cellar.

Owner: Joseph De Angelis and   Chef: Paul Rogalski
        Josef Mathes

Specialties
Salmon Filet on Creamed Savoy Cabbage, Pinot Noir Sauce
Ostrich Medallions Glazed with Blue Cheese, Portwine Sauce

139 17th Ave. S.W., Calgary, AB, T2S 0A1
PH: 403.228.5690 FAX: 403.228.4448
Website:www.calgarymenus.com/lachaumiere

S	M	T	W	T	F	S		AE	VC	MC	DC	ER	

B
L
D

The Dining Room
THE POST HOTEL

Set amidst the natural wonders of Banff National Park in the majestic Canadian Rocky Mountains, the Post Hotel dining room offers a menu of fresh market cuisine complemented by an award-winning wine list. With over 600 selections and an inventory of 16,000 bottles, the wine list was recognized by *Wine Spectator*, winning the Award of Excellence. Fine cognacs and hand-rolled Cuban cigars are also available in an adjacent smoking room.

Owners: André and George Schwarz   Chef: Wolfgang Vogt

Specialties
Alberta Beef, Alberta Rack of Lamb
Northwest Territories Caribou

200 Pipestone St., Lake Louise, AB, TOL 1E0
PH: 403.522.3989 FAX: 403.522.3966
Email:posthotl@telusplanet.net

Sooke Harbour House

"This morning, at sunrise we awoke to see the tide out, the first light hitting the water and, cozy in our bed, we watched a blue heron elegantly walk through the bay. The food is unforgettable and the mornings are magic." Our internationally renowned restaurant is a *Wine Spectator* Award of Excellence winner. We offer the best produce available, grown in our gardens, on nearby organic farms or harvested in the wilds around Sooke. We are located 45 min. SW of Victoria.

Owners: Frederique & Sinclair Philip

Specialties
Organic Vegetables, Greens and Edible Flowers
West Coast and Pacific Northwest Cuisine
Fresh Local Fish and Shellfish

1528 Whiffen Spit Rd., Sooke BC V0S 1N0
PH: 1.800.889.9688 or 250.642.3421
Website:www.sookeharbourhouse.com

Caffe de Medici

Tucked away from the bustle of the street, Caffe de Medici is artistically designed with high molded ceilings, muralled walls, serene portraits of the 15-century Medici family and plush drapery. The polished, unmistakably romantic interior is matched by rich, delicious northern Italian entrées and flawless, genteel service. On Robson Street, where the choices for dining out seem endless, Caffe de Medici helps you narrow the field.

Owner: Steve Punzo   Chef: James Bowen

Specialties

Northern Italian Cuisine
Extensive Award-winning Wine List

109-1025 Robson St., Vancouver BC V6E 1A9
PH: 604.669.9322 FAX: 604.669-3771
Website:www.medici.cc

Five Sails

Located in the Pan Pacific Hotel with a spectacular setting overlooking Vancouver's harbour and mountains, Five Sails is the recipient of numberous awards, including the prestigious AAA/CAA Five Diamond for the past four years. Executive Chef Ernst Dorfler and Sous Chef Cheryl Mishio create their own unique cuisine with a touch of European and Asian influence. An expansive wine list perfectly complements the menu.

Owner: Pan Pacific Hotel   Chef: Ernst Dorfler

Specialties

Basil Marinated Chargrilled Salmon Filet
Crispy Sea Bass
Roast Rack of Lamb

300-999 Canada Place, Vancouver BC V6C 3L5
PH: 604.662.8111 FAX: 604.662.3815

Imperial Chinese Seafood Restaurant

Hong Kong chefs deliver Cantonese cuisine with French service amid a breathtaking view of Coal Harbour in a sumptuous art deco setting complete with crystal chandeliers. Dim Sum is served daily. Whether you desire a light lunch, quiet cocktails or a grand dinner, the Imperial's staff will cater to your every need.

Owner: K.L. Wong

Specialties
Dim Sum
Seafood

355 Burrard St., Vancouver, BC, V6C 2G8
PH: 604.688.8191 FAX: 604.688.8466

Langdon Hall

Chef and gardener work in unison to produce masterpieces for the palate. Vegetables, fruits and edible flowers grown on the property are incorporated into every dish to create a fresh, seasonal, Canadian flavour. Guests may choose to dine indoors by soft candlelight, or under the Arbor amidst the beauty of three seasons. Healthy Spa Cuisine is an added feature for guests of the newly renovated Spa.

Chef: Louise Duhamel

Specialties
Freshly Grown Vegetables
Contemporary Canadian Cuisine

RR33, Cambridge ON N3H 4R8
PH: 519.740.2100 FAX: 519.740.8161

On The Twenty

A casual but sophisticated destination in the heart of Ontario's wine country, On The Twenty offers innovative cuisine in an area where orchards, vineyards and verdant fields give true meaning to the concept of regional bounty. Located in the charming village of Jordan, the restaurant is adjacent to Cave Spring Cellars, a leading estate winery, and The Vintner's Inn, a small but luxurious hostelry. A lovely day trip from Toronto or Buffalo, and close to Niagara-on-the-Lake and Niagara Falls.

Owner: Helen Young   **Chef: Michael Olson**

Specialties

**Potted Foie Gras in Ice Wine Jelly with Saffron Brioche
Quail with Sage, Pancetta and Sourdough**

3836 Main St., Jordan, ON, L0R 1S0
PH: 905.562.7313 FAX: 905.562.3348
Website:www.onthetwenty.on.ca

Hogan's Inn

Located in King City just minutes north of Toronto, Hogan's has been part of the local landscape since 1851. Chef Robert Steele is producing unique menus that reflect years of experience with culinary sensibilities from his Canadian heritage and a commitment to fresh local produce, meats and game. Everything from breads to desserts is prepared on the premises. With over two hundred labels respresented in our wine cellar, we can claim to have one of the finest cellars in the province.

Chef: Robert Steele

Specialties
**Warm Portobello Tart
Salmon, Leek and Spinach Strudel
Baked Seabass in a Sesame Cornmeal Crust**

12998 Keele Street, King City, ON, L7B 1A4
PH: 905.833.5311 FAX: 905.833.2912
Website:www.hogans-inn.com

The Inn at Manitou

A luxury lakeside spa and tennis resort 150 miles north of Toronto, The Inn at Manitou is a member of the Paris-based Relais & Chateâux chain renowned for excellence in cuisine. The restaurant features contemporary cuisine prepared by a brigade of 14 chefs from two and three Michelin Star restaurants in France. Menus emphasize fresh local and imported ingredients. Guests not staying at the resort are welcome, but must have reservations.

Owner: Ben Wise   Chef: Thomas Bellec

Specialties

Duck Liver Confit with Apricot Chutney and Port Sauce
Maine Lobster with Chanterelles and Asparagus

McKellar Centre Rd., McKellar, ON, P0G 1C0
PH: 705.389.2171 FAX: 705.389.3818
Open every day from May 10th to Oct. 19th
Website:www.manitou-online.com

360 Restaurant

Located atop the CN Tower in the heart of Toronto, the 360 Revolving Restaurant is one of the city's most spectacular dining experiences. With its awe inspiring panoramic view, 360 is a kaleidoscope of colour and fancy, complete with unique adornments throughout, and featuring original Canadian art. Chef Brad Long and his team have developed a reputation for innovation and unique presentation of regional market cuisine. Rich in flavour, textures and colours, signature dishes are complemented with an award-winning selection of International and Canadian wines and pastries.

Chef: Brad Long

Specialties

Almond Crusted Atlantic Salmon on Persian Rice
Venison Chops with Juniper Latkes and Pan Juices

301 Front St. W., Toronto, ON, M5V 2T6
PH: 416.362.5411 FAX: 416.601.4712

Biagio Ristorante

Historic St. Lawrence Hall is the backdrop for this classically elegant restaurant with an authentic Italian pedigree. Milanese cuisine, featuring traditional and unusual pasta dishes and daily specials are just the beginning; there are many more intriguing possibilities. An enchanting tree-covered patio is the perfect place for romantic rendezvous in the summer. Winner of *Wine Spectator's* 1997 Award of Excellence.

Owner: Biagio Vinci   Chef: Gianpiero Tondina

Specialties
Venison Braised in Truffle Oil
Saffron Risotto

155 King St. E., Toronto, ON, M5C 1G9
PH: 416.366.4040 FAX: 416.366.4765

Centro Grill & Wine Bar

Tony Longo and Marc Thuet's jewel of a restaurant is equally beloved by local and international fine dining connoisseurs. Visitors are drawn to a setting reminiscent of a modern Venetian palace with high ceilings, pillars and mezzanine resplendent with color and refracted light, and enhanced by attentive service, elegant leather armchairs and Rosenthal china. Patrons return for the innovative cuisine of Thuet and one of the best wine lists in North America, expertly assembled by Longo with over 450 selections.

Owners: Tony Longo and Marc Thuet   Chef: Marc Thuet

Specialties
Roasted Rack of Lamb

2472 Yonge St., Toronto, ON, M4P 2H5
PH: 416.483.2211 FAX: 416.483.2641
Website:www.centrorestaurant.com

Chiaro's

LE ROYAL MERIDIEN THE KING EDWARD

Chiaro's is the definition of superb dining with flair. Chef John Higgins' inventive cuisine reflects his classical European training and influences gleaned from his travels around the world as Captain of Culinary Team Canada. Higgins, who also worked for Britain's Royal Family at Buckingham Palace, stresses only the freshest and very best of ingredients in all his menus. Exquisite service and over 400 exciting wines, chosen by manager and Sommelier, Fergus O'Halloran, complete Chiaro's dining experience.

Owner: Le Royal Meridien Hotel   Chef: John Higgins

Specialties

Canadian Lobster Marrakech
Lavender-Rubbed Rack of Lamb on Goat Cheese Tian

37 King St. E., Toronto, ON, M5C 1E9
PH: 416.863.4126 FAX: 416.863.4127

La Fenice

Seasonal recipes and fresh fish grilled Mediterranean style are served with olive oil from our own olive grove. We have a great variety of pastas both imported and home-made, and many special surprises not on the menu. A modern approach characterises the ambience of the restaurant, which seats sixty-five guests. A beautiful lower level has its own menu and private elegance.

Chef: Luigi Orgera

Specialties

**Truffles in Season
Caribou, Venison, Quail and other Game
Fresh Pasta**

319 King St. W., Toronto ON M5V 1J5
PH: 416.585.2377 FAX: 416.585.2709

S	M	T	W	T	F	S	AE	VC	MC	CB	DC	ER

B
L
D

POUR:
*1 PART KAHLÚA,
1 PART CLOS DU BOIS*

ADD:
*1 PART CANADIAN CLUB,
1 PART BEEFEATER*

MIX IN:
*1 PART COURVOISIER,
1 PART MAKER'S MARK*

WITH:
*1 PART HARVEYS BRISTOL CREAM,
1 PART SAUZA*

Prego della Piazza

Sophisticated, confident and glamourous, Prego della Piazza looks onto a tented piazza nestled against the Church of the Redeemer at Avenue Rd. and Bloor. Owner Michael Carlevale has gathered a team of seasoned professionals providing first-rate service and a kitchen founded on the selections, ingredients, style and techniques of Italian cooking. Located in Toronto's upscale downtown shopping district, Prego della Piazza recently celebrated its tenth anniversary.

Owner: Michael Carlevale   Chef: Tim Ayiotis

Specialties
**Vegetable Antipasto • Spaghetti with Calamari
US Prime Beef • North Atlantic Fish**

150 Bloor St. W., Toronto ON M5S 2X9
PH: 416.920.9900 FAX: 416.920.9949

Signatures
HOTEL INTERCONTINENTAL TORONTO

Escape to the casually elegant surroundings of Signatures Restaurant in Yorkville's Hotel Inter-Continental Toronto. The restaurant has floor to ceiling windows that open onto a landscaped courtyard offering three styles of dining: cafe, restaurant and patio. Chef Jack Lamont creates menus that reflect North American regional cuisine with an international touch. Menus feature heart-healthy selections and are seasonally designed around fresh market produce.

Chef: Jack Lamont

Specialties
**House Cured Atlantic Salmon
Oven Roasted Provimi Veal Chop with Sage and Prosciutto**

220 Bloor St. W., Toronto, ON, M5S 1T8
PH 416.324.5885 FAX: 416.324.5920

Café Henry Burger

Welcome to a 75-year-old tradition of refined cuisine, impeccable service and elegant surroundings. As the oldest restaurant in the national capital region, and one of the oldest in Canada, we have followed a tradition of excellence set by Marie and Henry Burger. The Café has been the preferred rendez-vous of diplomats, politicians, artists and connoisseurs since 1922.

Owner and Chef: Robert C. Bourassa

Specialties
Grilled Heritage Smoked Salmon
Cider Braised Partridge with Cabbage and Apple Fricassee
Roast Loin of Venison
Herb Crusted Grilled Rack of Alberta Lamb

S	M	T	W	T	F	S	AE	VC	MC	DC	ER	J

B
L
D

69 Laurier, Hull, Québec J8X 3V7
PH: 819.777.5646 FAX: 819.777.0832

Beaver Club

Widely known as one of the top restaurants in the country, the legendary Beaver Club at the Canadian Pacific Queen Elizabeth Hotel is your ticket to a culinary adventure you won't soon forget. Experience the unique and innovative gourmet cuisine that has earned this respected establishment 1996, 1997 and 1998 Five Star *Mobil Travel Guide* ratings, the highest distinction awarded by this prestigious publication. Join us for elegant dinner and dancing every Saturday night.

Owner: CP Hotels **Chef: John K. Cordeaux**

Specialties
Magdalen Island Lobster Armoricaine
Mignons of Caribou Grand Veneur with Wild Cherries
Roast Rack of Québec Lamb with Parsnip Chips

S	M	T	W	T	F	S	AE	VC	MC	DC	ER	DS

B
L
D

900 René-Levesque Blvd. W., Montréal PQ
PH: 514.861.3511 FAX: 514.954.2256
Website: www.cphotels.com

Le Passe-Partout

Located 10 minutes from downtown in the charming Notre-Dame-de-Grâce area, Le Passe-Partout serves French *cuisine de marché* in intimate and elegant surroundings. The house-made breads, pâtés and smoked salmon, as well as an extensive selection of French raw-milk cheeses are available in the adjoining bakery. "A dining experience to treasure," says the *Montréal Gazette.*

Owners: James MacGuire and   Chef: James MacGuire
Suzanne Baron-Lafrenière

Specialties
Quenelles de Pétoncles Homardière
Filet de Canard aux Champignons Sauvages
Tourte de Pintade Grand Veneur

3857 Boul. Décarie, Montréal PQ H4A 3J6
PH: 514.487.7750 FAX: 514.487.5673
Toll free:1.877.487.7750

S M T W T F S   AE VC MC DC ER J
B
L
D

Le Piment Rouge

Le Piment Rouge is located in one of Montréal's celebrated landmark buildings in the heart of downtown, surrounded by major hotels. The restaurant has served world-class Szechuan cuisine to its loyal local and international clientele for nearly two decades. The atmosphere is elegant and relaxing; the service is courteous and efficient. We offer private reception rooms for large and small groups. Le Piment Rouge is the winner of the prestigious AAA CAA four diamond and *enRoute* awards.

Owners: Chuck & Hazel Mah   Chef: Chen Wha Pin

Specialties
Chinese Szechuan Cuisine

1170 rue Peel, Montréal PQ, H3B 4P2
PH: 514.866.7816 FAX: 514.866.1575
Email:cpmah@msn.com

S M T W T F S   AE VC MC DC ER J
B
L
D
Holidays Open For Dinner Only

La Marée

An internationally renowned seafood special-
ist, La Marée enjoys a well-deserved reputation among fish and seafood connoisseurs. A
number of awards attest to the quality of our
classic dishes, and our elegant Louis XIII
décor, refined service and cuisine are outstanding. La Marée has earned an AAA/CAA
Four Diamond rating, ranking it among the
most prestigious eating establishments.

Owner: Alfred Grilli   Chef: Norbert Lennartz

Specialties
Sautéed Lobster with Tomato and Fresh Basil
Braised Fish and Shellfish with Morels
Tournedos Poèle
Châteaubriand

404 Pl. Jacques Cartier, Montréal PQ H2Y 3B2
PH: 514.861.9794 FAX: 514.861.3944

Restaurant Les Halles

Restaurant Les Halles, an establishment
which recreates the atmosphere of the
famous Les Halles Parisian market, celebrated its 25th anniversary in 1996. Food critics
consistently rate it as one of Montreal's best.
Hosts Jacques and Ita Landurie invite you to
enjoy their lunch specials and superior table
d'hôte, always prepared with seasonal goods.
A choice of savory dishes à la carte and gastronomic Owner's Surprise or Surprise du
Patron will satisfy the most discriminating
palates.

Owners: Jacques & Ita Landurie   Chef: Dominique Crevoisier

Specialties
Red Deer in Season
Grapefruit Marie-Louise

1450 Crescent St., Montréal, PQ, H3G 2B6
PH: 514.844.2328 FAX: 514.849.1294

Auberge Hatley

Overlooking picturesque Lake Massawippi, in an exceptional country setting, you will discover one of the finest country inns in Canada. Given Five Stars by Québec Tourism, The Hatley grows salads and herbs in its own greenhouses, giving the cuisine a flavour worthy of the highest praise. Winner of the *Wine Spectator* Best of Award of Excellence and a member of Relais & Châteaux.

Owner: Robert Gagnon   Chef: Alain Labrie

Specialties
Escalope of Fresh Foie Gras
La Grande Assiette de Canard

325 Virgin Rd, North Hatley, PQ, J0B 2C0
PH: 819.842.2451 FAX: 819.842.2907
Email:hatley@relaischateaux.fr

B L D

AE VC MC

Weekdays: May 15-Oct. 31 only

Le Champlain

Inside the renowned Château Frontenac is the magnificent Le Champlain. This stately dining room overlooking the St. Lawrence River is steeped in Canada's illustrious French heritage. Under Chef Jean Soulard's enlightened direction, the freshest of local ingredients marry the flavours of the past with the sophistication of the present. Staff, outfitted in delightful period costumes, take guests a step back in time. On weekends, the soft tones of harp music enhance the atmosphere.

Owner: CP Hotels   Chef: Jean Soulard

Specialties
Caribou Medallions with Braised Chestnuts
Québec Rack of Lamb En Persillade

1 Rue des Carrières, Québec PQ G1R 4P5
PH: 418.692.3861 FAX: 418.692.4353
Website:www.cphotels.com

B L D

AE VC MC CB DC ER J
DS

Le Mitoyen

For 20 years, Le Mitoyen has evolved in quality and generosity, and has taken pleasure in serving their loyal clientelle. Le Mitoyen has intrigued the connoisseur who appreciates the art of fine dining. The restaurant has been recognised with numerous awards, including America's Top Tables. The restaurant's charms will enhance any business meeting; we have five salons with room for up to 80 people at our guests' disposal. It will be a pleasure to welcome you.

Owner and Chef: Richard Bastien

Specialties
Roast Rack of Québec Lamb with Fennel Purée
Médallions of Caribou with Raspberries & Cranberries

652 Place Publique, Ste-Dorothée,
Laval, PQ H7X 1G1
PH: 450.689.2977 FAX: 450.689.0385

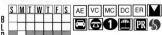

Estoril

Since its establishment in 1971, Estoril has been the chosen meeting place for the most interesting personalities of modern Mexico. Upscale cuisine, a blend of gastronomic cultures and the creative talent of the restaurant's founder supply the ideal frame for an impeccable business meal or an intimate dinner among friends in a refined environment.

Owner: Rosa Martin   Chef: Pedro Ortega

Specialties
Estoril Parsley
Chateaubriand Au Whiskey

Alejandro Dumas No. 24 Polanco
11560 Mexico, DF
PH: 011.525.2803414 FAX: 011.525.2809311

S M T W T F S   AE VC MC CB
B
L
D

La Cava

A palatial yet inviting restaurant with many vistas and exciting fare to offer. Some of the most famous Mexican cuisine is impeccably created and served here. Spanish, French, Italian and Mediterranean cuisine are also offered. The wait staff is personable, knowledgeable and willing to assist in any way to make your visit a memorable one.

Owner: Jordi Escofet   Chef: Demetrio Coloballes

Specialties
Caldo Verde Milpa • Flaming Skewered Quails
Roast Duckling in Aged Wine Sauce

Insurgentes Sur 2465, San Angel,
Mexico DF, 01000
PH: 011.525.5501106 FAX: 011.525.5503801

S M T W T F S   AE VC MC DC
B
L
D

Saint-Honoré

Our Limoges china, Riedel glasses and Saint-Hilaire cutlery enhance the delightful adventure of the palate at Saint-Honoré. The soft, inviting atmosphere of this 8-table restaurant is a beautiful environment in which to taste our caviar, salmon and French foie gras. We serve a selection of vintages fit for any wine lover, and offer a wide range of cigars.

Owner: Ernesto Pérez-Rea   Chef: Jorge Martinez

Specialties

Lentil and Foie Gras Soup
Fresh Lobster in Vanilla Sauce
Venison Filet with Grand Veneur Sauce

Av. Presidente Mazarik 341A, Polanco 11560,
Mexico City, DF
PH: 011.525.2811065 FAX: 011.525.2814048

Casa De Sierra Nevada

Built in 1580 and exquisitely restored, Casa De Sierra Nevada is one of the finest small hotels and restaurants in Mexico. Sitting on an ancient cobblestone street, the Casa blends the beauty of Colonial Mexico with the attentive service of the finest European hotels, and the result is a truly unique experience. Guests praise our gourmet restaurants noted for their contemporary international and Mexican cuisine.

Specialties

Rabbit 'Tacos' with Huitlacoche Sauce
Fish Stew Served in Coconut Shell

Hospicio 35, Santa Elena 2, San Miguel de
Allende, Guanajuato, Mexico, 37700
PH: 011.524.6520415 FAX: 011.524.1522337

Villa Jacaranda
HOTEL VILLA JACARANDA

Welcome to Villa Jacaranda, a small intimate hotel and restaurant in a restored colonial mansion. Our internationally acclaimed restaurant is nestled among the hotel's flowering patios, just two cobblestone blocks from San Miguel de Allende's central square. Located in Mexico's bountiful agricultural area, our menus are enhanced by fresh regional fruits and vegetables. Enjoy international cuisine and authentic Mexican fare harvested from the region's rich native and colonial past.

Owner and Chef: Don Fenton

Specialties
Chile en Nogada
Pollo Borracho

Aldama 53, San Miguel de Allende, GTO, Mexico
PH: 011.52.415.21015 FAX: 011.52.415.20883
Website:www.villajacaranda.com

Casanova

At Casanova, beautiful decor and a breathtaking view of the Pacific Ocean and the Bay of Acapulco provide a spectacular setting for an outstanding Northern Italian dinner. The menu offers an extensive selection of the best veal, lamb and fish. Pastas and baked goods are made in house, and are complemented by an expansive wine list. Casanova is located in the exclusive area of Las Brisas.

Owner: Arturo Cordova   **Chef: Esteban Aleman**

Specialties
Center Cut Veal Topped with Mushrooms
Grilled Veal Paillard

Av. Escencia Las Brisas 5256,
Acapulco, Guerrero
PH: 011.527.4846815 FAX: 011.527.4840035

Las Mañanitas

Exquisite gardens populated with exotic birds set the scene for this beloved restaurant. The incomparable International dishes are each "knock-outs" and compare favorably with the surrounding beauty. These characteristics have placed Las Mañanitas in a privileged position and have earned it a membership in the prestigious Relais & Chateaux chain. This international chain selects small, privately owned & managed hotels and restaurants whose Quality, Service, and Cuisine place them among the finest in the world.

Owner: Rubén Cerda   **Chef: Marcelino Araujo**

Specialties
Tortilla Soup
Mañanitas Duck

Ricardo Linares 107 Col Centro Cuernavaca,
Morelos, 62000
PH: 011.527.3141466 FAX: 011.527.3183672
email:roy1@infoscl.nc1.mx

El Asador Vasco

Located in the heart of Oaxaca, a Spanish colonial city designed by UNESCO as a World Cultural Patrimony, El Asador Vasco Restaurant emphasizes Basque and Spanish cuisine, featuring a variety of local and international dishes. Visitors enjoy the idyllic climate on the terrace overlooking the Zocalo (main square) and savor the delicacies prepared with traditional care.

Owners: Ugartechea Brothers   **Chef: Juanita Hernandez**

Specialties
Fish Robalo au Basque
Mole Negro

Portal de Flores #11 Centro
Oaxaca, Oaxaca Centro 68000
PH: 011.529.5144755 FAX: 011.529.5144762

Blue Bayou

Blue Bayou was the first Cajun restaurant in Mexico, and is still the only such restaurant in Cancun. The restaurant features authentic and creative Cajun and international dishes in a five-level hanging garden with a waterfall. Blue Bayou offers a romantic and cozy atmosphere, and a one-of-a-kind dining experience. Live jazz music nightly.

Chef: Marco Cazares

Specialties

Mayan Blackened Seafood
Rack of Lamb Lafayette

Zona Hotelera km 10.5, Cancun QR
PH: 011.529.8830044 FAX: 011.529.8831514
Website:www.cancun.hyatt.com

Index (restaurant, city, state, page numbers)